Philosophy, the Good, the True and the Beautiful

ROYAL INSTITUTE OF PHILOSOPHY SUPPLEMENT: 47

EDITED BY

Anthony O'Hear

CAMBRIDGE
UNIVERSITY PRESS

PUBLISHED BY THE PRESS SYNDICATE OF THE UNIVERSITY OF CAMBRIDGE
The Pitt Building, Trumpington Street, Cambridge, CB2 1RP,
United Kingdom

CAMBRIDGE UNIVERSITY PRESS
The Edinburgh Building, Cambridge CB2 2RU, United Kingdom
40 West 20th Street, New York, NY 10011–4211, USA
10 Stamford Road, Oakleigh, Melbourne 3166, Australia
Ruiz de Alarcón 13, 28014 Madrid, Spain

Printed in the United Kingdom at the University Press, Cambridge
Typeset by Michael Heath Ltd, Reigate, Surrey

*A catalogue record for this book is available
from the British Library*

Library of Congress Cataloguing in Publication Data

Philosophy: the good, the true, and the beautiful/edited by Anthony
O'Hear
    p. cm.—(Royal Institute of Philosophy supplement: 47)
Includes index
ISBN 0 521 78511-1
1. Philosophy. I. O'Hear, Anthony. II. Series.
B29.P447 2000
150—dc21   00–029244
                                                        CIP

ISBN 0 521 78511 1 paperback
ISSN 1358-2461

Contents

Contents

Notes on Contributors

Sebastian Gardner is Lecturer in Philosophy at University College, London.

Paul Horwich is Professor of Philosophy at University College, London.

Ronald Hepburn is Professor Emeritus of Philosophy at the University of Edinburgh.

John Haldane is Professor of Philosophy at the University of St Andrews.

John Leslie is Professor Emeritus of Philosophy at the University of Guelph.

Roger Fellows is Senior Lecturer in Philosophy at the University of Bradford.

David Evans is Professor of Philosophy at Queen's University Belfast.

T. L. S. Sprigge is Professor Emeritus of Philosophy at Queen's University Belfast.

A. W. Price is Reader in Philosophy at Birkbeck College, London.

Jonathan Dancy is Professor of Philosophy at the University of Reading.

David Wiggins has recently retired as Wykeham Professor of Logic at the University of Oxford.

David McNaughton is Professor of Philosophy at the University of Keele.

Piers Rawling is Professor of Philosophy at the University of Missouri at St Louis.

Robert Hopkins is Senior Lecturer in Philosophy at the University of Birmingham.

Notes on Contributors

Anthony Saville is Professor of Philosophy at King's College, London.

Stephen Mulhall is Fellow of New College, Oxford.

Preface

After perhaps some decades of neglect, the topic of value is once more centre stage in philosophy. We have moved away from the crude idea that all talk of value is merely a reflection of the speaker's emotions. But the precise epistemological and ontological status of values remains a matter of philosophical controversy.

This collection of essays derives from the Royal Institute of Philosophy's annual lecture series of 1998–9. In it the contributors explore how questions of value arise in many areas, including epistemology, ethics, aesthetics, fundamental metaphysics and spirituality.

I should like to thank all the contributors to both the lecture series and the book, and also James Garvey for preparing the index and for the indefatigable editorial assistance.

Anthony O'Hear

Preface

Anthony O'Hear

Value and idealism

SEBASTIAN GARDNER

1 This paper is concerned with the attempt to base a general theory of value on an idealist metaphysics. The most explicit and fully developed instance of this approach is, of course, found in Kant, on whom I shall concentrate, though I will also suggest that the account I offer of Kant has application to the later German idealists. While the core of the paper is devoted to commentary on Kant, what I thereby wish to make plausible is the idea that Kant's endeavour to base a general conception of value on an idealist metaphysics is of contemporary, not merely historical, interest. Specifically, my suggestion will be that a correct understanding of what is demanded by our ordinary, pre-philosophical grasp of value shows there is reason to think that something along the lines of Kant's transcendental idealism (or, like absolute idealism, developed from it) is required for a fully adequate metaphysics of value. Essential to the case I will make is a distinction between Kant's moral theory and his broader account of value, my claim being that, whether or not Kantian moral theory is ultimately dependent on any metaphysics, the broader conception of value to be found in Kant cannot be detached from his doctrine of transcendental idealism.

2 Transcendental idealism enters Kant's theory of value in the form of his double claim, first, that the empirical, natural world of which we have theoretical knowledge is in his special sense 'mere appearance', and second, that what we enter into relation with in the sphere of moral value is a non-empirical, supersensible realm, a realm of things in themselves. These claims are two parts of a single strategy. Because, for Kant, the only kind of value that can be squeezed out of the empirical world – goods based on desire, inclination – is inadequate to our true rational purposes, Kant holds that the only kind of legitimation which judgements of value can receive is one that refers beyond nature to the supersensible, and that this reference can be achieved only on the basis of an ontological devaluation of the objects of empirical knowledge. Reducing empirical reality to 'mere appearance' is, on Kant's account, a precondition for the reality of value.

Kant's theory is therefore relatively complex in comparison with the more obvious way in which idealism may be applied to yield a metaphysics of value, namely the Berkeleyan strategy of reducing the empirical world to appearance in a sense that will allow the value-qualities that things are naively experienced as having to rank alongside all of their other, primary and secondary qualities. This strategy requires us to suppose that the natural order is capable of containing elements that are conceptually remote from objects as conceived in modern natural science. Kant does not pursue this strategy because on his account – here concurring with error theory forms of scientific naturalism, though not necessarily sharing their reasons – empirical experience is too heterogeneous with experience of value for us to be able to pretend that the natural world, as given in our immediate experience of it, is hospitable to us.

The interpretation of transcendental idealism which I will adopt in what follows is the strong ontologically committed one which is immediately suggested by Kant's texts, as opposed to the 'negative', non-ontological interpretation, several versions of which are found in commentary on Kant. Ontologically committed transcendental idealism maintains that the concept of things in themselves is no mere cipher or thought-function, but has reference, either to objects distinct from empirical objects, or to the real but unknowable con-stitution-in-itself of empirical objects. Whatever may be said in other contexts either for or against this interpretation of transcen-dental idealism, if the account given here is correct, then only the ontologically committed version can do the work that Kant regards as necessary for the theory of value.

3 The attempt to resurrect transcendental idealism as a way of grounding value may initially seem unpromising on three counts.

First, there is the fact that transcendental idealism, considered as a metaphysical doctrine, is widely regarded as dead and buried. Second, the enormous amount of work that has gone on under the general heading of Kantianism in recent moral and political philos-ophy makes virtually no use of transcendental idealism, tending on the contrary to distance Kant's practical philosophy as far as possi-ble from his idealist metaphysics. Third, it may be thought, partic-ularly by those who are out of sympathy with Kantianism in moral and political philosophy, that Kant's general conception of value is for reasons which are plain to view so limited, that the attempt to articulate a defence of it can hardly be right-minded.

The first point, concerning the supposed incoherence of tran-scendental idealism, cannot be addressed properly in the present context, but it can be deflected by pointing to the recent emergence of a large body of work which shows at the very least that the case against transcendental idealism is not closed. Also, it should be emphasised that, on Kant's own account, a central part of the rationale for transcendental idealism lies in its unique implications for value,[1] so the dependence of Kant's theory of value on his idealism which I propose to defend may be considered to contribute to the case for transcendental idealism.

Regarding the second point, concerning the general anti-metaphysical tendency of contemporary work on Kant's moral and political philosophy, it will become clear that no disagreement with this approach is entailed by what I wish to claim. Of course, if it is held that the assumption of individual freedom at the centre of Kantian ethics presupposes transcendental idealism, then necessarily there is a disagreement with the anti-metaphysical bent of contemporary Kantians such as Rawls. However, as said above, the focus here will be instead on the way in which transcendental idealism is integral to Kant's conception of value as a whole, as opposed to its role in the more narrowly circumscribed task of providing morality with a justification. On the account that I will give, there is another pressure, aside from questions of human freedom, forcing the theory of value into an alliance with idealist metaphysics, which has to do with our need to conceive ourselves in teleological terms and our interest in being able to sustain under reflection our ordinary sense of purposiveness; this, I will argue, gives rise in Kant to the idea of the supersensible as providing us with a purpose. The question of what metaphysical grounds, if any, are required by the conception of freedom presupposed in Kantian moral and political philosophy is an altogether different issue.

The third objection, that Kant's conception of value is evidently impoverished to a degree that makes it not worth salvaging, is a notion that this paper aims to take issue with. It is, of course, possible to regard the Kantian landscape in a way which makes it seem profoundly bleak: Kant may appear to reduce the natural world to a bare Newtonian machine from within which the only value to which we have any access consists in grim adherence to the

---

[1] *Critique of Practical Reason*, 5:6, in Kant, *Practical Philosophy*, trans. and ed. M. Gregor (Cambridge: Cambridge University Press, 1996), p. 141. Julian Young, in *Willing and Unwilling: A Study in the Philosophy of Arthur Schopenhauer* (Dordrecht: Martinus Nijhoff, 1987), pp. 6–7, refers to Kant's statement that 'the antinomies [of each of the Critiques, including that of practical reason] compel us against our will to look beyond the sensible to the supersensible' (*Critique of Judgement*, trans. W. Pluhar [Indianapolis: Hackett, 1987], §57, 341) as showing that 'from the perspective of, at least, the third *Critique*, transcendental idealism is itself a postulate of practical reason'. This point is insufficiently considered in discussion of transcendental idealism.

moral law, at the expense of natural inclination, with the result that everything exhibiting a trace of human warmth is abandoned to the valueless, Newtonian side of reality. The thought that Kant's philosophy is at root hostile to human life recurs in the history of later philosophy: in an extreme form, in Nietzsche's critique of Kant, and in a more moderate form, in Schiller's *Letters on Aesthetic Education*, which contain an extended criticism of Kant as having erected an opposition between duty and inclination which is at once insupportable and unnecessary.

Against this historically well-entrenched view, I will argue that the complaint that Kant is indifferent or hostile to human life as such can be met up to a point, provided Kant's system is grasped in its entirety.

4 The elements of Kant's practical philosophy which provide the main reference points for my discussion are the following. What I will call the *first part* of Kant's practical philosophy comprises his analysis of morality in chapters one and two of the *Groundwork of the Metaphysics of Morals* and the Analytic of the *Critique of Practical Reason*, followed by its justification in the third chapter of the *Groundwork* and the Deduction of the second Critique. Kant's analysis of morality comprehends his theory of moral motivation – his account of the good will – and his derivation of the categorical imperative, in its various formulae, as the supreme principle of morality. Kant's justification of morality presupposes his division of our reason into two spheres, the theoretical and the practical, and it proceeds by arguing that the supreme principle of morality is necessarily connected with the concept of freedom, and that moral thinking, because it belongs to the sphere of practical reason, has a right to employ the idea of freedom that, according to the first Critique, theoretical reason cannot employ constitutively.

What I will call the *second part* of Kant's practical philosophy consists in his attempt to derive from the moral law, which he assumes to have been sufficiently justified, what he calls a *moral theology*: namely, belief in God and the immortality of the soul, grounded on consciousness of the moral law. This is presented in the second Critique where Kant argues that there is no other way of resolving the conflict between the demands of morality and those of desire, what he calls the antinomy of practical reason. In the *Critique of Judgement* Kant attempts to derive in addition a *moral teleology*, which will be discussed shortly.

The second part of Kant's theory is where most contemporary Kantian moral and political theorists stop seeking to follow him.

5 What I want to consider is the transition from the first to the second part of Kant's practical philosophy. With the moral theology, we are put into a cognitive relation with things in themselves. Kant engineers this relation on the basis of his transcendental idealism, so if his moral theology is an essential part of his theory of value, then his theory of value depends on transcendental idealism.

The best way to see this is to ask what the first part of Kan't practical philosophy alone gives us by way of a conception of value. The relevant question is: What kind of value are we left with, if we truncate Kant's system in this way?

We remain unconditionally subject to the moral law, and bound to regard the moral will as for us the unique unconditional good, and ourselves as ends in themselves, as per the second formula of the categorical imperative. So the first part of Kant's practical philosophy establishes a good independent of desire, namely ourselves *qua* moral beings or bearers of good wills.

What is absent from the first part of Kant's practical philosophy, however, is any *teleological* representation of our practical situation. It of course allows us to have teleological relations to *individual* chosen empirical objects, but it ascribes no teleological character to our practical existence *as such* and *as a whole*.

This requires some clarification, in view of the fact that the first part of Kant's practical philosophy does, as just said, provide us with an end in itself. The absence of teleology consists in two things. First, the moral law represents itself to us simply as bare practical necessity. And, second, the recognition of ourselves as ends in themselves is not a cognition of real intrinsic value – an apprehension or intuition of human beings as in themselves possessing intrinsic worth – but derives in a purely formal manner from our consciousness of the moral law as requiring that we make our wills conformable to universal principles.

On the first count, the moral law's being simply a case of rational necessity, the point, which Kant makes repeatedly, is simply that we do not grasp the moral law in its primary, underived form as referring to any end. This is clear in Kant's account of respect: the moral law is given to us as unconditionally valid, but its value is expressed solely in thoughts of practical necessity, of certain actions as ones that either must or must not be performed. The non-teleological character of consciousness of the moral law is similarly clear in Kant's account of the 'fact of reason', which again hinges on the idea of an apprehension of bare necessity.

On the second count, the point is that what Kant has shown by deriving the formula of ends, is that we must *represent* ourselves as ends in themselves, in order to be able to will in a universal fashion,

5

not that we *really are* beings that possess intrinsic value; to determine one's action in accordance with the formula of ends is merely to grasp oneself as having to reason practically on the assumption that persons must be regareded as ends in themselves. Thus, as regards the formula of ends, and all of the other formulae of the categorical imperative, our practical situation exactly mirrors our theoretical situation: the necessity of representing ourselves as ends in themselves is of the same kind as the necessity of our representing empirical objects as, for example, causally ordered. Both are transcendental necessities, necessities of representation, rather than cognitions of reality in itself: causality is a transcendental necessity deriving from *a priori* elements of our mode of cognition, and the formula of ends is a transcendental necessity deriving from our representation of ourselves as free rational practical beings. As a transcendental necessity, the self-representation of persons as ends gives a teleological character to the intra-wordly exercise of practical reason, but not to practical reason as such and as a whole – to our very being in the world as practical reasoners. This it would do only if representing ourselves as ends were at the same time cognition of reality in itself.

Now it is just this absence of teleology which is at the root of the antinomy of practical reason. Here Kant says that practical reason discovers a contradiction between its unconditional commitment to the moral law, and the demand for happiness which stems from our empirical natures.

Some commentators have puzzled over this, and Kant has drawn the objection that, if he is to succeed in building his antinomy, then he must be construed as conceding here that moral consciousness, as theorised in the first part of his theory, is not after all motivationally self-sufficient, and the moral law not after all supreme, contradicting his earlier claim to have provided morality with a justification. Otherwise, so the objection goes, it is impossible to see why there should be any motivational problem with morality, and why any further motivational incentive to it should be needed.

There is, however, a way of understanding Kant here which releases him from contradiction. What is at issue in the antinomy is the purposiveness of practical reason, the relation of moral necessity to teleological order. The antinomy consists in an opposition between, on the one hand, the non-teleological character of moral consciousness, as Kant has up to this point analysed it, and on the other, the demand of practical reason to be fitted out with a teleology. The solution to the antinomy consists, accordingly, in supplying the moral subject with further thoughts that give a teleological character to moral consciousness, without contradicting the categorical, non-instrumental character of morality.

In the *Critique of Practical Reason* Kant does this by arguing that the requisite teleological thoughts should be supplied in the form of the highest good. The solution, Kant argues, is to suppose for ourselves an afterlife, in which we may attain, through moral striving, a condition of complete virtue, rewarded with proportionate happiness – the highest good. The highest good, as an object of hope, yields the postulates of practical reason – the immorality of the soul, and the existence of God as the apportioner of happiness corresponding to virtue – as objects of moral belief.

In the *Critique of Judgement* Kant proposes, as said earlier, something additional to the moral theology. Part two of this work, the 'Critique of teleological judgement', is intended to harmonise the view of nature as a product of mechanical causality with the apparently contradictory view that some natural objects are fit objects of teleological judgement. Kant argues that this is achieved by treating teleology as a principle of reflective judgement, rather than a constitutive principle of objects. And as part of this reconciliation of mechanism with teleology, Kant asserts that we can think of there being a single supersensible source of both mechanical and teleological causality – we can think of the mechanical and teleological orders of the world as having a single, supersensible explanation.

The extension of Kant's philosophy to teleological judgements contributes to an adequate theory of natural science, but its other dimension, which is far more important in Kant's overall scheme, is that it allows the moral subject to regard the nature *in herself* as purposive. By virtue of the teleological perspective, we can think of nature in its totality as having as its end man *qua* moral being, not merely as the ultimate or *last* end of nature – an end which is not related to any further end – but as its *final* end – an end which *could not* be referred to any further end because it is an *absolute* end. Equipped with the idea that nature is a teleological unity which serves a final end, the moral subject can, at a stroke, regard her own empirical psychology and existence as a natural being, and human life in its entirety, to the extent that it conforms to the moral law, as intrinsically purposive.

The difference between the second and third Critiques, then, as regards their respective resolutions of the antinomy of practical reason, is that the second leaves the moral agent confronting the nature in herself as something to be overcome or bullied into conformity with the moral law, and the purpose of morality located outside the natural world and independent from natural psychology; while the third Critique, without withdrawing the postulates of practical reason and hope of attaining the highest good, extends the scope of purposiveness to include oneself as a natural being. Both

Critiques tell us to conceive the supersensible in terms which are such as to render our adherence to the moral law purposive, but the third Critique grants, as the second does not, that the nature in us, our desiring, has a positive and not merely a negative relation to our supersensible purpose.

Kant makes it entirely clear that the necessity of teleological self-representation provides the key to the transition from the moral law to his supersensible teleology in the Preface to his *Religion within the Limits of Reason Alone*. Having reminded us that, 'for its own sake morality needs no representation of an end which must precede the determining of the will', Kant adds: 'it is quite possible that it [morality] is related to such an end, taken not as the ground but as the sum of the inevitable consequences of maxims adopted as conformable to that end'.[2] An 'end does arise out of morality', Kant affirms, because the question, '*What is to result from this right conduct of ours?*', and the question of 'towards what, as an end [...] we might direct our actions' so as to be in harmony with that end, 'cannot possibly be matters of indifference to reason'. Why can our reason not be indifferent to them? Because, Kant says, the idea of a 'final end of all things' which provides the unifying focus for all our ends, and thereby gives reality to the union, 'union of the purposiveness arising from freedom with the purposiveness of nature', 'arises out of morality' – the need for such an end ('a final end for his duties, as their consequence') is 'morally effected' in the subject. Morality 'thus leads ineluctably to religion'.

6 Now the key question is whether Kant is within his rights to do this – to move to the moral theology of the second Critique.[3] Why

---

[2] Kant, *Religion within the Limits of Reason Alone*, trans. T. Greene and H. Hudson (New York: Harper, 1960), pp. 4–5.

[3] Kant certainly thinks that he is no less within his rights to make this move than he is to make his earlier move from the moral law as fact of reason to the reality of transcendental freedom. The latter turns on a conceptual connection between the moral law and transcendental freedom: analytically, a principle of pure practical reason in application to a finite, sensible being is a principle applied to a subject with transcendental freedom, such that, if I know the moral law to apply to me, as Kant's account of the fact of reason affirms, then I know myself to be transcendentally free. Kant's further move, from the moral law to supersensible teleology, is intended to consist similarly in unpacking what is presupposed in moral consciousness: though there is not the same kind of direct conceptual relationship – the concept of a practical law that is unconditionally valid for me does not contain that of a purposive relation to the supersensible – there is in its place, Kant supposes, a necessity of practical reason: if I am to represent the law that binds my will as maximally rational, as rational in all respects, then I

should it be thought that teleological representation is an overarching requirement of practical reason, rather than just an ultimately contingent feature of our outlook, an ultimately contingent, merely psychological accompaniment to human agency? Only if the demand for purposiveness is rationally necessary, does Kant have any business *requiring* that moral consciousness be recast in teleological form.

The answer that I will give comes in two parts. The first refers directly to claims embedded in Kant's philosophical system, and the second to a consideration which, I will argue, supports them.

On Kant's conception, the faculty of reason is intrinsically teleological, in two senses. First, reason is bound to consider its objects in terms of their ends. This is part of what distinguishes it from the understanding. Thus, when reason considers itself – as required by Kant's famous call for reason to put itself before its own tribunal – it is bound to consider the question of its own end, and since reason, on Kant's conception, has before it in all contexts the task of thinking totality (attaining the unconditioned, complete systematicity, subordination of all to a single principle), it is bound to consider the question of its own *final* end. So reason cannot avoid asking if it has a final end.

It is worth indicating that one option which might seem to present itself here, namely reason's identifying *itself* as a final end, is unacceptable to Kant, for all of the reasons that separate his transcendental idealism from the absolute idealism of his successors.[4] Because Kant thinks of reason in Copernican terms, as the cognitive power of a finite being, and as known exclusively from within the sphere of representation, he cannot regard the reflexivity of reason – the self-relation that it achieves in moral consciousness – as the realisation of a final end; this would require a different, non-finite, absolute view of human reason. Thus for Kant, reason's self-fulfilment in morality does not answer the question of its final purpose; and so leaves room for this to be discovered in reason's relation to something distinct from itself.

Second, Kant thinks of all rational activity as intrinsically end-directed. His view is that the exercise of reason involves necessarily

[4] It is to be noted that the anti-metaphysical school of Kantian ethics, to the extent that it may be attributed with any view of reason's teleology, appears to endorse the identification of reason as its own final end.

must bring it under a further description – I must reconceive it in a way that gives my moral will a purposive character; thus, if I know the moral law to apply to me (as, again, Kant's account of the fact of reason affirms), and if I exercise the rights of my reason, then I can know myself to be purposefully related to the supersensible.

the representation of an end. This is a corollary of his conception of reason as spontaneous: necessarily we represent our rational activity not as the effect of empirical causality, but as undertaken for the sake of something, whether or not that something is determinate. This conception is expressed in Kant's doctrine of practical reason in the second Critique. Here Kant raises the question of the ground on which practical reason is entitled to its practical postulates, and answers that practical reason has in general a right to advance its interest even when they are of indifference to theoretical reason, provided it does not conflict with interests of the latter, because practical reason is the *more fundamental* faculty – every exercise of theoretical reason being first and foremost a doing, a practical undertaking.

Reason is, therefore, bound to raise the question of its own final end, and because rational activity as such presupposes ends, reason *must* be able to discover itself to have a final end, on pain of being forced to think itself purposeless and thereby put into permanent practical contradiction with itself.[5]

At this point, Kant's naturalistic critics might say the following: So much for Kant's overloaded conception of reason; if Kant's identification of reason with absolute purposiveness leads off into the supersensible, then what is shown is simply the importance of learning to make do with a less grandiose conception of reason.

But it is not easy, I believe, to charge Kant with arbitrariness at this point. Kant's view of rational beings as saturated with teleological expectation does not depart from our ordinary self-understanding. We do represent our desires, and our attempts to realise them, as purposive.[6] We think, not that our *desires* make it *seem* to us as if there is a purpose to realising them, but rather that we seek to realise our desires *because* there *is* a purpose to their being realised. This, at any rate, is true of all desires that do not appear to us as alien, of all desires that we endorse and identify with. We suppose our desires to be grounded on and enclosed within purposiveness, not the other way around. Again, this is part and parcel of our spontaneity, our image of ourselves as the authors of our actions: when we act, we take up incentives supplied by our sensuous nature and other contingent sources, and this 'taking up' (converting desires into reasons for action) is something that we must represent as done

[5] It is irrational – contradictory – for reason to do what there is no point in doing; and if reason has no final end, then there is nothing to validate its non-final ends, i.e. it has no end at all.

[6] And this representation is composed of something over and above desire: to represent one's desires and activity of desiring as purposive is not equivalent to merely *desiring* that one's desires be fulfilled.

for a purpose, not as something which is *effected* in us by the desires themselves; we cannot intelligibly think of desires as *making* us take them up without alienating ourselves from our own practical existence. Purposiveness is, therefore, an assumption built into the perspective that we necessarily have on our desires, and which cannot, for that reason, be regarded as an effect of desiring. If the purposiveness of ordinary rational consciousness is, on the contrary, really just a function of its having desires, a kind of feeling effected in us by the pressure of desire, then ordinary practical consciousness is subject to a profound illusion.

7 The philosopher who saw with unparalleled clarity what follows if this part of our ordinary self-understanding is philosophically negated is of course Schopenhauer. Schopenhauer never tires of insisting that our ordinary self-image is turned upside down by the absence of a final end, as implied by the identification in his philosophical system of ultimate reality with blind will. This identification implies that purposes are relativised to, and can only be thought to exist within the perspective of a desiring agent: because the ground of desiring agency is nothing but will, which lacks any intrinsic teleological character, there can be nothing outside the agent that underwrites or even resonates with the agent's setting of ends for himself. The sense of purpose is thereby reduced to an *effect* of will, with no correlate in reality. As Schopenhauer puts it, the motives (reasons for action) of human beings do no more than 'set in motion' the 'individual manifestations' of will and 'alter the direction of the will's effort': 'being accompanied by knowledge', i.e. taking the form of reasons for action, is a mere 'circumstance' of the will.[7]

The view that Schopenhauer's anti-teleological metaphysic of will offers of human agency is precisely a description of what follows if the relation of desire and purpose is inverted and the sense of purposiveness reduced to an internal effect in consciousness of desire. Teleological self-representation is needed, therefore, in order to avoid having to think of our desires and practical existence in the same terms as Schopenhauer describes the individual manifestations of blind will.

[7] Schopenhauer, *On the Will in Nature: A Discussion of the Corroborations From the Empirical Sciences that the Author's Philosophy Has Received Since its First Appearance*, trans. E. F. J. Payne, D. Cartwright (ed.) (Oxford: Berg, 1992), p. 20; *The World as Will and Representation*, trans. E. F. J. Payne (New York: Dover, 1966), vol. I, pp. 294, 105.

8 One way of expressing the point at issue – that the absence of teleology from the moral law matters from the point of view of reason and demands rectification – is to say that, while the first part of Kant's practical philosophy supplies us with an abundance of reasons for *action* – of the strongest variety – it supplies nothing by way of a reason for *existence*. It leaves us in the position of knowing that, *given* that we exist with such and such empirically given incentives to action, our pursuit of their objects must have such and such a form, but it gives no reason to affirm the fact that we exist as rational agents. It leaves, therefore, no rational obstacle to thinking that our existence – practically irrevocable as it may be – is a matter of regret, or at least, that the incarnation of oneself *qua* rational being in empirical form, i.e. one's humanity, is something which it is appropriate to regret. Without the moral theology, Kant would not, therefore, have shown anything rationally amiss with the image of human existence as reason imprisoned in nature, and of all desire as, from the point of view of reason, a kind of permanently recurring burden.

9 It may be asked whether teleological thinking need be considered more than a transcendental necessity, a necessity of representation on a par with the formula of ends. In other words, is there any reason why it should be thought that there *really is* a supersensible teleology, rather than just that we must *represent* ourselves as having one?

The answer, in Kant's terms, is that this is a condition of regarding human value and purposiveness as anything more than quasi-real. If teleological thinking is only a necessity of representation, then there is no difference between the kind of reality that human value and purpose possess, and the kind of inferior reality possessed by empirical objects, 'mere appearance'. And if human value and purposiveness reduce to mere appearance, then, whatever interpretation is adopted of Kant's concept of appearance, it would have to be conceded that we cannot have any reason for thinking that the value which things appear to us to have is anything more than a function of our point of view – returning us, in effect, to a Schopenhauerian understanding of our practical predicament. So if ordinary, pre-philosophical belief in the reality of value is to survive philosophical reflection, it must be thought that there really is a supersensible teleology, rather than just that we must represent ourselves as having one.[8]

[8] Note that this argument aims to defend the general concept of a supersensible teleology, rather than the specific conception of it expressed in Kant's postulates of practical reason; in the present context, what matters is not the specific formulation of our thoughts of the supersensible but their general warrant.

In this way Kant's practical philosophy emerges as asymmetrical with his theoretical philosophy: value emerges as real in a sense that Kant denies to empirical objects. Kant makes it clear in numerous places that this is exactly his intention. The fundamental rationale of the asymmetry is straightforwardly that, whereas in the theoretical sphere, we have no business asking for more than that our beliefs should be consistent, grounded in necessity, and sceptic-proof, any further thoughts of unconditional reality being surplus to requirements, in the practical sphere, by contrast, necessarily it does really matter whether we are capable of grasping and realising values that are truly, unconditionally real. It makes not a practical difference – in the sense of a difference to what we decide to do – but a teleological difference – a difference to the view that we take of what we do, and thereby, a difference to the reflective spirit in which we act.

If this is correct, then transcendental idealism, in an ontologically committed form, is a prerequisite of Kant's teleology, which is in turn founded on the demands of ordinary practical consciousness. At the same time, the place of morality in Kant's system as a whole becomes clear. Far from contracting the sphere of value to moral value, Kant's justification of morality is undertaken for the sake, not just of morality, but of value in general, and the privileged position which Kant accords to morality is warranted by the consideration that it alone offers a secure window to the supersensible and, thereby, a proper basis for value in general.[9] Kant's picture of value is not, therefore, as minimal as the common criticism would have it, and one of the reasons why his practical philosophy is metaphysically committed is because Kant recognises Schiller's problem of finding an adequate conception of the value of human life.[10]

10 At this point I wish to refer, though extremely briefly, to a deep criticism of Kant's project found in Hegel's *Phenomenology of Spirit*.[11] Hegel brings into the open an aspect of the connection of Kant's theory of value with transcendental idealism which has not yet been discussed, attention to which also allows one to see how

---

[9] This is what we find in Kant's aesthetics, where morality supplies the ground of aesthetic value but no reduction of aesthetic to moral value is made.

[10] See *Critique of Judgement*, §83, 434 n29 (321).

[11] G. W. F. Hegel, *Phenomenology of Spirit*, trans. A. V. Miller (Oxford University Press, 1977), §§596–632. Also relevant is §60 of *The Encyclopaedia Logic*, trans. T. F. Geraets, W. A. Suchting and H. S. Harris (Indianapolis: Hackett, 1991), 104–5. I will not attempt to evaluate Hegel's criticism here.

Hegel's own absolute idealism may be regarded as inheriting the motivation which I have attributed to Kant's transcendental idealism.

In the sections of the *Phenomenology* where Hegel discusses what he calls the moral world-view, Hegel argues that Kant is impaled on a paradox concerning the reality of the moral law. The paradox is that Kant both claims that the moral law is something real, and denies it reality by reducing it to a mere postulate: 'its truth is supposed to consist in its being opposed to reality, and to be entirely free and empty of it, and then again, to consist in its being reality'.[12]

The point at the root of Hegel's criticism is that Kant holds that the ground of all value exists solely in the form of the moral 'Ought', and requires us to think of the moral Ought as set over and against all reality – as 'postulated *beyond* reality'.[13] So when we ask, as we must, What kind of reality does the moral Ought itself have?, Kant's answer must be, in Hegel's words, that it has postulated, or demanded, reality: 'it is *thought of* as something that necessarily *is*, i.e. it is *postulated*',[14] it is 'a *postulated being*' which 'is not actually *there*' and which 'is to be thought of merely as an absolute task'; while yet 'at the same time its content must be thought of as something which simply must *be*, and must not remain a task',[15] as 'a beyond that ought to be actual'.[16] This same peculiar status, Hegel shows, flows from duties to all of the various objects that Kant constructs for practical reason – the unity of freedom and nature, the highest good (final purpose of the world), the holy will, God. In each case, Hegel insists, we have a contradiction: the object is thought as necessarily having being *and* as necessarily having being only in thought – a contradiction which, Hegel says, pushes Kant to the fatal confession that the status of the object is that of a mere object of imagination.[17]

---

[12] *Phenomenology of Spirit*, §630.

[13] Ibid., §609.

[14] Ibid., §602.

[15] Ibid., §603.

[16] Ibid., §613.

[17] Hegel's line of thought might be glossed as follows: What *ought* to be presents itself to us as necessarily distinct from, and set over against, what *is* the case in nature (as per the famous passage from the first Critique where Kant says that it is as absurd to ask what ought to happen in the natural world as to ask what properties a circle ought to have; *Critique of Pure Reason*, trans. P. Guyer and A. Wood (Cambridge: Cambridge University Press, 1998), A547/B575); but according to Kant all that we *know* determinately to be the case is contained in nature; so the question is, How can the moral law be thought to have any sort of reality, given that it presents itself in a form essentially distinct from and opposed to that in which only

Now, as Hegel recognises, Kant is not without a solution to this problem, and the solution is provided by transcendental idealism. A supersensible realm may be thought to be what gives reality to the moral law. This supersensible realm may be thought, furthermore, to exist in the form of a unity of fact and value.[18] This allows it to be thought that morality, although it is not *what is the case* in the sphere of nature, is – in some sense that we cannot determine – identical with *what is the case* supersensibly (and so that what *ought* to be is, in some sense that we cannot make determinate, identical with what *is*); a claim which Kant can make coherently because the very distinction of theoretical and practical reason, and so of fact and value, is regarded by him as ultimately merely a feature of our cognitive constitution.

Hegel is aware that Kant's response to his criticism is to refer to a supersensible unity of fact and value. He rejects it, however, because, in his own words, the upshot is to leave consciousness 'in a nebulous remoteness where nothing can any more be accurately distinguished or comprehended', where 'consciousness surrenders itself altogether'.[19] Hegel here evinces his fundamental dissatisfaction with Kant's subjective treatment of reason, and with Kant's general Critical strategy of bringing philosophical explanation to an end with the recognition of incomprehensibility and merely making incomprehensibies comprehensible. Whether or not Hegel's attitude to Kant's philosophical solutions is justifiable, he does not expose any inconsistency in Kant's system.

What is brought to light by Hegel, though, is the question of whether there may not be some other way of applying idealism to achieve the same ends as Kant, one which has the advantage of leaving nothing uncomprehended. And this is what Hegel himself aims at. The difference between Kant and Hegel thus comes to this, that, while both conceive reality as in some sense identical with value, Kant's Critical philosophy locates this identity outside the scope of human knowledge, while Hegel regards it as something that we must be able to grasp conceptually.

If this is correct, then absolute idealism is not, as has been alleged, based on a kind of romantic greed for value. Nietzsche said

[18] See *Critique of Judgement*, §77, esp. p. 408 (292). This conception is prefigured in Kant's early *Dreams of a Spirit-Seer Elucidated By Dreams of Metaphysics*, in Kant, *Theoretical Philosophy, 1755–1770* (Cambridge: Cambridge University Press, 1992), trans. D. Walford with R. Meerbote.

[19] Ibid., §622.

---

the objects that we can determine as real present themselves? If this question is not answered, then there will be a kind of antonomy in reason – not in practical reason taken individually, but in reason as a whole.

of Hegel that his 'silver-glistering idealism' is intended to put everything 'in as beautiful a light as possible', to 'deify the universe and life'.[20] Instead it should be said that, while it is true that Hegel's intention is in some sense to identify the world *in toto* with value, his endeavour to do so is driven by a concern, founded ultimately in the nature of practical conciousness, for the reality of our small, ordinary values.

11 In conclusion, something may be said about why one might, from our present philosophical vantage point, consider that a metaphysics of value like Kant's has strengths not shared by other, currently more favoured positions.

Looking out over the contemporary philosophical landscape with an eye to the metaphysics of value, two very broadly defined positions, or clusters of positions, stand out. Both regard themselves as naturalistic, but they are naturalisms of opposite kinds. The one accepts the conception of reality fashioned by the natural sciences, and analyses value in terms of a conception of agents as, in a corresponding sense, natural beings. The other disputes the identification of reality with the world as represented by natural science, and contends that reality can be thought to contain *sui generis* value features, and that this can be done without importing any substantial non-natural metaphysical basis for value.

Regarding the first, scientific kind of naturalism, while there are of course many ways in which scientific naturalism can uphold the objectivity of attributions of value, its conception of value is wholly desire-based, which means that it leaves our relation to our desires in the same terms as those defined by Schopenhauer's metaphysics of will. Scientific naturalism can, therefore, claim to provide a fully adequate conception of value only if it repudiates the idea that such a conception requires a non-Schopenhauerian relation to desire. Whether or not this challenge can be met, it can hardly be claimed that scientific naturalists have made noteworthy attempts to do so.

Regarding the second, non-reductive form of naturalism, matters are different. Non-reductive naturalism avoids the Schopenhauer problem, because it affirms the reality of non-desire-based value. Moreover, it can hope to avoid the kind of problem concerning the reality of value which Hegel raises for Kant, in so far as it can hold that moral value is given, not in the form of a pure Ought, but as

[20] F. Nietzsche, *Daybreak: Thoughts on the Prejudices of Morality*, trans. R. J. Hollingdale, intro. M. Tanner (Cambridge: Cambridge University Press, 1982), p. 190; *The Will to Power*, §95, trans. Walter Kaufmann and R. J. Hollingdale (New York: Vintage, 1968), p. 60.

part of the fabric of nature, in a semi-perceptual mode, akin to that in which aesthetic value is given.

Non-reductive naturalism has, then, those advantages. But a different problem confronts it. The claim that the natural world can contain *sui generis* moral properties is tenable only if an adequate response to the question of why the natural world should have such a character can be provided. The demand for an explanation of nature's being such as to contain value features, rather than its being the limited, value-free kind of thing affirmed by the scientific naturalist, is wholly reasonable; there is, on the non-reductive naturalist's account, no necessity to the world's containing value features.

It is hard to see what sort of answer to the question non-reductive naturalism can give that does not involve the kind of substantial metaphysics that will upset its claim that values belong to a single world order which can be contentfully described as natural. The scientific naturalist, by contrast, has no difficulty explaining why the world should be, in the particular sense that he affirms against the non-reductive naturalist, value-free.

The non-reductive naturalist may decline to attempt to meet the demand for explanation directly: he may instead respond by offering a diagnosis of scientific naturalism as lying in the grip of a false picture of reality; or appeal to a philosophical methodology which licences his value-rich conception of nature by disallowing the relevant explanatory question. But it is unclear that either defensive strategy will achieve more than a temporary holding position, unless the diagnosis or methodology is advanced in tandem with a positive account of the nature of reality, at which point the need for a substantial metaphysics seems to reappear.

If this is correct, then there will always be a tendency for scientific naturalism to trump non-reductive naturalism from the point of view of explanation. This does not render non-reductive naturalism inconsistent, but it does make it permanently vulnerable on one crucial front, while suggesting that the best that non-reductive naturalism can hope for in its engagement with scientific naturalism is a stalemate. The idealist alternative, by contrast, outflanks scientific naturalism by allowing reflection on the nature of value to play a fundamental role in determining our basic conception of reality, rather than accepting the idea of nature as an independent parameter on what is philosophically plausible, antecedently to reflection on value.

The notion that scientific naturalism is a powerful position which needs to be met by an equally substantial, anti-naturalistic metaphysics of value, is strongly present in Kant, as indicated when it was pointed out that Kant does not take the quick, Berkeleyan

17

idealist route to defending the reality of value. The same outlook, according to which there is no middle position to be occupied between a substantial metaphysical account of value and a scientific naturalism which is, at the highest level of reflection, practically insupportable, can be detected in absolute idealism.[21]

It should not be pretended that either of the two naturalisms can be shown to lose out to an idealist metaphysics of value by an easily agreed common measure. What is decisive, I have argued, is the demanding view of practical consciousness that I have attributed to Kant. If this interpretation of practical consciousness is rejected, then one is free to regard Kant and his successors as having failed to grasp how an adequate account of value can be based upon a conception of ourselves as fully part of the natural order. But if it is accepted, then the all-or-nothing picture of our philosophical situation taken by Kant and his successors should be recognised as manifesting a clarity of philosophical vision which is missing from the attempt to reconceive nature as enriched with value.[22]

[21] See for example Fichte's opposition of 'dogmatism' and 'idealism' in the First Introduction to *The Science of Knowledge*, trans. and ed. P. Heath and J. Lachs (Cambridge University Press, 1982), and Book One, 'Doubt', of *The Vocation of Man*, trans. P. Preuss (Indianapolis: Hackett, 1987).

[22] I would like to thank Christopher Hamilton for comments on an earlier draft of this paper.

Norms of Truth and Meaning

PAUL HORWICH

It is widely held that the *normativity* of truth and meaning puts a severe constraint on acceptable theories of these phenomena. This constraint is *so* severe, some would say, as to rule out purely 'naturalistic' or 'factual' accounts of them. In particular, it is commonly supposed that the *deflationary* view of truth and the *use* conception of meaning, in so far as they are articulated in entirely non-normative terms, must for that reason be inadequate.[1]

I want to oppose this point of view. I am not going to deny that there are correct norms concerning truth and meaning – we rightly value true belief, and we rightly take it that the meaning of a word determines what it ought, and ought not, to be applied to. But I want to argue that these normative facts can easily be reconciled with complete accounts of truth and meaning that are wholly *non*-normative. Thus my conclusion, in a nutshell, will be that although truth and meaning do indeed have normative *import*, they are not *intrinsically* normative. By this I mean that they are not to be analysed in terms of, or constituted from, or reduced to, blatantly normative concepts such as 'ought', 'rational', or 'good'. Putting it more generally, I mean that the explanatorily fundamental theories that specify the natures of truth and meaning will not deploy such explicitly normative notions. So those of us who are attracted to the deflationary view of truth and to naturalistic analyses of meaning (in terms of 'dispositions of use', for example) have nothing to worry about, at least as far as normativity is concerned.[2]

[1] I am here concerned with the meanings of terms *in thought*, as well as the meanings associated with sounds in public languages. Thus the scope of the discussion will encompass the normativity of *mental* content.

[2] It might be thought that proponents of non-normative theories of truth or meaning would have nothing to worry about even if these phenomena *were* intrinsically normative. For, it might be thought that normative properties can be reduced to non-normative properties. However, there is no plausible *conceptual* (i.e. definitional) reduction of normative to non-normative notions; and a weaker (merely constitutive) reductionism could not help those who advocate non-normative accounts of our *concepts* of truth and meaning. Moreover, there is absolutely no reason to think that any of the plausible non-normative *non-conceptual* accounts of truth or meaning (such as the use theory) could possibly result from combining a normative theory of truth or meaning and a reductive analysis of normativity.

Paul Horwich

Many philosophers have urged the point of view that I will be opposing in this paper; but let me single out Michael Dummett and Saul Kripke as especially influential examples. Dummett has complained that the redundancy theory of truth is inadequate – too weak – on the grounds that it leaves out the value we attach to truth. And his point applies with equal force to other versions of deflationism.[3] In his 1959 paper, 'Truth',[4] he compares the making of true statements to the winning of a game such as chess. He points out that we could describe the rules for how to move the various pieces and we could specify which positions count as winning the game – but still something vital to the concept of winning would have been left out: namely, that one *tries* to win. And according to Dummett the same goes for truth: the deflationary theory merely identifies the circumstances in which things are true; it tells us, for example, that the proposition *that dogs bark* is true if and only if dogs bark; but it leaves out the vital fact that we *want* our beliefs to be true; this is how they are *supposed* to be.[5]

Another philosopher who has made much of the normative character of language is Saul Kripke. In his *Wittgenstein: On Rules and Private Language*[6] Kripke emphasises that, for example,

'+' means PLUS →

    one *ought* to apply '+' to
    the triple <68, 57, 125>

[3] The redundancy theory says that 'The proposition *that p* is true' means the same as simply 'p', whereas certain more recent forms of deflationism about truth – including the 'minimalism' defended in my *Truth*, 2nd edition, (Oxford University Press, 1998) – propose to define the truth predicate by means of our commitment to the *material biconditional*, 'The proposition *that p* is true ↔ p'.

[4] M. Dummett, 'Truth', *Proceedings of the Aristotelian Society* n.s. 59, pp. 141–162 (1959).

[5] Something like this position has been re-iterated by Crispin Wright in his book *Truth and Objectivity* (Cambridge, Mass.: Harvard University Press, 1992). He maintains that deflationism is wrong on the grounds that truth is a goal, hence a genuine property, not merely a device of generalisation. See the Postscript of my *Truth* (2nd edition) for further discussion of Wright's argument. Bernard Williams has also expressed sympathy for the view that redundancy-style accounts of truth cannot do justice to its value. See his 'Truth in Ethics', *Ratio* 8, 227–42 (special issue, *Truth in Ethics*, ed. B. Hooker). For similar ideas see Hilary Putnam's 'Does The Disquotational Theory of Truth Solve All Philosophical Problems?' and 'On Truth', both reprinted in his *Words and Life*, edited by J. Conant, (Cambridge, Mass.: Harvard University Press, 1995).

[6] S. Kripke, *Wittgenstein: On Rules and Private Language* (Oxford: Blackwell, 1982). See especially pages 11, 21, 24 and 87.

and maintains that any account of the underlying nature of this meaning property – any reductive theory of the form:

x means PLUS $= P(x)$

– would have to accommodate that normative implication. But he goes on to argue that no behaviouristic, mentalistic, or otherwise naturalistic account can meet this constraint and, consequently, that no such account can be correct. So, for example, one might be tempted to suppose that meaning PLUS by a symbol is simply a matter of being disposed to apply it to certain triples of numbers (including <68, 57, 125>) and not others. But that cannot be right, Kripke says; for how could the existence of any such *factual* disposition determine what I *ought* to say?[7]

In one form or another Dummett's and/or Kripke's sentiments have been endorsed and elaborated by many philosophers (for example: Bernard Williams, Hilary Putnam, Crispin Wright, John McDowell, Robert Brandom, Paul Boghossian, Simon Blackburn, and Allan Gibbard[8]); but I want to suggest that these sentiments are incorrect. As I said at the outset, I do not wish to deny the normative *import* of truth and meaning: there certainly are norms governing truth and meaning. More precisely, I agree with the following principles:

(T) We ought to believe only what is true

and:

(M) If a sentence means that dogs bark, we ought to accept it only if dogs bark; and if a sentence means that killing is wrong we ought to accept it only if killing is wrong, ..., and so on

But it remains to be seen whether these commitments should lead us to the conclusion that truth and meaning are intrinsically normative.[9]

---

[7] Some other philosophers influenced by Kripke and sympathetic to the intrinsic normativity of meaning are John McDowell ('Wittgenstein on Following a Rule', *Synthese*, 1984), Allan Gibbard ('Meaning and Normativity', *Philosophical Issues* 5 – *Truth and Rationality*, edited by E. Villanueva, (Atascadero CA: Ridgeview Publishing Company, 1994, 95–115), Robert Brandom (*Making It Explicit* Cambridge, Mass.: Harvard University Press, 1994), Paul Boghossian ('The Rule Following Considerations' *Mind* 98, 1989, 507–50), and Simon Blackburn ('The Individual Strikes Back', *Synthese* 10, 1984, 281–301).

[8] For references, see footnotes [4] and [6].

[9] Here I am simplifying the issue in a couple of respects. First: I am focusing on why it is desirable, if one has a certain belief, for that belief to be true rather than false; and I am not explicitly considering the desirabil-

After all, it is fairly clear that something *can* have normative import without being intrinsically normative. Surely, human happiness might well be valuable – something one ought to promote – even if (as is plausible) the state of happiness is characterisable in purely mentalistic or neurological terms. Similarly, there would seem to be no incoherence in fundamentally valuing the preservation of an endangered species (e.g. giant pandas) even though the existence of these animals is in itself a non-normative state of affairs. So the issue of whether truth and meaning are intrinsically normative is not settled simply by calling attention to their normative implications: that is, to principles (T) and (M).

Indeed it would seem that something's having normative implications provides simply no reason at all to suspect that it is intrinsically normative. And this might be regarded as a sufficient defense of non-normative accounts of truth and meaning against the critique under consideration (namely, that (T) and (M) can hold, and can be recognised as holding, only if truth and meaning are intrinsically normative). However, it is one thing to show that this critique is not well motivated, and another thing to prove it wrong. The latter can be done only through a detailed investigation of precisely how the normative implications of truth and meaning are to be accounted for. Does the actual explanation of principles (T) and

---

ity of believing something because it is true. I allow myself this simplification (a) because the latter 'pursue truth' norm must be qualified to take account of the fact that most truths are too trivial to be worth bothering about; and (b) because the two norms, though logically distinct from one another, seem likely to be explicable along similar lines.

Second: it might be that what we *ought* to do, strictly speaking, is not *actually* to avoid false belief, but rather to *aim* to avoid it, by conforming to the canons of epistemic justification. In other words it may be that, in so far as we have no *direct* control over our conformity with the norm of truth, it should not be thought to specify what we *ought* to do but, rather, what is *valuable*. I shall ignore this complication in what follows. (Although there is a very brief further discussion of epistemic justification in footnote 13.)

Note that it is our deployment of these more immediate epistemic canons that reveals our acceptance of the two truth norms. Clearly, one's concern for truth cannot be manifested by a tendency, once one has come to appreciate that a belief would be true or that it would be false, to then strive, respectively, either to have that belief or not to have it. Rather, one's acceptance of the 'pursue norm' is manifested in curiosity, in a proclivity for investigations, in the frequent deployment of one's techniques of discovery and confirmation. And one's acceptance of the 'avoid falsity' norm is manifested in self-criticism, in the practice of scrutinising, refining and improving one's methods of inquiry.

(M) (or of our commitment to them) require that the notions of truth and meaning be cashed out in terms of explicitly normative concepts (such as 'ought'); or can one manage with wholly non-normative theories of truth and meaning? Let us see.

To begin with, we can simplify the problem considerably by recognising that (T) and (M) are more intimately related to one another than they might at first appear to be. It might seem that we are confronted with two distinct norms – one regarding truth and the other regarding meaning. But on reflection we can see that they are basically the same: the norm (T) is nothing more than a generalisation whose particular instances are equivalent to the various elements of (M). More specifically, (T) generalises the particular norms of belief:

(B) We ought to believe that dogs bark,
   only if dogs bark
We ought to believe that killing is wrong,
   only if killing is wrong
... and so on

which, modulo the schematic linking principle:

(L) u means that p →
   we accept u only if we believe that p[10]

is equivalent to (M). Thus the concept of truth, as it appears in (T), is serving merely as a device of generalisation. Since this is precisely the role that is stressed by deflationism, it would be surprising if principle (T) could yield an objection to that point of view.

To confirm these claims let me first review the deflationary account of the *function* of our concept of truth. Generalisation normally proceeds according to a very simple rule. For example, we can generalise:

That raven is black

by saying:

Every raven is black

And similarly we can always construct a generalisation from a statement about a particular object by replacing the term referring to the object with a (possibly restricted) universal quantifier: thus, 'a is H' becomes 'Every G is H'. However there is an important class of

[10] Accepting a sentence u is, to a very first approximation, a matter of uttering it to oneself. More accurately it involve relying on that sentence in theoretical and practical reasoning. For a little further discussion see footnote 16.

generalisation that cannot be constructed in this way: for example, the one whose instances include:

(a) Either snow is white or it is not the case that snow is white
(b) Either there are infinitely many stars or it is not the case that there are infinitely many stars
(c) Either capital punishment is wrong or it is not the case that capital punishment is wrong

In this example, and in various others, the usual strategy does not work. How then can the generalisation be formed? What is the single proposition that captures all these particular disjunctions?

The deflationist's claim is that it is merely in order to solve this sort of problem that we have the concept of truth. More specifically, what is needed is the equivalence schema:

The proposition *that p* is true $\leftrightarrow$ *p*

For in the light of its instances we can convert our original list, (a), (b), (c), etc., into an obviously equivalent one:

The proposition *that either snow is white or it is not the case that snow is white* is true
The proposition *that either there are infinitely many stars or it is not the case that there are infinitely many stars* is true
The proposition *that either capital punishment is wrong or it is not the case that capital punishment is wrong* is true

in which the same property (namely, '*x* is true') is attributed to objects of a certain type (namely, propositions of the form, 'Either *p* or it is not the case that *p*'; that is, '*pv–p*'). So this second list can be generalised in the standard way, as

Every proposition of the form, '*pv–p*', is true

The deflationist's contention (which is founded on an informal survey of linguistic usage) is that whenever we deploy the concept of truth non-trivially – whether in logic, ordinary language, science, or philosophy – it is playing this role: a device of generalisation. Moreover, its doing so requires, as we have just seen, no more and no less than the equivalence schema. Thus the basis for our use of the truth predicate is our acceptance of the instances of that schema, and *not* any definition of the traditional explicit form:

For every *x*: *x* is true $\equiv$ *x* is such-and-such

where 'such-and-such' is spelled out in terms of correspondence, coherence, verification, utility, or some other substantive property[11].

Let me now return to the main line of thought. Remember that the agenda is to account for the normative principles (T) and (M) without assuming that truth and meaning are intrinsically normative. And what I said I wanted to do first was to simplify this problem by showing (in light of what we have just seen about the generalising function of truth) that (T) and (M), despite their superficial difference in topic, really amount to the same thing. – Or, more precisely, that the truth norm (T) is just the generalisation whose instances are the belief norms (B), which are themselves equivalent, modulo the linking principle (L), to the meaning norms (M). To verify that this is so, consider the belief norms again

(B) We ought to believe that dogs bark,
   only if dogs bark
   We ought to believe that killing is wrong,
   only if killing is wrong
   ... and so on

or a little more formally:

O [Bel *that dogs bark* → dogs bark]
O [Bel *that killing is wrong* → killing is wrong]
... and so on

(where 'O' means 'It ought to be the case that', and 'Bel *that p*' means 'We believe that *p*'). What is the general principle of which these claims are instances? Well this is just one of those problematic cases in which the normal method of arriving at a generalisation does not immediately work. As explained above, the solution is provided by our conception of truth, in virtue of the fact that it is governed by the schema:

The proposition *that p* is true → p

For this enables us to recast each component of (B) into a form that *is* susceptible to generalisation in the normal way. Given the apriori known instances of the equivalence schema: namely:

(The proposition) *that dogs bark* is true ↔ dogs bark
(The proposition) *that killing is wrong* is true ↔ killing is wrong
... and so on

the components of (B) are equivalent to:

[11] For a more detailed discussion of truth as a device of generalisation, see my *Truth* op. cit.

O [Bel *that dogs bark* → *that dogs bark* is true]
O [Bel *that killing is wrong* → *that killing is wrong* is true]
... and so on

which generalises in the standard way to

(x) O [Bel x → x is true]

Or, in English:

We ought to believe only what is true

This is the generalisation of (B) that we were looking for. Modulo the truth schema, every component of (B) is entailed by it.

Moreover, given the above-mentioned linking schema

u means *that p* → (Acc u → Bel *that p*)

(where 'Acc u' means 'We accept utterance u') our belief norms (B) entail our meaning norms (M). For example,

O [Bel *that dogs bark* → dogs bark]

together with the necessary truth of

u means *that dogs bark* → (Acc u → Bel *that dogs bark*)

yields

O [u means *that dogs bark* → (Acc u → dogs bark)]

which, given that we *know* what we mean by u, entails

u means *that dogs bark* → O (Acc u → dogs bark)

And in a parallel way we can explain *every* instance of:

u means *that p* → O (Acc u → p)

Thus we may conclude that there is indeed a single norm here, an instance of which is:

We ought to believe that dogs bark, only if dogs bark

or:

If a sentence means that dogs bark, then we ought to accept it only if dogs bark

and that the concept of truth enters the picture only as a way of generalising such examples. Therefore Dummett could not be more mistaken: not only does the norm of truth reveal no inadequacy in the deflationary conception; on the contrary, that norm provides a paradigm for the deflationist's view of truth as merely a device of generalisation.

So far so good. But we are still only part of the way to our destination. I have argued that there is really just one norm here rather than two or three different ones. And in so doing I have defended the deflationary view of truth. But it remains to explain that single norm. For I still need to show that it can hold even if meaning-properties (such as, '*x* means that dogs bark' and '*x* means that killing is wrong') are constituted in wholly factual, naturalistic, non-normative terms – in the way proposed by, for example, certain versions of the use theory of meaning.

My strategy will be to begin with a purely *pragmatic* explanation. The basic idea is simply that we ought to ensure that our beliefs are true (or, equivalently, that we accept only those sentences whose truth conditions are satisfied) because we can see that we are more likely to get what we want if our beliefs are true that if they are not. In other words, true belief is evidently conducive to practical success, and that is why it is valuable.

Here is an explicit reconstruction of the elementary reasoning that vindicates this claim. Suppose I want X, and I believe that if I do A, then I will get X. In that case (assuming that A is a possible action under my control) it is likely that:

I do A

Moreover, *if my belief is true* then:

If I do A, then I will get X

Therefore, by modus ponens,

I will get X

Thus:

I will get what I wanted

So I should try to ensure that my beliefs of the form, 'If I do A, then I will get X', are true. But such beliefs result from inferences that I take to be truth preserving. Therefore I should try to ensure that all premises of such inferences are true. But I have no belief that might not at some point be employed as a premise in such an inference. Therefore I should ensure that *all* my beliefs are true. In particular:

(B)   O [Bel *that dogs bark* → dogs bark]
       O [Bel *that killing is wrong* → killing is wrong]
       ... and so on[12]]

And, as we have seen, given the linking principles:

[12] For a more elaborate version of this explanation, see *Truth*, chapter 3, (op. cit.) and Barry Loewer's 'The Value of Truth' in E. Villanueva, ed., *Philosophical Issues* 4, (Atascadero, Cal.: Ridgeview Publishing Company, 1993).

(L)   *u* means that dogs bark →
        (we accept u only if we believe that dogs bark)
        u means that killing is wrong →
        (we accept u only if we believe that killing is wrong)
        ... and so on

then we have also explained

(M)   *u* means that dogs bark →
        (we ought to accept u only if dogs bark)
        u means that killing is wrong →
        (we ought to accept u only if killing is wrong)
        ... and so on

So there we are. It turns out that we *can* explain (B) and (M) without making any assumptions at all about the underlying nature of meaning – leaving it completely open, for example, that we could find an analysis in terms of regularities of use. And we can then go on to explain (T) on the basis of the deflationary theory of truth. Therefore Dummett, Kripke, and their many followers are mistaken: the normative character of truth and meaning may easily be squared with entirely non-normative accounts of them.[13]

[13] In this essay I am concerned to show that the norms (T), (B), and (M), provide no basis for the claim that truth or meaning are intrinsically normative. Granted, there are *other* language-related norms in light of which such a claim might be made:

(a) Norms to the effect that a member of a given community *ought* to attach certain meanings to certain words
(b) Norms of deference to 'experts' in the uses of words
(c) Norms of epistemic justification, specifying what we might reasonably accept, either *a priori*, or in light of available evidence

However, it is relatively easy to see that these bases for the claim of intrinsic normativity are defective:

(a*) The value of my meaning the same as everyone else in my community is pragmatic – providing the benefits of smooth communication. It has no tendency to show that the valued state is itself intrinsically normative.
(b*) What determines my meaning what I do by a given word may be, in part, my accepting correction from certain other people. But in that case what is meaning-constituting is *not* that I *ought* to accept such correction, but rather the fact that I *do* accept it. And this is a non-normative fact.
(c*) Policies for the acquisition of belief are means to an end: namely, truth. Therefore one ought to comply with a given policy only to the extent that truth is valuable. Thus the normative force that attaches to certain canons of justification derives from (T), which we have already dealt with.

But we are still not home and dry. For the position, as it now stands, contains some significant weaknesses, which should and can be rectified.

First objection: Consider a man whose evidence points in the direction of a belief that would make him miserable – e.g. that his wife is having an affair. If the value of truth were merely pragmatic then the question of whether he ought to adopt that belief would have to be settled by weighing the unhappiness that it would cause him against the practical benefit he could expect to derive from having a correct view of the situation. But this is clearly not how we think of such cases. We tend to feel that, however unpleasant the reality might be, the man *should* ideally face up to it. We think he would be displaying a *virtue* if he did. Therefore this 'should' cannot be simply pragmatic. Rather, we recognise a *moral* principle to the effect that one ought to value the truth.

I agree with this point. Commitment to truth, alongside kindness, courage, and so on, is indeed a moral virtue. But I do not think that this concession obviates the need for the pragmatic story I have just sketched, because this virtue is, in a certain sense, 'grounded' in the utility of truth. After all, an important discovery is not useful merely to the person who makes it, but to all the rest of us to whom it is communicated. Thus it is beneficial to each member of a community that the other members pursue the truth. And this, I would conjecture, explains our endorsement of the moral norm.

But one must be careful not to neglect the distinction between our moral *commitments* and the moral *facts* – in this case, the distinction between *our attaching* a moral value to truth and truth *actually being* morally valuable. The pragmatic account I have just mentioned directly addresses only the first of these things; it explains why we should *adopt* the moral norm about truth. But it remains to be seen how that account can help us to understand why that norm is *correct* – why the pursuit of truth really is a virtue. And surely *that* is the explanation we have to articulate in order to confirm that meaning need not be intrinsically normative.

One possible response to this point is to offer a realist-cognitivist analysis of *the correct moral norms* as (very roughly speaking) 'the policies whose general endorsement within a community would be pragmatically advantageous'. On the basis of some such analysis our above demonstration of truth's utility would yield an explanation of its moral value.[14]

[14] For an elegant and more sophisticated account of moral virtue along realist lines, see Judith Jarvis Thomson's 'The Right and the Good', *Journal of Philosophy* 94, 1997, 273–98.

Paul Horwich

However, a more plausible view of (T)'s explanatory status, in my opinion, comes out of the emotivist–expressivist view of normativity. According to this view: (a) the predicate, '*x* ought to be implemented', has *no* naturalistic analysis; (b) its meaning is fixed implicitly by the principle (very roughly speaking): 'To believe that *x* ought to be implemented is to approve of *x* being implemented'; and (c) only our normative *commitments* are susceptible of explanation, and never the normative facts themselves.[15] If this perspective on normativity is correct, then it follows trivially that there can be no pressure, coming from the need to explain the *correctness* of (T) and (M), to suppose that truth or meaning are intrinsically normative; for *nothing* explains their correctness. As for the question of why we *accept* the norms (T) and (M), the pragmatic account, sketched above, provides a perfectly good explanation.

Now it might well be that neither of these two general accounts of normativity is correct. None the less it is reasonable to suppose that whatever the explanation of (T) and (M) may be (if there is such a thing) it will not invoke normative analyses of truth or meaning. For there are no plausible candidates for such an explanation. There are not even any *implausible* candidates, as far as I know! Thus there is a huge onus of proof on those who would maintain that (T) and (M) require the intrinsic normativity of meaning, to show how this could possibly be so.

Second objection: From a purely pragmatic point of view, not all false beliefs are worth trying to avoid. For it may be extremely unlikely that certain propositions will ever play a role in deliberation (e.g. certain propositions regarding ancient history, aesthetics, set theory, sports trivia, etc.). So if we have, for whatever good or bad reason, some inclination to believe such a proposition, the cost of making sure that the belief is correct may well exceed the small expected loss that would attach to uncritically relying on it. We must there-

[15] The emotivist-expressivist position is traditionally taken to include the view that there are no normative facts and that normative pronouncements do not have a truth-value. And in that case it would be obvious that there can be no explaining why truth is morally valuable. But deflationism about truth suggests that what is distinctive and defensible in the emotivist-expressivist position is merely the identification of normative commitment with a kind of desire or pro-attitude, and that the existence of normative truth is not thereby precluded. If this is right, then we can equally recognise normative facts (in a deflationary sense of 'fact'). However, these facts will not be part of the causal order and will not be susceptible of naturalistic explanation. For further discussion see *Truth* (op. cit.) and my 'Gibbard's Theory of Norms', *Philosophy and Public Affairs* 22, 1993, 67–78.

fore acknowledge that the pragmatic norm (T) is something of an oversimplification – no more than a fairly reliable rule of thumb. But in that case, how can we explain the fact that the *moral* norm to which we subscribe asserts that false belief, *no matter how trivial*, is wrong? Why do we maintain this, rather than a more qualified and more accurate version of it, along the lines of:

> (T*) When it matters pragmatically, one ought to ensure that one's beliefs are true

The answer, I would suggest, is that it will often be extremely difficult and time-consuming to judge, for any given proposition, just how much hangs on getting its truth-value right. Therefore the unqualified (T) is much easier to apply than the qualified (T*). But if a norm is to be socially useful, it must be widely followed; and if it is to be widely followed it must be relatively easy to apply it. Therefore, from a pragmatic point of view, it is better to teach people to rely on the simple unqualified (T) than to attempt to deploy the more complicated and cumbersome (T*).

Third objection: What was supposed to be shown has not really been shown: namely, that the normative principles (T) and (M) can hold even if truth and meaning are intrinsically non-normative. For my main explanatory premise was the general instrumental (means-end) norm that one should decide to do what will be conducive to the satisfaction of one's desires. But this is itself a normative principle which adverts to the propositional contents of beliefs and desires. So, in so far as it was suspected that the normativity in (T) and (M) requires the intrinsic normativity of meaning, it might equally well be suspected that the general instrumental norm has that implication too.

Granted, the instrumental norm is assumed in explaining why one *ought*, from a pragmatic point of view, to ensure the truth of one's beliefs. However, that means–end norm is *not* assumed in the explanation of why we are *in fact* inclined to pursue the truth and to want others in our community to do so too. In the latter case, what is needed was the *fact* that we tend to do what we take to be conducive to the satisfaction of our desires. There is no need to assume that there is a correct norm to the effect that we *ought* to act in that way. Consequently, the means–end norm is not involved in the explanation of why we regard the love of truth as a virtue. Nor is it involved in explaining the fact that the love of truth is a moral virtue. For, given the emotivist–expressivist view of normativity, there is no such explanation. And, given the realist-cognitivist view of normativity, that fact derives from the expected utility of concern for the truth.

None the less, I agree that it would be desirable to have some account of the general instrumental (means-end) norm – an account that will show that this norm is not dependent on meaning being a normative notion. And I think it is plausible that this can be done. I can see two possible strategies.

First, the norm as it is usually articulated – as a principle governing our attitudes to certain *propositions* – might be explained as the consequence of a parallel norm, which instead governs our relations to the *sentences* that express those propositions. More specifically, we can begin with the norm:

[S desires* '*v*' & S believes* 'If I do *k*, then *v*']
    → O [S decides* 'I do *k*']

concerning sentences. We can add to this that

'I do *k*' means that he does *A*
'*v*' means that *q*

Then infer that

S desires* '*v*' ↔ S desires that *q*
S believes* 'If I do *k*, then *v*' ↔
    S believes that if he does *A*, then *q*
S decides* 'I do *k*' ↔ S decides to do *A*

And thereby explain why

[S desires that *q* &
S believes that if he does *A*, then *q*] →
    O [S decides to do *A*]

Thus we can explain, independently of assumptions about the underlying nature of meaning and content, why it is rational to do what is conducive to the satisfaction of our desires; and hence, why we ought, from a pragmatic point of view, to pursue the truth and avoid false belief.[16]

---

[16] The present strategy does of course leave us with an unexplained norm, and it might be alleged (a) that this norm can hold only if belief* (i.e. sentence acceptance) and desire* are intrinsically normative; and (b) that meaning must be explained in terms of those notions; therefore, (c) that meaning is intrinsically normative. I agree with (b). Therefore, in order to meet this challenge, I would elaborate the following three pronged criticism of (a):

(1) repeat my earlier examples of notions that are obviously not intrinsically normative, but which are none the less governed by norms;

A second strategy for dealing with the present objection would be to invoke, once again, the emotivist-expressivist account of normativity. As we have seen, this is an account according to which the belief that policy X is a correct norm consists in a certain sort of pro-attitude towards X; this pro-attitude (hence that belief) is possible no matter what X may be; and the fact that X is a *correct* norm, *if* it is, is not amenable to explanation. If this is right, then although we will not be able to get an explanation of the instrumental norm, showing its independence of the underlying nature of meaning – we will have something which, given our purposes, is just as good. For if there is *no* explanation of the norm's correctness, then its explanation cannot require the intrinsic normativity of meaning.[17]

I have been developing the following explanatory picture: that certain non-normative (e.g. use) facts constitute the meanings of words and hence of sentences; that these meanings then trivially engender the truth conditions of sentences – via the schema 'u means *that* p → (u is true iff p)'; that true belief is valuable, both pragmatically and morally; that, in other words, we *ought* to accept sentences only when their truth conditions are satisfied; and that, as the means to this end, our use of language should respect specific canons of justification. The speculation I've been opposing (namely, that meanings are somehow founded on *norms* of use) could be sustained only it were incorporated within a better overall explanatory

---

[17] One might wonder, if we ultimately need to rely on the emotivist-expressivist view, what the point was of any of the preceding argument. For couldn't we have invoked that view at the very beginning of this essay in order to dispose of any suspicion that the explanation of (T) and (M) requires that truth and meaning be intrinsically normative? In fact, the emotivist-expressivist view of (T) and (M) does not undermine the point of my pragmatic explanation of their adoption, because that explanation provides support for the emotivist-expressivist view. For it shows that these normative claims do not depend on our having in mind some analysis of 'ought to be done'; whereas, from the realist-cognitivist perspective, the belief that something ought to be done would have to be justified in light of some account of what ought-to-be-done-ness amounts to.

---

(2) be prepared to apply the emotivist-expressivist view of norms;
(3) provide a functional account of belief* and desire*: a non-semantic, psychological theory that simultaneously implicitly defines belief* – i.e. sentence acceptance), desire*, observation, and action by means of principles that relate these notions to one another, to behavior, and to environmental conditions. (For the beginnings of such an account see my *Meaning*, chapter 3, pages 94–96.)

model than mine – one containing a plausible alternative account of
the origin of the relevant norms. But it is hard to see what such an
alternative could possibly be.[18]

[18] The present paper is also published in *What Is Truth?*, edited by
Richard Schantz (Gruyter: Berlin, New York). I would like to thank him
and Anthony O'Hear for allowing the paper to appear in both volumes.
Many of the ideas in it derive from Chapter 8 of my *Meaning*; but I have
revised and extended that discussion in order to address a variety of problems. I am grateful to Paul Boghossian, Wolfgang Kuenne, Michael
Martin, David Owens, Barry Smith, Helen Steward, and Albert Visser for
bringing some of these problems to my attention.

Values and cosmic imagination

RONALD HEPBURN

I

I shall mean by 'cosmic imagination', first, the mental appropriating of objects, events, processes or patterns perceived in nature-at-large (or 'widest nature'), so as to apply them in articulating our own scheme of values (as we seek to establish, or to revise, these), and in our quest for self-understanding. I shall apply the phrase also to the synthesising activity of the mind in our appraising of items in wider nature itself or as a whole – whether we believe nature to have no value save what we choose to confer or project on it, or take it to have a value that sets limits on our appropriation, benign or exploitative.

I start with brief critical examinations of two undoubtedly lively exercises in cosmic imagining – one from Wordsworth's autobiographical poem, *The Prelude*, and the other from a book published in 1995 by the contemporary revisionary theologian and philosopher of religion, Don Cupitt, which he entitled *Solar Ethics*.

First, Wordsworth. I know of no passage in English literature that illustrates more splendidly 'cosmic imagination' in one of its aspects, and shows the unwitting ingenuity and unconscious resourcefulness that its exercise can involve – its proneness to illusion, also. It is from a well-known passage in Book XIII of *The Prelude* – Wordsworth's ascent of Snowdon. What is vividly displayed there is the poet's belief that his imagination's operations are exalted in their dignity, if they can be seen as mirroring an activity *which nature on the grand scale* is also seen to manifest. The poet's life and work are in this way revealed to have value and dignity by being so connected to nature's ultimate, indeed quasi-divine powers and doings. In this passage, Wordsworth shows us imagination (as he believes) in the act of receiving that enhancement and validation.

Wordsworth's aim was to see the sunrise from the summit of Snowdon. The summer's night was close and warm with a 'dripping mist/Low-hung and thick'. Some way up the hillside, the ground brightened, 'a Light upon the turf/Fell like a flash...' 'The Moon stood naked in the Heavens, at height/Immense above my head, and on the shore/I found myself of a huge sea of mist,' – mist at the level of Wordsworth's 'very feet'. A little way off was a 'blue chasm; a fracture in the vapour,/ A deep and gloomy breathing-place thro' which/Mounted the roar of waters, torrents, streams/ Innumerable...'.

In his later 'meditation' Wordsworth discerned a powerful analogy ('a genuine Counterpart', he called it) between the poetic imagination, on the one hand – its transforming and constructive powers – and (on the other hand) the transforming, on the scale of the sublime natural landscape, of the normal appearance of that landscape, by the mist and the moonlight; and the making of that 'fracture' in the mist that generated the chasm whose awesomeness prompted Wordsworth to call it the 'Soul, the Imagination of the whole':

> ...and it appear'd to me
> The perfect image of a mighty Mind,
> Of one that feeds upon infinity, ...
> ...   .
> One function of such mind had Nature there
> Exhibited by putting forth, and that
> With circumstance most awful and sublime,
> That domination which she oftentimes
> Exerts upon the outward face of things...
> So moulds them, and endues, abstracts, combines,... [1]

The analogy, then, which ennobles Wordsworth's conception of his own 'imaginative' vocation, affirms that human imagination relates to that transforming of experience which characterises poetry, as nature's transforming power or mighty Mind (in the role of Imagination) relates to the transforming of natural objects so as to yield experiences such as Wordsworth's on Snowdon.[2] Now, what I want to add is the following: that Wordsworth's own imagination was active not only in the first portion of that diagram of analogical relationship – but also and equally vitally in the second. It is *Wordsworth's* imagination which interprets the natural scene on Snowdon, which takes or reads effects of mist and moonlight as transformations of what *would* have appeared, had the mist and moonlight *not* been there. 'Nature had transformed nearly everything', writes his commentator. Yes, but here where nature transforms nature – the transforming agency and what is transformed are equally nature, and the decision what to think of as un-transformed and as transformed nature is itself the work of imagination – *our*

---

[1] *The Prelude*, Book XIII, lines 10–116.

[2] See J. A. W. Heffernan, *Wordsworth's Theory of Poetry* (Cornell University Press, 1969), chapter 4, particularly pp. 102–5. 'For the rest of his life, [Wordsworth] firmly believed that when a poet transforms the visible universe by the power of his imagination, he imitates the creative action of nature herself' (p. 105).

imagination, or in this case Wordsworth's. To put my point crudely: the differentiating of the landscape *without* mist and moonlight from the landscape *with* these present, each being the effect of natural forces, must be wilful, *our* artefact, and can scarcely bear univocally the momentous interpretation Wordsworth seeks to put upon the experience. For that interpretation involves the thought of the operation of a distinct power of nature, or mighty Mind, analogous to the (unified but finite) human imagination.

'Wordsworth,' says his critic, '... finds evidence in nature for ... a "Power" which behaves like the human imagination.' No, I want to say: ironically, though he seeks confirmation for the power and near-divine dignity of imagination, and believes – with wonderment – to have been given it on Snowdon; in order to set the stage, as it were, for that apotheosis of imagination, he has had to *employ* it, and on the grandest scale, in differentiating – from the sheer flux of natural events – a transforming Power (on the one side) from elements transformed (on the other); and so appear to furnish imagination with its ennobling cosmic counterpart. Or in other words, nature is made (by the poet's imagination) to set up its own stage-scenery by which to 'write-large' the cosmic significance of imagination. The Snowdon-experience furnishes the 'perfect image', 'the express/Resemblance [of our 'glorious' imagination], in the fulness of its strength/Made visible'. But, of course, the active agent here is Wordsworth himself, or the poet's own imagination, interpreting, projecting.

Alternatively, if we dwell on the metaphor of 'projection' (and the passage richly illustrates the phenomenon), Wordsworth, all the time, has his eye upon the *poet's* imagination in relation to the subject-matter it seeks to transform and to mould. He then projects, in his meditation, that picture on to nature, and so sees it again there 'writ large'. This is not nature displaying imagination at work on a cosmic scale, from which the poet can accept ennoblement for his own *lesser* imaginative powers, but Wordsworth receiving an epiphany of his own imagination's contriving. In less noble language, imagination here has been pulling itself up by its own bootstraps.

I leave Wordsworth now, as a somewhat detached, perhaps admonitory, preface, and I shall jump, without further comment, from 1805 to 1995 and to the theologian, Don Cupitt, in his short book, *Solar Ethics*.[3] There he makes rather spectacular use of cosmic

---

[3] Don Cupitt, *Solar Ethics* (SCM Press, 1995). In discussing Cupitt I shall make use of material of mine first published in *Studies in World Christianity*, edited by J. L. Mackey, Vol. XX, No. 1 – with the editor's kind permission.

imagery in commending a way of life for mankind. I want to sample this imagery. He invites his reader to see the human self as 'a miniature counterpart of the world'. Like the cosmos as a whole, 'it too burns, pours out and passes away. We should', he claims, 'burn brightly, all out'. Human fulfilment is to be found 'not by giving the human self a special metaphysical status and delivering it from the world, but rather by melting it down into the flux of the world', in its 'spontaneous and joyful' self-affirmation – life's 'solar self-outpouring'. It will be a lifestyle of 'pure expressive freedom', of 'all out religious expression', an acceptance and celebration of contingency and transience: like the sun, we live 'by dying as we go out ... into expression', in 'heedless prodigal self-expenditure'. As the sun is 'its own outpouring self-expression', its 'headlong process of self-exteriorisation', so with ourselves – 'there is nothing left for ethics to be but that we should love life and pour out our hearts'[4].

'The world empowers you, pouring into you its own Dionysiac flux of upwelling energies; and you in complementary response go out into linguistic expression, into the action and the consciousness' which impart to the world its '... dazzling all-human beauty'. For Cupitt, there can be no conflict between such a choice of life-style and the imperatives of an objective moral law, for he denies that there exists such a law. The moral realism that once underpinned such notions, he says, with its attendant vocabulary, 'is dead'.[5]

Where, if anywhere, does our salvation lie? 'I have found salvation when I have found something that I can give my heart to'. And thereby we experience 'the highest love of life and the purest love of death as being simply identical'. What, then, *do* people give their hearts to? It may be their homeland, their own 'image', ... or, for a teacher, a brilliant pupil. The object 'does not matter very much', so long as it acts as catalyst. 'Love...hustles us rejoicing towards death'.[6]

Cupitt's ethics, in this book at least, comes close to being a new version of 'Follow nature' – *naturam sequi*: Be headlong, self-outpouring as the sun is.[7] The analogy on which Cupitt relies is with the sun's energy, imagined as a glorious, chaotic out-pouring, a burning self-expenditure. But surely (I want to respond – in less headlong fashion) the operations of nature cannot be definitively *summed up* in such terms, as if those terms captured a uniquely essential character, normative for ourselves: or indeed as if cosmic imagination could in this way confirm or validate any single, practical style of life for man.

[4] Cupitt, *Solar Ethics*, pp. 2, 3, 4, 13, 14, 48, 8, 9, 14, 15, 16, 19.
[5] Ibid., pp. 27, 45. On Cupitt's dismissal of realism, see my comments in *Studies in World Christianity* – footnote 3, above.
[6] Cupitt, *Solar Ethics*, pp. 58, 59.
[7] Ibid., pp. 8, 9.

Other aspects of nature offer imagination other analogies *no* less valid, from which we could read off very different possible implications for the living of human life. Nature is also rationally intelligible order, the evolving of complex organisms, structures hierarchically scaled and nested, up to the intricacy of our own brains. Let imagination brood upon these other aspects of nature, and we could derive strong pointers to such values as unity, integration, harmony, to an appreciative wonderment at the slowly and precariously emergent modes of awareness, rationality, sense of beauty, personhood: perhaps also a sense of ecological responsibility. Religious values do indeed suggest themselves here, but concerned with less frantic, less vertiginous experiences than those Cupitt proclaims: of which more soon.

Of course, if an ethic one-sidedly ignores the ideals of self-expression and self-fulfilment, it does present an impoverished life-plan. But no less distorted is an ethic that one-sidedly *celebrates* them, fails to build in checks to modes of self-fulfilment that harm others. To respect the needs and rights of others necessarily limits the individual's 'heedless prodigal self-expenditure' – as Cupitt puts it. And his cosmic imaginings do nothing to promise such a needed balance. If it really doesn't matter very much what I can give my heart to, and supposing that the 'catalyst' turns out in my case to be the pursuit of personal power over others (their bodies or their beliefs), it is only an acknowledged unconditional moral obligation to respect the freedom of others that can prevent my venture into 'solar ethics' having a disastrous outcome. Or suppose we take seriously Cupitt's Romantic linking of love and death ('Love consumes us ... hustles us rejoicing towards death'; '...the highest love of life and the purest love of death ...[are experienced as]...simply identical'), at the very least this will again deflect us from that form of love which affirms and respects the value of the other, and from the self-love which, while acknowledging the reality of death, fights any self-destructive fantasies we may harbour. The pursuit of peak experiences, vivid but doomed, short-lived, followed by a fall-away (Icarus-like) into non-being – here is an 'ethic' sadly, though today familiarly, off-balance. It exemplifies, dramatically, both the power and the fallibility of cosmic imagination: but to proclaim it, or to preach it, would be a doubtful service to the ethically perplexed.[8]

[8] To be fair to the author, there are places in the book where Cupitt does acknowledge other and very different values. For instance, 'It now appears that we humans are ... social animals who must co-operate...' and must 'procure enough co-operation for survival', and deal with our 'discordant impulses' (45). But in *Solar Ethics* he does not indicate that much needs to be said about these; nor does he claim that we shall need a reasoned moral scrutiny of the 'catalysts' or the styles of life they may instigate.

Ronald Hepburn

In a word, that same image of the sun with the thought of its burning-up, or indeed any powerful image of huge cosmic energies expending themselves, pell-mell, unplanned and uncontrolled, could equally well be coupled with altogether contrary normative judgements. '*That*', we may say, 'is the nature of the impersonal cosmos around us. *We*, however, within the world of *I* and *Thou* (while not denying ourselves the awesome spectacle those energies provide) must live in altogether different style, by altogether different laws, laws that counsel the cherishing, not the indifferent destroying, of the structures on which personal life depends; and the quiet furthering of life, so far and so long as we can fruitfully sustain it.' Only our autonomous, reasoned judgements of value, working upon the equivocal visions of cosmic imagination, can determine which interpretation to accept and endorse.

II

So, ventures in cosmic imagination can be exciting (indeed, intoxicating), puzzling and illusion-prone. After those extended examples, I would like, more soberly and on a more general level, to explore some of the roles of cosmic imagination in relation to value – moral and religious. This has to take us back to the level of basic value-theory, where I have much more sympathy with current moral realism or cognitivism than has Cupitt. In the context of a single lecture, these basics, however, can only be affirmed, not argued out.

When I say that I am drawn to a cognitivist-realist account of the most fundamental human values, I have the following familiar thoughts in mind: that such values as beneficence, justice, respect and our commitment to them cannot be adequately accounted for as expressions of feeling or emotion; that our emotions are themselves proper objects of our moral self-monitoring and not final moral arbitrators; and that, besides, there is such a thing as moral *authority* – not itself reducible to strength of feeling. Now, I can accept for many moral judgements what has been called a 'procedural' realism: that is to say, some version of universalising procedure. But it is not sufficient for the grounding of all values. Those procedures which limit my permitted action have their grounding in the value of the 'persons' who are to be respected. The worth of persons must be affirmed in a value-judgement at the end of the line of justifications, and such a terminal value-judgement requires of us either a lapse back to an emotivist analysis, or a realist-cognitivist account of a different kind. Opponents of moral realism will scorn an analysis of the latter sort as a lapse into an outmoded intuitionism, and take that as sufficient rebuttal. I see it differently: – we can opt either for an easy-to-grasp, broadly Humean, view of reason and its limits and an ultimate appeal to *de facto* 'humanity' or sympathy; or accept that our experience of moral authority demands something else – something still cognitive, still seen as a discerning of what can in principle challenge any appeal to feeling or sentiment – though certainly at the cost of a much less tidy analysis.

III

On the appropriate *objects* of value-judgements, the simplest position would be to see values as belonging purely to the human life-world, the world of *I* and *Thou*, of perceptual (or 'secondary') qualities and emergent human 'meanings'. Should the activities of cosmic imagination, then, be dismissed as a misconceived extension of the proper domain of human concern? That does not seem right either – for all their proneness to illusion. Whatever analysis of them we shall find ourselves giving, we do venture value-judgements – some hesitantly, but others very confidently – that go far beyond those life-world confines. We do so whenever we look at the heavens with awe or with dread, and ponder the benignity or oppressiveness or menace or beauty of the world: and we do so when we ponder how we ought to appraise and respond to items in wider nature itself (both sentient and non-sentient) – with indifference, or with respect. Whatever we decide in the end about these, it is hard to expel the thought that to exclude such reflection from the start – because all value-matters are internal to the life-world of persons – amounts to a serious self-diminishing.

There can be an oscillation in our thinking between what may be called an 'over-distancing' and an 'under-distancing' of the realm beyond the *I-Thou* world. We may so distance the realm beyond, that a comet is no more to us than a bright smudge in the night sky: a meteor-shower, a flicker of light-points only.[9] The thought here is this – our values pertain to *our* world alone. Vast cosmic distances may have frightened Pascal, but, being altogether outside the value-world of *I* and *Thou*, they have no authority to trouble us, snug as we are within our life-world. 'Snug' is of course absurd: but it may play a momentary role as I develop my claim that imaginative self-confinement to the *I-Thou* world does indeed 'diminish' humanity,

---

[9] There is an echo here of F. P. Ramsey's often quoted remark that the stars are no more to us than three-penny bits, *The Foundations of Mathematics*, p. 291: also a distant memory of Antony Flew and R. W. Hepburn, 'Problems of Perspective', BBC Third Programme, Sept. 1955.

through an *over*-distancing of the objective world. We may thus be lured into so insulating ourselves as to ignore environmental obligations and responsibilities, as well as denying ourselves rich possibilities of *aesthetic* experience. It is as if we were indulging a wish to remain in a child's universe, refusing to allow our imagination to grow up: as if all value-matters could be settled before we peep beyond our person-with-person lives. But perhaps not even serious self-understanding and self-evaluation are feasible without *attempts* at wider connecting, whatever the risk of illusion in the operating of cosmic imagination.

Now it is equally easy to *under*-distance the world beyond the world of *I* and *Thou*. To do that is to see – or to think we see – messages, values to assimilate, everywhere in nature, though in reality we are mostly anthropomorphising, unwittingly projecting upon nature aspects of our own life, values we have already autonomously deliberated upon and endorsed. That, I agree, is certainly the case in many instances, with many innocent cosmic imaginings in aesthetic mode. But that cannot be the whole story. For one thing, projecting of feelings cannot be the whole story about our moral relations with *non*-human sentient beings. The vagaries of sentiment cannot cover the sense that it would be morally wrong of me to ignore a suffering animal which I am uniquely placed to help – even when I am low in sympathetic feeling towards it: morally wrong also, more broadly, to acquiesce in policies that lead to the destruction of species. And this is not basically because (with Kant) I see such concern as good for the strengthening of my own moral relations with *human* beings, who alone, as rational, are the real objects of moral concern. The animal too, as a sentient other, is a no less real object of direct moral concern. We are constrained, then, to extend our cognitivist or realist account over other sentient life, in acknowledging that the valuing (respecting) of non-human animals is a genuine recognition of their otherness as it impinges on our awareness, and is not our own anthropomorphising construction. Rather, it *cuts through* all such construction. It is a common experience to become aware that we have been anthropomorphising about some bird or beast, to realise that we have apprehended it primarily as an item of our life-world furniture or fantasy (under-distanced, that is), and that 'behind' that there is something to be grasped (at least approximated to in understanding) – namely what it is actually like to *be* that sentient creature. The tension here signals that projection is *not* all. The thought of *another consciousness*, other sentience, cannot be reduced simply to elements in our own life-world sensibility.

Must we not go a step further still? Is not a similarly cognitivist-realist account required for the claim that the natural world itself and as such ought properly to be an object of our 'respect', not of our proprietorial manipulation? For instance, our moral judgement against arrogant destructiveness in its various environmental forms surely again transcends our contingent and variable feelings (and precedes any projecting or gilding) as much as any parallel judgement in the domain of *I* and *Thou*.[10]

None of this denies that we *also* very commonly project and gild, as was amply illustrated by Wordsworth on Snowdon. That being so, my *overall* picture has to be one of a constant and complex interweaving of the different sorts of value-judgements (requiring more than one theoretical treatment – cognitivist in some cases, projectionist in others) in the reflective and imaginative human life. Given the presence of *some* realist judgements about wider nature, there is no case for confining serious value-deliberation to the *I* and *Thou* domain. We cannot dismiss as morally irrelevant our sensed affinities and antipathies with nature-at-large: rather, they must be scrutinised and appraised case by case.

It is another question, however, whether we can validly derive from our perception and reflection concerning wider nature alone any judgements about our own lives – about their 'significance' or lack of it, or about particular life-choices that we ought to make. Are there in nature discernible patterns that we ought to imaginatively appropriate (*because* they are there in nature?) and on which we should model some of our own patterns of life? Answers have swung between the poles of a Wordsworthian view of nature as man's 'educator' and a position like that of J. S. Mill, who subjected the maxim, 'Follow nature', to a sustained critique and repudiation. As I suggested earlier, I have to go along with Mill – though I would put the point in a more Kantian way, as an insistence upon autonomy.[11]

Only in a (vain, ultimately incoherent) effort to deny that autonomy, can we speak (looking back to Cupitt, and quoting him again) of 'melting down [the human self] into the flux of the world'[12]. Images from wider nature keep us mindful of the context in which we act and try to appraise the significance and worth of our lives. But most often they are ambiguous or multi-interpretable, and they

[10] I pick up the topic of respect again, below, pp. 47–49.

[11] It will be clear that I am not working with a conception of autonomy which equates autonomy with a kind of individual relativism – each moral agent as fashioning his or her set of values. Rather, I take it to involve a refusal to let the determining of my moral action pass out of my rational deliberation – and a concern to grasp values I do not make but discover.

[12] Cupitt, *Solar Ethics*, p. 3.

lack overriding authority. Despite the fact that we are *embodied* beings, and are, in that sense, one with physical nature, it is those factors that make for our *distinctiveness* that are decisively relevant in our life-planning, namely our freedom, language and reasoning power. Wider nature, lacking these, has no imperatives for us – certainly no *moral* imperatives.

So: the pervasive feature here is ambiguity. We ponder, for instance, the fact that many of the processes governing the universe display rationally intelligible and often aesthetically remarkable fundamental principles and structural forms. Can we see this as carrying an unambiguous implication for values? I think not. We *might* respond by feeling more at home in the universe. Alternatively, however, we could feel awed, but disturbed and dismayed that nevertheless the bodily vehicles of our own rationality and personal existence are so fragile and ephemeral, and that we are treated by nature-at-large – for all its rational aspects – with ultimate indifference as finite individuals. (Similar ambivalence can readily characterise our responses to cosmic 'fine tuning'.)

Suppose we were to become strongly aware of nature as indifferent or 'callous'. To read that expression on the face of nature can neither annihilate human values, nor (obviously) vindicate them. Love, compassion, justice, can be affirmed, harmoniously with, or despite, their wider context.

Nature, then, itself provides no resolution to the ambiguities – nor unequivocal 'support' to the basic principles by which we might seek resolution. So we are thrown back on our own normative resources, to accept or reject the promptings and suggestions of images drawn from wider nature.

In his essay, 'Platonism and the Gods of Place', Stephen Clark reminds us of the often-reproduced photograph of the Earth seen from orbit, on its own in space. 'We all live,' that image tells us, 'within a single, beautiful and isolated world...' We go away from home, and we 'look back and love it. Seeing the Earth, and so ourselves, from outside, we can realise who and what we are.'[13] We may well conclude that we have a solemn duty to tend or 'shepherd' the Earth. Here again is cosmic imagination in vivid action. Nevertheless, it is not the image itself that generates on its own those moral judgements, not the image that has the moral authority to urge us to cherish the Earth, not despoil and plunder it. As far as the image alone is concerned, we might see it as expressing a desolate and hopeless isolation, or a cosmic absurdity, rather than an

[13] Stephen R. L. Clark, 'Platonism and the Gods of Place', in T. D. J. Chappell, ed., *The Philosophy of the Environment* (Edinburgh University Press, 1997), pp. 19f.

exquisite, and exquisitely vulnerable, centre of value. *Qua* cosmic imagining, each interpretation is as good as (as true to experience as) the others. We can distance ourselves from a cosmic-imaginative slant, acknowledge that it is there, presenting itself but not necessarily receiving our value-commitment. That is to say, we can slip in a wedge between 'seeings-as', interpretations of cosmic imagination, and reflective, mature evaluation of the same item: between the positive, wondering interpretation of the Earth-in-space picture and a value-judgement that the Earth needs to be cherished.[14]

IV

In defining cosmic imagination, two main questions were distinguished. There is, first, the question about the items and ongoings in wider nature which may be thought relevant to our deliberation about how best to live. To that, I respond, in effect, that the sub-personal cannot instruct us in the conducting of personal existence. The normative basis of our moral lives cannot be found there. Powerful *illustrations*, analogies, metaphors, yes – but ambiguity also.

Second is the question about valuing items in wider nature itself and deliberating about appropriate attitudes of response. We have already strayed into its territory. The most seriously defensible exercises of cosmic imagination that I know tend to be answers to that second question, outwardly directed from our situation to wider nature, towards which we may come to see ourselves as hav-

---

[14] Something has to be said about the distinction between what I have been calling the '*I-Thou*' context of value-deliberation and -judgement and 'wider nature'. For a start, it is tempting to label the former, 'the (human) life-world' – and of course (whether or not anchored close to Husserl) the term is often enough used. But the concept of life-world has an unfortunately determinate ring to it. It is easy to see, however, that the distinction between what belongs to the life-world and what is supposed to lie beyond it can be made in many ways.

It is a matter of degree how far we modify our unschooled common-sense view of the world to take account in perception and belief of what we know of the world as it is beyond that common-sense view of it: the light- and sound-waves that cause our seeing and hearing, our planetary position in relation to sun, galaxy and beyond. Instead of any concept of life-world, we could work with a spectrum of degrees of 'cognitive revision' or 'adjustment'. The scope and the limits of our knowledge may determine whereabouts on that spectrum we stabilize our 'reading' of our world: but will, choice, decision may also play a part.

ing serious responsibilities. Those environmental philosophies
which attempt today to rework moral, aesthetic, and religious attitudes to nature make it their chief concern. So will the remainder of
this essay.

'Moral, aesthetic, and *religious*' – the word 'religious' at once risks
misunderstanding. I mean it in a very broad, but not empty, sense:
its presence signalled by both formal and substantial factors. Formal
– as involved in the most comprehensive imaginative syntheses, in
global and *totalising* evaluation and *ultimate* values; substantial – as
taking account of such attitudes and emotions as respect, wonder
and awe. These owe much of their meaning to their place in the
development of traditional religions, but do not have to be restricted to those contexts, nor does their applicability necessarily depend
on the soundness of the metaphysics that underlies those religions.

Is it possible, then, to argue for some specific ways in which value-
thinking and imagination may be deployed – ways that are not vulnerable to the kind of criticisms I made earlier – in support of such
a cosmic orientation? We resolve not to forget the ambiguities, not
to be one-sided – for instance, neither frantic nor unrealistically
euphoric, neither demonising nature nor divinising it, but concerned to contemplate and celebrate nature as it is, so far as that is
a coherent objective. And we do seek to unify and stabilise our attitudes and appraisals as far as we can, but not at all costs and not in
ways that falsify experience.

Ambiguous nature presents us not only with the image of headlong process towards extinction, but also with that of *equilibrium* –
in both the inanimate and animate domains. If we dwell only on the
former of these, the image of 'burn, all out!' works one-sidedly
towards exalting the ephemeral and expendable in the human enterprise. It could intensify destructive and self-destructive urges. In
the field of the arts, for instance, it could prompt hostility to valuable ideals of continuity, tradition and measured change, which
together enormously expand our expressive range.

But, I am saying, as well as 'headlong' self-outpouring, there is
equilibrium: forces in balance that permit and sustain form and
complex structure, that allow our personal, rational and purposive
mode of existence to 'ride' upon the impersonal and material, and
the physical laws of nature. Closely connected are the aesthetically
enlivening images of the 'still centre', and of a *contemplative* equilibrium, such as facilitates and sustains our present reflection itself.
All of that can elicit wondering appreciation.

We pledged ourselves, however, not to forget the ambiguities, not
to let the quest for unity falsify how things are; so the bright

thought of equilibrium must be qualified by poignant awareness of its (living) instances as fragile and contingent: ephemeral and minute in a vast universe. 'Ephemeral and minute' – certainly. But there is yet another aspect to bear in mind. Scientific cosmologists have been arguing that there can be no spots of equilibrium and no life, *without* those daunting spatial and temporal immensities: a fact which makes a difference to our imaginative grasping and responding to these. Learning that to create and sustain life, the universe *had* to be old and huge may well help to mitigate the more desolate and value-undermining responses that otherwise we are tempted to make to its indifferent emptiness.[15]

Would it then still be feasible to postulate a single unifying appraisal concept that – rising above the ambiguities – could regulate our attitudes and actions towards nature as a whole? Or would it show only a blind commitment to the monistic? I spoke tentatively of venturing a cognitivist account of an obligation to *respect* nature-at-large. But what could we mean here by 'respect'? Can a single sense of the word apply to all we know of nature?

The principle of **mutual love** [wrote Kant] admonishes men constantly to *come closer* to one another; that of the **respect** they owe one another, to keep *at a distance* from one another...

... a duty of free respect towards others is ...analogous to the duty of Right *not to encroach* upon what belongs to anyone.

...The duty of respect for my neighbour is ... *not to degrade* any other man to a mere means to my ends ...[16]

Kant is writing about 'rational beings', and obviously we cannot transfer this *in toto* to relations with *im*personal, non-human and non-living nature: yet there are tempting analogies, and we can extend the scope of respect under their tutelage. Respect for widest nature too requires *distancing* – as acknowledgement of the variety of beings and modes of being, and accepts these as setting a *limit* on our action, our 'encroachment'. The concept of 'degradation' is also readily extendible to some of our dealings with non-human nature. Respect refuses to treat nature as unlimitedly exploitable, unchecked by any principle superior to human self-interest.

[15] Cf. John D. Barrow, *The Artful Universe* (London: Penguin Books, 1995), pp. 38, 39: 'Billions of years are needed to produce elements like carbon, which provide the building blocks for complexity and life. Hence, a universe containing living things must be an old universe. But, since the universe is expanding, an old universe must also be a large one.'

[16] Kant, *The Metaphysic of Morals* (The Doctrine of Virtue), part II, chapter 1, section I, divisions 24f. The italics are mine.

Ronald Hepburn

'Distancing' acknowledges otherness, and others' desire or striving to persist in their own modes of being. Respect in this sense requires us to realise the fragility of processes and ecological inter-dependencies necessary to effects that we have reason to value. To respect is to steer clear of policies that may result in blundering into such harm.

But can we move, from this minimal though vital 'hands off!' requirement, to any stronger sense or senses in which nature-at-large is to be the object of our respect – and stably so? I doubt it. To speak of nature is (necessarily) to speak of the only ultimate source of all development, creativity, conscious life and freedom: yet the same nature can of course be indifferently destructive of long-evolving species, through climatic change, competitive defeat or impact of bodies from beyond the Earth. The highest organisms we know can be brought down by minute viruses; nature has no built-in means whereby to protect its own created hierarchies.

Recall the huge destruction of potentiality in nature – potentiali-ties of individual lives started and quickly brought to a frustrated end; as well as the suffering inflicted endlessly by one living thing on another. We have to incorporate in our would-be unified nature-respecting orientation an element of sadness and regret concerning the predatory entanglements of animals – deeply built-in, and with-out which they would have to be utterly different in anatomical structure, behaviour, habitat, and so in identity.

When we are checked, for instance, by reflecting that the well-being of some particular creature depends upon its preying success-fully on others for which we have no less respect and no less com-passion, a familiar instability enters our search for an fitting sustain-able attitude. Perhaps then we are simply confirming that there is to be no 'rising above ambiguity' in our attitudes to nature: no single fundamental guiding principle. Respect is checked by the inextrica-ble tangle of creative-destructive in nature. 'Respect for nature' will stave off our damaging ecological meddling, but if we allow the con-cept to advance any way towards resuming its richer positive conno-tations, we find 'respect' ill-matched to nature's operations. Of course we anthropomorphise if we call those operations 'callous' or 'stupid': but 'respect' seems poised to err in the other direction.

As in moral philosophy we may well end with an irreducible plu-rality of fundamental concepts, so here too: though there is room only to suggest what these might include. *Wonder* may not have to back down as, it seems, respect has to in some contexts. While respect, in all but its minimal sense, involves an element of acquies-cence or approval, wonder – in both questioning and appreciative modes – can be free of ontological and evaluative presuppositions.

Again, where sentient and suffering nature is concerned, our overall orientation cannot be without *compassion* as one of its key concepts. Nature-at-large cannot provide it: *we* cannot withhold it.

Respect, wonder, compassion: I suggest, then, that we need such a cluster of concepts – at least these – rather than entrust the guiding of attitudes to a single one, to be inevitably over-stretched and attenuated.[17]

V

In the first group of topics, we saw ourselves as over-against nature, and we looked to nature for 'messages' of instruction or inspiration: the emphasis was ultimately on *ourselves*, to be instructed or inspired. The second group put the emphasis upon *nature* – still seen as over-against us and distinct from us, the object of our respect, wonder, compassion. Thirdly, however, we may become aware that our situation is *not* in fact properly described as 'over-against' nature. I am not thinking of the fact, important as it is, that we exist as part and parcel of nature, not as opposed to it; but of the fact that we *create* as well as *discover* in our cognitive relation with wider nature, that we partly *constitute* the nature we experience and come to know.

Iris Murdoch showed herself sympathetic to the position that man 'saves or cherishes creation by *lending a consciousness to nature*'.[18] I would like to develop that intriguing and potent thought in my own way: we are privileged to be able to *add* to nature as it would be without us, by causing it to burgeon forth in the light of our consciousness. We organise the elements of our perceptual field – say a landscape – by way of our bodily standpoint, our selective colour-vision, our imagination's synthesising power and limits, our phenomenal 'feels' and associations, memories shared and un-shared, all of which make our experience a rich, complex and unique addition to the world.

I spoke earlier about the 'self-diminishing' that occurs if we try to limit or proscribe the flight of imagination. The point I am now

[17] There is a many-sided discussion of closely related issues in Alan Holland, 'The Use and Abuse of Ecological Concepts in Environmental Ethics', *Biodiversity and Conservation,* 4, 812–26 (1995).

[18] Iris Murdoch, *Metaphysics as a Guide to Morals*, p. 252. Timothy Sprigge has discussed overlapping topics, e.g., in *The Philosophy of the Environment*, ed. T. D. J. Chappell, p. 127. Relevant also is Mikel Dufrenne *Phénoménologie de l'expérience esthétique* (Presses Universitaires de France, 1953), II, ch. IV.

making can be seen as combating a further and serious means of self-diminishing. This takes the form of understanding the 'life-world', the un-revised world of everyday human perception, as no more than a meagre selection from the fullness of the objective world, the result of our perceptual filtering, limiting, reducing. Of course, these reductions constantly occur; but (to repeat) the range of conscious experience thereby made actual constitutes also an individual, distinctive *positive* contribution to the diversity of the world. Our experience of colour, for instance, adds a qualitative diversity that is not present in the objective-level quantitative gradation of wave-lengths of light, even though its diversifying goes on only within a very limited range.

The relationship is a symbiotic one: it is on *nature's* provision that we exercise our own perceptual-creative-imaginative efforts. Nature and ourselves are indissolubly co-authors, for instance, of our *aesthetic* experience. For we do not *invent* the features of nature-as-it-ultimately-is, by virtue of which we – with our own distinctive perceptual apparatus – can experience nature as beautiful. There is still a strong element of givenness and contingency there. More generally, the task is to avoid self-diminishing without lurching to the opposite error of exaggerating our creative role.

VI

Given an exuberant metaphysical-religious imagination, a writer may be strongly tempted to 'go over the top' and to see the human subject's contribution, great as it is, as greater still – and beyond what sober reason could endorse. We can see – and enjoy – an example of such a lyrically enhanced account in C. G. Jung's *Memories, Dreams, Reflections*, where Jung recounts his visit to an African game reserve:

> To the very brink of the horizon we saw gigantic herds of animals: gazelle, antelope, gnu, zebra, warthog … Grazing, heads nodding, the herds moved forward like slow rivers. … This was the stillness of the eternal beginning… … There the cosmic meaning of consciousness became overwhelmingly clear to me. … I, in an invisible act of creation, put the stamp of perfection on the world by giving it objective existence.
>
> Now I knew … that man is indispensable for the completion of creation; that … he is the second creator of the world, who alone has given to the world its objective existence – without which, unheard, unseen, silently eating, giving birth, dying, heads nod-

ding through hundreds of millions of years, it would have gone on in the profoundest night of non-being ... Human conscious-ness created objective existence and meaning, and man found his indispensable place in the great process of being[19]

Although it is necessarily true that before the coming of 'human consciousness' no-one had had the experience Jung describes, he is not – surely not – entitled to say that we have given 'objective exis-tence' to the world. He could – and did – speak of our *completing* the world – a completion in which the animals, their visible forms, sounds, the course of their lives, are brought together, synthesised by our imagination, understood, grasped and valued. As I have been claiming, *that* vision, together with its appreciation, *is* uniquely our work.

Nevertheless, it is surely better to risk some lyrical hyperbole than to acquiesce in a wasteful abandoning of religious values and attitudes and responses which, wrongly, we may judge to be brought down – all of them – along with the metaphysics of theism.[20]

[19] C. G. Jung, *Memories, Dreams and Reflections* (Fontana Press 1995), pp. 284f.

[20] I am grateful to members of the audience at the meeting of the Royal Institute of Philosophy on 9 October, 1998: their comments have been helpful to me in revising the lecture for publication.

On the very idea of spiritual values

JOHN HALDANE

'Vain is the word of that philosopher which does not heal any suffering of man'

Epicurean saying

I

It is unusual for an academic philosopher in the Anglo-American tradition to discuss the subject of spirituality. Not so long ago this fact might have been attributed to a general view of philosophy as the practice of conceptual analysis and the theory of logic. However in a period when the discipline has developed to a point where almost every aspect of human life has been made the subject of some department of 'applied philosophy' it could hardly be said that the subject of spirituality, in so far as discussion of it may have normative implications, lies outside the sphere of reasonable philosophical enquiry. Yet it is almost entirely neglected.

There is, of course, another reason why academic philosophers might not think to explore the area of spirituality, or having thought of it might then make a detour around it. For 'spirituality' smacks of religion, and not of the interesting metaphysical aspects that form the subject-matter of natural theology, but rather of those devotional and pietistic preoccupations that are felt to belong to the affective domain, if not to the sphere of irrationality.

Occasionally a passing philosopher will, so to speak, stop at the church door, muster his resolve and march up to the credulous man in the Clapham pew in order to point out what nonsense talk of spirituality really is. One such exercise was recently performed by Anthony Flew. In an essay entitled 'What is "Spirituality"?' he begins by looking at several terms with which the word is linked: these are '*spirited, spirit, spiritist, spiritual* and *spiritualist*'.[1] With a few brief passes of the hand he distributes these into various categories: psychological disposition (*spirited*), incorporeal substance (*spirit*), those believing in the latter (*spiritists* and *spiritualists*), and then that pertaining to higher human characteristics, or to non-earthly matters (*spiritual*). As a confirmed atheist who regards

[1] A. Flew, 'What is "Spirituality"?' in L. Brown, B. Farr and R. Hoffmann (ed.), *Modern Spiritualities: An Inquiry* (New York: Promethius Books, 1997).

John Haldane

immaterialism as absurd (i.e. as worse than false) Flew barely lingers over the incorporeal, but he dwells a while to denounce modern educationalists who favour policies of spiritual development in 'the (state) maintained school system'. Readers familiar with Professor Flew's spirited writings may feel that by this point he had been joined in the aisle by a couple of restless hobby horses.

Certainly, when educational theorists talk about 'spiritual development' they are usually either struggling to take a last dip in the shallows of the ebbing tide of faith, or engaged in the practice of aggrandising the ordinary, or else doing both at once. The appreciation of art and music and the cultivation of a concern for the feelings of others are worthwhile educational activities, but their point and value is made less and not more clear by describing them as parts of 'spiritual development'. Yet increasing numbers of educationalists are adopting this way of speaking, and requiring teachers to act upon it, specifying the need, for example, to induce in children experiences of awe and wonder.[2]

One may well ask, 'At what?'. The question that arises, of course, is whether such attitudes and others grouped under the heading of the spiritual are intelligible, save as focused upon transcendent phenomena. Even putting the point in terms of *intentional* objects and appearances, the question is whether the spiritual can be anything other than the religious. That indeed is one way of introducing the subject of this essay: Can there be non-religious spirituality? and, If so what might be its forms?

II

Within properly religious domains the 'spiritual' certainly has definite meanings. Theologically its uncontested home is Christianity in which it refers to matters concerning the indwelling of the Holy Spirit, the third person of the Trinity, whose gifts are courage, knowledge, reverence, right-judgement, understanding, wisdom and wonder and awe, and whose fruits are specified by St Paul in his *Epistle to the Galatians*. Widening out from this one may say that the spiritual life is that given to the search after an inner awareness of God, a condition pursued through prayer and meditation and attained through grace. Although this is the stuff of mystical theol-

---

[2] In this connection see *Spiritual and Moral Development – Discussion Paper* (London: National Curriculum Council, 1993) and *Social and Cultural Development* (London: Office of Standards in Teacher Education, 1994)

ogy it is not without philosophical interest for it may bear upon at least one issue that is of current concern in the philosophy of mind and action, namely the problem of mental causation. Having a mind seems to make a difference in the life of human animals: action is an expression of rational agency and there are dependencies between successive stages of psychological development. How can this be so?

Theologians (used to) write of the efficacy of 'infused' or 'sanctifying' grace by which the soul is given supernatural life, and of 'actual' or 'occasional' graces by which that life is maintained and strengthened. They were usually concerned to explain that neither violates free human agency, but rarely have they had anything to say about the nature of the (divine) causality involved. Thinking about the causal relevance of mind and of grace I have come to the conclusion that the issues are closely analogous and that an understanding of both must involve setting aside the usual mechanistic view of causation and put in its place something like the Aristotelian notions of formal and final causality. Reason and grace make a difference not by pushing or pulling but by introducing normatively significant potentialities into behaviour; potentialities the actualisation of which is discernible from a third person perspective, but which the agent is in a unique position to avow or reject. The efficacy of reason and of grace is then expressed by behaviour that is both voluntary and rational, or 'gracious'.[3]

My concern here, however, is not with the theology of grace nor with the metaphysics of causation. Rather I am interested in the possibility of non-religious spirituality, and in the thought that this may not just be philosophically credible but that it is a central aspect of philosophy itself. So far as that second idea is concerned let me say immediately that I intend it not as a sociological remark but as a philosophical one, an identification not of what academic philosophers *do* but of what philosophy itself *is*, and hence of what those who aspire to practice it *ought* to do.

III

Contemporary philosophy in the main English language countries consists overwhelmingly of logic, metaphysics, epistemology and ethics. Since there is so much of the last of these and an increasing amount of it is practically oriented, it might seem that this is the

[3] For some discussion of these ideas so far as the issue of mental causation is concerned see John Haldane, 'A Return to Form in the Philosophy of Mind, in D. Oderberg (ed.), *Form and Matter* (Oxford: Blackwell, 1999).

place to look in the expectation of finding something relevant to my interest. In fact, however, contemporary ethics is remote from the sort of thing I have in mind in thinking about non-religious spirituality. It was not always so, however, and the ancient world especially engaged in styles of reflection about conduct that bear the mark of spiritual meditations.

Before coming to that, however, let me say more about the contemporary scene. First, it is helpful to conceive moral philosophy in terms of three familiar levels of thought and discourse. At the bottom there is ordinary pre-philosophical moral thinking involving judgements in various modalities and of varying degrees of specificity about what is good and bad, right and wrong, and virtuous and vicious. At the next level there are more or less systematic structures of justification of these first level judgements (such moral theories as utilitarianism, Kantian deontology, and so on). At the third, top-most level there are philosophical accounts of the status of first-order claims and of second-level justifications (metaethical theories). The last of these levels draws on general arguments and theses in logic, metaphysics and epistemology and is not distinctly ethical in content, whereas the second is. Interestingly, however, the growth area in recent moral philosophy has been in 'applied ethics' which consists in deploying particular moral theories in relation to the problems that feature in first-order moral thinking. It is a downward movement from theory to practice.

Since I am a member of the only department of Moral Philosophy in the United Kingdom what I am about to say should not be taken as an uninformed or prejudiced dismissal, and the emphasised qualifications '*generally*' and '*often*' should be noted: applied ethics is *generally* of little intellectual value, and is *often* corrupting of the spirit of true enquiry into value and requirement. So far as the first defect is concerned, this style of thought is largely automatic. It contributes little to the identification of moral dilemmas and problems than that already accomplished by those whom they affect, and it rarely questions the adequacy of the moral theories it applies. In recent years I have often found myself involved in public discussions of first-order moral questions, and my experience has been that while philosophers *may* provide an unusual degree of conceptual organisation it is often others who have the liveliest sense of the real moral difficulties involved and the prudence to deal with them. In *general*, and for so long as my concern was practical, I would much prefer to hear from a good doctor, or priest, or school teacher, or social worker than from a professional ethicist.

The second defect – the tendency to intellectual corruption – arises from the applied nature of the exercise. There is a real sense in which the philosophical work has already been done, and this means that the applied ethicist is just working out the conclusion of a series of syllogisms whose major premises express the favoured moral theory and whose minor premises are provided by the facts of the case. This leaves out of the account the possibility that looking hard at the situation and at related ones may itself disclose moral features not previously conceptualised within the theory. In this sense applied ethics prejudges moral issues and thereby disposes the practitioner to exclude the possibility that he or she might learn something new and of general *moral* interest from attending to cases.

In this respect it differs from traditional causistry with which it is sometimes equated, for the causists were generally alive to the possibility that particular departments of human activity might have area-specific moral features whose adequate characterisation requires the formation of concepts that are not specifications of broader ones defined within a general moral theory. Certainly there are philosophers who think hard and well about moral, political and cultural issues and who make imaginative and helpful contributions to thinking about them, but this activity is not essentially philo-sophical and similar styles are often adopted by high-grade journal-ists and social commentators.[4]

What we have within contemporary academic philosophy is a good deal of necessarily technical epistemology and metaphysics, some of it deployed in metaethics; a fair amount of subtle moral theory; and considerably more applied ethics. In almost none of these areas taken individually or collectively is there scope for, let alone evidence of, anything that begins to look like spirituality. In order for that to seem surprising, however, I need to show why one should expect philoso-phy to have anything to say about this aspect of human experience.

IV

Let me offer two pathways towards this expectation: one *phenome-nological* the other *historical*. Thoreau wrote that the mass of men lead lives of quiet desperation.[5] This is a sad thought, and though it

[4] For further discussion of these matters see John Haldane, 'Applied Ethics' in N. Bunnin and E. Tsui-James (eds), *The Blackwell Companion to Philosophy* (Oxford: Blackwell, 1996). For examples of recent contributions from non-philosophers see various of the papers in John Haldane (ed.) *Philosophy and Public Affairs* (Cambridge: Cambridge University Press, 2000)

[5] Incidentally the *Oxford Dictionary of Quotations* reports that in the same year, 1854, as Thoreau first published this dictum in *Walden*, George Sand wrote (in her *Histoire de ma vie*) of Chopin as being in a state of '*dés-espérance tranquille*'.

is difficult to assess its truth there is evidence provided in imaginative literature, in the press, in doctors' surgeries, through personal acquaintance, and by knowledge of one's own circumstances, all of which suggest that many people are ill at ease with the human condition as they experience it. Many of us are desperate and many of us are sad, and the sources of our distress are not easily removed.

Certainly many privations may not befall one, but their very possibility casts a shadow across human lives. Those who are betrayed or bereaved, those who long for recognition or for love, those who experience rejection, those who fear their own impulses, those who are ill or dying, those who are clinically depressed, those who fear creeping insanity, those who feel used, those who labour with mental or physical handicaps, or who struggle with sufferers, those who are victims of injustice, all are in a position to see into the frailty of the human condition, and to see beyond the possibility of immediate and temporary relief to the facts of unredeemed suffering, weakness, solitariness and death. In the face of all of this human beings often ask whether there is any spiritual truth that might counter, alleviate or otherwise help deal with these facts, and they often suppose that it might be the task of non-religious philosophy to identify such a truth or to show that there is none. Clearly this supposition is related to the still popular belief that philosophy has something to do with the meaning of life. Such, however, is the growing ignorance within the profession of the broad history of the subject, and such has been the extent of specialisation with accompanying technicality, that many philosophers are genuinely puzzled when they encounter these expectations. The fact that 'philosophy' means love of wisdom (*philo-sophia*) will be set aside as being of purely antiquarian interest.

However not all academic philosophers are as unwelcoming to questions about the possibility of finding meaning in life (or even of finding *the* meaning of it). One who has taken them seriously is David Wiggins, who explored the first of these themes in an important lecture given some 20 years ago to the British Academy. Entitled 'Truth, Invention and the Meaning of Life', this has been the subject of some discussion but mostly for the bearing of parts of it upon certain metaethical issues. As interesting, I believe, are Wiggins' attempt to give structure to the quest for meaning and his suggestion that progress towards discerning it calls for a phenomenology of value. He writes:

Working within an intuitionism or moral phenomenology as tolerant of low-grade non-behavioural evidence as is literature (but more obsessively elaborative of the commonplace, and more theoretical, in the interpretative sense, than literature), [the theorist] has to appreciate and describe the quotidian complexity of what is experientially involved in a man's seeing a point in living. It is no use to take some existing moral theory – Utilitarianism or whatever it is – and to paste on to it such *postscripta* as the Millian insight 'It really is of importance not only what men do but what manner of men they are that do it'. ... If life's having a point is at all central to moral theory [as Wiggins had suggested it is] then room must be made for these things right from the very beginning.[6]

It is a matter of regret, I think, that Wiggins has not pursued this aspect of his important essay further. One reason for his not doing so is perhaps the thought expressed at the end of the lecture, that it is not for the theorist *qua* theorist to say what meaning consists in but only to say what finding meaning is. As a corrective to a tendency to end up preaching, this may be appropriate. However, it also suggests a residual attachment to the view that philosophy can only be conceptual analysis, and it assumes a distinction between describing an activity and engaging in it which is in some tension with the recommendation to the *theorist* (not the non-philosopher) to adopt the method of moral phenomenology. It also puts severe strain on the idea associated with Wiggins' metaethical epistemology, that certain concepts are only available to one who shares the evaluative interest they express. In other words describing what it is to find meaning may require evaluative concepts fashioned in the effort to describe the constituents of meaning itself. The two tasks may not be distinct.

More to the present point, however, is the assumption made at the very beginning of Wiggins' text, and maintained throughout it, that the issue of the meaning of life is among the central questions of moral philosophy. Whether that is true or not depends upon the scope of the expression 'moral philosophy'. One of the definitions of the term 'spiritual' identified by Flew is 'of or pertaining to the higher moral qualities'. Noting that this is offered in explanation of one of the earliest uses of the term, Flew speculates that the word '*moral*' should be interpreted as it was in the old contrast between moral and physical sciences; in other words as pertaining to higher human faculties. I am sure this is right and it is a closely related sense that survives in the title of the department at St Andrews. Unsurprisingly, therefore, courses in 'Moral Philosophy' there include the philosophies of mind and action, aesthetics and the

---

[6] 'Truth, Invention and the Meaning of Life' in D. Wiggins, *Needs, Values, Truth* (Oxford: Balackwell, 1987), pp. 136–7.

philosophy of religion as well as moral problems, moral theory, meta-ethics, political philosophy and the philosophy of law. In this very wide sense the meaning of life may be a subject for moral philosophy, but it is clear from what he writes that Wiggins in thinking more narrowly and locating it within *moral theory*.

Let me suggest that this is inappropriate and that one consequence of placing the topic there is that it is unlikely to receive the attention it needs. This indeed may be part of the reason why this aspect of Wiggin's lecture has not been pursued by moral theorists. The relevant point is best developed by returning to the attempt to identify non-religious spirituality as a subject for philosophical attention. Hearing that someone was interested in this a philosopher might well direct them to ethics, or perhaps to aesthetics having in mind experiences of the sublime. But, if I am right, spirituality is not to be located entirely within either or these domains or even in their union. If we confine ourselves to these fields, we shall not make much progress in answering the question of whether there is anything philosophy can offer to cure, alleviate or confirm the quiet desperation felt by many as they experience what life brings before them, or to validate the sense that some have that all can be well.

V

I have already indicated why one might not hope for much from applied ethics or from metaethics. For while the latter is substantial it is not itself normative but analytical and ontological, and while the former is normative it does not provide a theory of value but presumes one or another such account. Moral theory itself may seem more promising, but while it is certainly concerned with value and requirement its domain is essentially that of right conduct in relation to moral subjects, and this is only a part of spirituality and perhaps then only *per accidens*.

I might have said, less carefully, that morality concerns norms of conduct regulating *interpersonal* relations. That would have passed muster at one time, but now it would be judged question-begging so far as concerns the rights of animals and duties to oneself. Of course, neither of these examples is uncontentious, yet they can probably be accommodated by speaking of intersubjective relations. I would say that so far as the first is concerned if we now believe that non-human animals have rights that is because we have come to view them as members of an enlarged community of moral subjects. One might attempt the same analysis with regard to non-sentient nature; but that is certainly more strained, which I take to be reason for thinking that the extension of rights to trees and valleys is untenable. This is not to say, of course, that there are no environmental values. The idea of duties to oneself is more problematic. Some sense might be made of it by regarding people as temporally and aspectually structured objects. Thus one might contend that the claim that Oliver has a duty to himself, to stay sober say, is to be analysed as holding that Oliver at t^1 has a duty in respect of Oliver at t^2; or again that Oliver *qua* party guest has a duty to Oliver *qua* driver. (Intoxication rarely being instantaneous this latter analysis will also involve temporal slices or indexes.) But this dubious ontology is a high price to pay for saving a notion that may have little to recommend it.

The idea that morality is definable in terms of interpersonal conduct, intersubjective relations or, in my preferred account, right conduct in relation to moral subjects, is given support by the form and content of moral theories. This is not the occasion for an exhaustive survey so allow me to refer only to the two main categories, namely consequentialism and deontology. Although they differ in their account of the primary objects of assessment – the former favouring effected states of affairs, the latter actions; they share a list of the candidates for evaluation, namely intention, action and outcome. In short they agree that a moral theory is a theory of *conduct* and they offer as guiding principles the well-being (happiness) or standing (autonomy) of those included within the scope of action.

At this point someone might agree that neither of the dominant styles of moral theorising seems suited to make sense of those fears and anxieties that constitute the quiet desperation of mankind, let alone to alleviate or to confirm them or again to make sense of the hopes men have that the cultivation of spiritual values may bring peace of heart and mind. Yet they may suggest that I have omitted an important range of moral theories that are designed to embrace this sort of thing, namely *virtue ethics*.

The merit of the appeal to virtue, as it was made first in analytical philosophy by Elizabeth Anscombe and related neo-Aristotelians, was in part that it suggested a way of acknowledging that not everything is down to the maximisation of happiness, while also allowing that what one should feel and do are not duties of pure reason or cosmic prescriptions, but may be grounded in naturally discernible facts about what is of benefit to rational animals. A further aspect of its merit and the one most emphasised in recent years is the suggestion that an ethic of virtue is not committed to codifiable and abstract rules of conduct but can locate the ethical in the broader constitution of human agency, taking account of character, emotion, social context and even of fortune and misfortune.

John Haldane

All of this is to the good but it does not alter the fact that contemporary virtue theory is presented by its advocates as an account of *morality*, which is to say it is offered as an alternative to consequentialism and deontology as providing an account of right conduct. In emphasising the importance of emotion and of character generally, and in allowing reasoning about action to give equal place to the interests of the agent, it is certainly a much richer theory, but it remains a normative account of practical reasoning primarily in the sphere of intersubjective relations. Whether others are involved in one's actual deliberations is a contingent matter but a moral theory has, of its nature, to be able to give account of rightness and wrongness under such social headings as charity, justice and honesty. That is what virtue theory claims to do and that is why it remains first and foremost a theory of *morality*.

My suggestion, however, has been that there is a further area of human existence, the spiritual, which is not essentially concerned with action in relation to the rights and interests of others and which has something to do with how one experiences the world and with what one makes of that experience. It is, I suggest, primarily a matter of what *personal demeanour* or mode of being one develops in the face of reality as one understands it in some more or less philosophical way. Earlier I mentioned that in antiquity the existence of such matters was recognised and catered for within philosophy and I shall touch on this shortly, but first let me anticipate and set aside another attempt to reduce the spiritual to a more familiar category of value.

VI

A focus on experience and on the contemplation of it, instead of on conduct, may prompt the thought that what I am looking for is in fact already a subject of extensive study within the area of philosophical aesthetics. No doubt part of what is liable to be included within spirituality, such as a cultivation of the sense of the glory of nature, overlaps with the proper business of aesthetics. As with the attempt to locate spirituality in moral theory, however, much will be left behind if one hives off what can plausibly be dealt with under the heading of the theory of beauty and related categories. Meanwhile an expansion of the idea of the aesthetic to include the philosophy of adversity, despair, reconciliation and hope, etc. will undermine its claim to have a well-defined subject matter. To one side lies the error of inappropriate aestheticisation, and to the other lies the danger of a loss of identity for aesthetics itself.

Of course, these remarks presuppose some account of the aesthetic. It is that which, notwithstanding various challenges, has occupied the central ground since the subject was born in the eighteenth century. Abstracting from detail, the aesthetic involves pleasure or disgust taken in the contemplation of things regarded as objects of experience not essentially connected with practical interests.[7] One may certainly view events in one's life and recurrent aspects of the human condition in that way, but since life is something to be lived, or for some poor souls something to be abandoned, to view it in that way is to be disengaged from it. Spirituality as I am concerned with it, however, and the meaning of life as that exercised Wiggins, are certainly not to be identified with disengagement. Stepping back may be in order but the point of it will typically be to step forward again so as to make some readjustment in one's demeanour and in the pattern of one's living.

To summarise: there seems little difficulty in understanding the idea of spirituality and of the spiritual life within the context of religious thought. In Christianity especially these are given definite content by reference to the indwelling of the Holy Spirit and to practices of prayer, meditation and devotion by which the soul progressively partakes in the life of God – not substantially but relationally as an adopted child might increasingly partake in the life of a family.[8]

When we turn to (non-religious) philosophy, however, a question arises whether any form of spirituality can find a home there. Yet even the most cursory reflection upon human experience, and on the efforts of great writers and others to give expression to it, suggests that there is a domain of thought, feeling and action that is concerned with discerning the ultimate truth about the human condition and with cultivating an appropriate mode of being or demeanour in response to that truth. The phenomenology is compelling, the concerns are intelligible, and for some reason intelligent people persist in supposing that it must be a central part of philosophy to deal with these matters and therefore look to it to do so.

Philosophers themselves, at least academics in the dominant

[7] Although this type of account of aesthetic attitude and experience is associated with Kant and other Enlightenment and post-enlightenment authors it is anticipated in the middle ages. Aquinas, for example, writes that 'good means that which simply pleases the appetite, while the beautiful is something pleasant to apprehend', *Summa Theologiae* (London: Washbourne, 1914) Ia, IIae, q.17, a1 ad 3.

[8] I use the analogy of participation in the life of a family rather than that of a parent given that in Christian mystical theology partaking in the life of God involves entering into the mutual Divine life of three persons.

John Haldane

Anglo-American tradition, either ignore such appeals as one might the entreaties of a door-to-door evangelist; suggest they are confused in ways similar to those in which some metaphysicians suggest that people are mixed up when they ask about first or ultimate causes; or else, if they are inclined to grant something to the claim that questions of non-religious meaning and spirit do arise and call for attention, they point to moral theory or possibly to aesthetics as being the relevant departments to visit.

I have argued that while this last option has the merit of recognising that there is something to be catered for, it makes a mistake in consigning it to moral philosophy as this is now understood, for that is concerned essentially with rightness of conduct, and first and foremost with conduct bearing upon other moral subjects. Notwithstanding its welcome breadth, contemporary virtue ethics remains a version of moral theory and as such is concerned principally with action. Likewise, aesthetics is concerned principally with disinterested contemplation of objects of experience. Spirituality involves intellect, will and emotion and is essentially contemplative, but the process of discovering the nature of reality, evaluating its implications for the human condition and cultivating an appropriate demeanour in the face of these is not reducible to ethics, nor to aesthetics. Yet unless philosophers can show this enterprise to be confused or exclusively religious they are open to the charge of neglecting something of fundamental, indeed perhaps of ultimate human importance.

VII

Earlier I commended Wiggins for at least engaging the question of life's meaning. Let me next draw upon an interesting essay (again originating in a lecture as it happens), by Anthony Quinton entitled 'Character and Will'. In his perceptive and witty discussion Quinton practices what he allows may have the appearance of 'lexicographical needlework' in familiar Oxford style, sorting out the differences between the closely related concepts of *personality*, *temperament* and *character*. Then he turns to consider the 'distinctly marginal, even furtive, role [of character and will] in organised [i.e. philosophical] thinking about morality'.[9]

What Quinton says about character is very useful for my purposes and it suggests that while he locates the formation and reformation of the self within the domain of moral philosophy he might be

[9] Anthony Quinton, 'Character and Will', in *From Woodhouse to Wittgenstein* (Manchester: Carcanet, 1998) p. 39.

persuaded, as I hope might Wiggins, that it is better to mark out a new field of study bearing the title the philosophy of spirituality (I might have preferred 'the philosophy of spirit' but that is already taken and has particular and not necessarily helpful connotations).

Quinton relates *personality*, *temperament* and *character* in point of their depth, stability and malleability within the structure of the human psyche. In this scheme *personality* lies on the surface, being a matter of manner or style, though clearly linked to something deeper. *Temperament* is the most stable element within personality and consists in broad orientations towards optimism and pessimism, sociability and solitariness, and so on. *Character* is more deeply rooted than personality and may be viewed as an enduring (though not unchangeable) structure of acquired habits of feeling and choice. I would add that it includes, at least in its deepened form, tendencies towards and away from significant recurrent features of human life. Indeed, strength of character is central to what I have called 'demeanour'.

Quinton's discussion harks back to the normative psychology of Plato and Aristotle, and in keeping with that tradition he considers the relation between character and virtue, concluding that while character takes on habits of affection and will, it is not as such virtuous or vicious in the sense that one does not know simply on account of knowing that someone has a character (as of necessity they will have) whether it is a good or bad one. Good character is one whose habituated dispositions are toward things of positive value; bad character one whose habits are orientated towards the negative.

For my own purposes I have chosen to speak of positive and negative *values* rather than of good and bad *ends*, because the latter are too readily interpreted in moral terms. More to the point, although Quinton refers these issues to moral philosophy he notes that his favoured notion of character comprises *three* of the four main Platonic virtues – prudence, courage and moderation – but expresses some doubt about the inclusion of justice conceived of as 'the self-denying supression of one's own interests for the sake of people other than oneself'.[10] The point, of course, is not to deny the value of justice but to question whether it is central to the subject of study, viz. *character*. I share this doubt and I am now in a position to suggest why it is apt. For justice is centrally a matter for moral philosophy, i.e. for moral theory, while the study of character theory is principally the philosophy of spirituality.

[10] Ibid., p. 42.

John Haldane

VIII

I promised some historical support for the claim that quiet desperation and other non-eccentric conditions of the soul or psyche are proper subjects for philosophy and I mentioned the period of classical antiquity. Plato and Aristotle have already made a brief appearance but of greater relevance are the Stoics. In the ages of Greece and Rome, Stoicism came in three phases: (i) the *Old Stoicism* of Zeno, Cleanthes and Chrysippus, the last of whom provided its most systematic formulation; (ii) the *Middle Stoicism* of Posidonius; and (iii) the *Late Stoicism* of Seneca, Epictetus and Marcus Aurelius. Like the Epicureans the Stoics were concerned with *ataraxia* (untroubledness), though their diagnoses of its causes, the form of their remedies and the exact understanding of good psychic health, all differ. Also there are significant and sometimes understated differences between Stoics of the three periods. In general, whereas the early practitioners were materialistic monists of atheist or pantheist orientation, Stoicism of the late period seems to accommodate the suggestion of a transcendent deity and to be dualistic. What unites the various strands, however, is a view about the tasks of philosophy and the need to cultivate inner peace.

The French classical scholar and historian of philosophy Pierre Hadot has made a series of very interesting studies of the aims and methods of the six ancient schools of philosophy, *viz. Stoicism, Epicureanism, Platonism, Aristotelianism, Cynicism* and *Pyrrhorism*, arguing that each reflects and in turn seeks to develop a permanent possibility of the human spirit. These studies have been collected and translated into English under the title *Philosophy as a Way of Life* and I strongly recommend them.[11] I shall not even attempt to summarise his many conclusions but I do want to extract one or two points so as to advance my own discussion.

First, then, Hadot discerns in the various ancient traditions, but especially in the Stoics, a distinction between '*philosophy*' (*philosophia* conceived of as the formation of the soul; or in Quinton's terms the deep structure of character, with the addition of an orientation towards the good), and *discourse about philosophy* (understood as the investigation of the nature of things, and to a lesser extent our knowledge of them). This, of course, is related to the more familiar distinction between practical and speculative philosophy. But whereas modern, recent and contemporary thought has invested greatest effort and talent in the pursuit of speculation in the form of epistemology and metaphysics, the ancients, and again

[11] See P. Hadot, *Philosophy as a Way of Life: Spiritual Exercises from Socrates to Foucault* (ed. A. I. Davidson) (Oxford: Blackwell, 1995).

I am focusing on the Stoics, give priority to thinking about practice, and within that to the cultivation of wisdom and the development of the spiritual life. Epictetus observes that 'the lecture room of the philosopher is a hospital'[12] which is to say that his work is the cure of souls. Later he writes:

> How shall I free myself? have you not heard it taught that you ought to eliminate desire entirely? ... give up everything ... for if you once deviate from your course, you are a slave, you are a subject.[13]

Hadot's reading of such texts is both informed and imaginative. It also encourages him to make three claims of great interest. First, he construes much more of the writing of antiquity as belonging to philosophy, in the sense of the practice of wisdom, than has been common among historians of ancient philosophy. More precisely and more strikingly he argues that these texts concern and in some cases *are* spiritual exercises. Second, and in direct opposition to the assumption which I mentioned at the outset that the notion of spirituality is in origin a religious one, he claims that in fact Christianity appropriated this area of reflective practice from pre-existing philosophical traditions, and even that it took over 'as its own certain techniques of spiritual exercises as they had already been practiced in antiquity'.[14] Third, he implies that the historical interest of all of this is perhaps its least significant aspect. In an essay responding to Foucault's use of his earlier work Hadot writes:

> I think modern man can practice the spiritual exercises of antiquity, at the same time separating them from the philosophical [metaphysical] or mythic discourse which came along with them. The same spiritual exercises can, in fact, be justified by extremely diverse philosophical discourses. These latter are nothing but clumsy attempts, coming after the fact, to describe and justify inner experiences whose existential security is not, in the last analysis, susceptible of any attempts at theorisation or systematisation. ... It is therefore not necessary to believe in the Stoic's nature or universal reason. Rather as one lives concretely according to reason. In the words of Marcus Aurelius 'Although everything happens at random, don't you, too, act at random'. In this way, we can accede concretely to the universality of the cosmic perspective, and the wonderful mystery of the presence of the universe.[15]

[12] *The Discourses of Epictetus* (ed.) C. Gill (London: Everyman, 1995) 3, 23, 30.

[13] Ibid., 4, 4, 33.

[14] Hadot, *Philosophy*, p. 206.

[15] 'Reflections on the Idea of the "Cultivation of the Self"' in Hadot, *Philosophy*, p. 212.

John Haldane

This passage is full of promise, but a few comments are called for. First, the exercises he refers to, what Foucault called '*pratiques de soi*' (practices of the self)[16] are designed to liberate one from (inappropriate) attachment to exterior objects and the pleasures deriving from them. By regular self-examination one keeps a check on the tendency to exteriority, and by contemplating the impermanence of things one seeks to master or to possess oneself, attaining happiness in interior formation. Writing-up this examination, or better, perhaps, examining through writing is one form of spiritual exercise.

Where Hadot takes issue with Foucault is in claiming with the ancient authors (including Plotinus) that the movement toward interiorisation is 'inseparably linked to another movement, whereby one rises to a higher psychic level, at which one encounters another kind of exteriorisation, another relationship with the 'exterior' – or what one might term the 'real'.[17] Without necessarily wishing to reject it, one may reasonably call for further specification of this transcendent movement. A major direction of development is likely to lead to the inexpressibility of the mystical encounter with the 'One', but other possibilities suggest themselves, including moderate versions of Platonist ontology and even naturalistic Aristotelianism. I shall comment on this in a moment, but first let me voice a reservation about the claim that spiritual formation may proceed independently of the truth of the accompanying philosophical discourse (metaphysics).

Presumably even Hadot thinks there are some limits to just how wrong one can be at the speculative level while keeping on track in the practice of wisdom. Also there is reason to tie the two together as constituent components of a single enterprise, such that the content of spiritual formation is dependent upon its metaphysical compliment. The argument for this is quite straightforward. I have spoken at various points of spirituality as involving an appropriate demeanour. It may now be asked 'appropriate to what?'.

One reason for my believing that the issue of spirituality arises within philosophy is reflection on a parallel relationship between religious belief and practice. Suppose someone was persuaded by philosophical or historical arguments that the God of Christian theism exists, but that he or she then seemed wholly unmoved by this acceptance. One would be inclined to say, I think, that religiously speaking the thing (conversion) has not yet begun. For *that* belief requires the formation of a demeanour appropriate to its content. Likewise I wish to say that a reductive materialist who really

[16] See M. Foucault, *History of Sexuality,* trans. R. Hurley (New York, 1984) Vol. III.

[17] Hadot, *Philosophy*, p. 211.

believes that his philosophy gives the ultimate truth about reality should be moved (by reason) to ask how in the face of this immensely significant belief he or she should compose themselves. It seems unintelligible to suppose that *nothing* follows for the enquirer from arriving at a fundamental view of reality be it physicalist or theist. Not only does the question arise of how to compose one's spirit in the face of this, but the content of the metaphysical belief must condition the character of the resulting demeanour. The believer in Christian theism will be moved towards familiar Christian religious practices, and the reductive physicalist whose metaphysics is after all not so very different from that of the Old Stoics may wish to explore their spirituality. I think, therefore, that Hadot is wrong to try to loosen the link between philosophy and philosophical discourse; spirituality and metaphysics go together as I believe the writers of antiquity would agree.

IX

Finally, and briefly, I turn to the themes of consolation or abandonment. Both terms refer to books each great in its own way and each well worth reading for the wisdom they contain. The first is, of course, Boethius' *Consolation of Philosophy*, a work of the early sixth century inspired by stoicism and Neo-Platonism. The second is far less well-known. It is the *Self-Abandonment to Divine Providence* of Jeanne Pierre de Caussade, a French Jesuit of the seventeenth and eighteenth centuries. In fact the *Abandonment* was never written as a book but was composed posthumously from a series of works and letters addressed to members of a community of Visitation Nuns in Nancy for which Caussade acted as a spiritual director.[18]

I have written about Boethius' Consolation elsewhere[19] and here I can only pick up one thread. This is the idea familiar from Platonism that whatever the contingencies that affect us, however bogged down we may become in material things, we have the power to engage intellectually with transcendent realities outside of space and time. Whether these be numbers or geometrical forms, essences or universal natures, they lie beyond fortune and misfortune, and in coming into contact with them we too are raised up, if not wholly or permanently at least for so long as intel-

[18] Jeanne-Pierre de Caussade, *Abandonment to Divine Providence* (trans. J. Beevers) (New York: Image, Doubleday, 1975).
[19] John Haldane, 'De Consolatione Philosophiae', in M. McGhee (ed.), *Philosophy, Religion and the Spiritual Life* (Cambridge University Press, 1992).

John Haldane

lectual contemplation endures. That is one kind of spirituality. Whether we can avail ourselves of it depends on the truth of its metaphysics; but, even if we can, happiness through intellection is surely redemption for the few.

Caussade by contrast is concerned to emphasise the universal accessibility of the spiritual values offered by Christian theism.

> If the business of becoming holy seems to present unsufferable difficulties, it is merely because we have a wrong idea about it. In reality, holiness consists in one thing only: complete loyalty to God's will. Everyone can practice this loyalty, whether actively or passively.
>
> To be actively loyal means obeying the Laws of God and the Church and fulfilling all the duties imposed on us by our way of life. Passive loyalty means that we loyally accept everything God sends us at each moment of the day ... To be passively loyal is even easier since it implies only that we accept what often we cannot avoid, and endure with love and resignation things which could cause us weariness and disgust. Once again this is what being holy means. ... But what is the seecret of finding this treasure? There isn't one. The treasure is everywhere. It is offered to us all the time and wherever we are. All creatures, friends or foes, pour it out in abundance, and it flows through every fibre of our body and soul until it reaches the very core of our being. ... This is the true spirituality which is valid for all times and for everybody ... It is the ready acceptance of all that comes to us at each moment of our lives.[20]

Of course, whether in the form in which it is provided it is valid for all times and for everybody depends on the truth of certain religious doctrines and this is not the place to assess those. However, I will end with two related questions. If the form of this spirituality seems attractive even to the non-religious can some version of it be refashioned on a non-theological world view? There is some reason for thinking that this may be possible. Suppose, however, that is not. This raises the second question. If it should seem after all that the necessary condition for the possibility of spirituality is some religious truth, and if the need and possibility of spirituality should seem compelling, then might we have the beginnings of an argument for religion?

Academic philosophy has travelled far from the concern of its founding fathers to provide a guide to life. Along the way it has lost sight of the very idea of spiritual values, and in its current phase it may have difficulty recovering or refashioning this idea. This very

[20] Caussade, *Abandonment*, pp. 24–6.

70

fact deserves to be examined and that examination might itself mark the beginning of a form of philosophical-cum-spiritual exercise: nothing less than an assessment of the value of what we currently practice in the name of philosophy.

The divine mind

JOHN LESLIE

I

By 'a blank', let us mean a situation including no actual existents: nothing beyond such platonic realities as that three groups of five apples, were there to exist such groups, *would contain* fifteen apples in total. Now, why is there a world and not a blank?

Could God be the reason? How could God be more than a reasonlessly existing magician, his acts of wishing for things just chancing to be followed by their leaping into being?

One way out of this maze is to deny that the realm of existents – of whatever possibilities have been actualised, for instance actual apples – is anything to get excited about. There had either to be no existents or else one or more of them. The second of these alternatives happens to be the case. That is what many philosophers now say. They typically add that this second alternative, the presence of some existents, could not have been in any way forced. 'Necessary being' is a nonsensical phrase, they maintain, unless applied merely to the shadowy kind of being possessed by platonic realities you simply could not get rid of, such as the reality concerning the three groups of possible apples.

For years I have defended another approach. Platonic realities are no less real for being 'shadowy'. Among them are realities of *ethically required existence*. In an ethical way, it can be required that this or that actually exist instead of just being a possibility. Whether or not there was anything in existence, the existence of various things could be ethically needful. An absence of all existents would be tragic because there might have been a good situation instead. Now, a situation which was sufficiently good – one which would not be rather a shame because something far better could be there in its place – might have an existence *required ethically and with creative effect*. Without contradiction or other absurdity, something's goodness might bear responsibility for that something's being more than merely possible.

This creation story is suggested in Book VI of Plato's *Republic*. The Form of the Good, we are told, 'is itself not existence but far beyond existence in dignity', for it is 'what bestows existence upon things'. Here are some ways in which the story could be developed:

73

(i) An absence of all existents truly would be tragic. Do not protest that it could be in some respects fortunate, for I am not concerned to deny that here. It too could be true. Yes, in the absence of all existents an ethical requirement could still have been fortunately fulfilled, namely, the requirement that there *not* exist an atrocious situation, of immense negative value: a world, perhaps, consisting solely of people in torment. But this just helps show that even in a blank there could be real ethical requirements. You do not need to have someone actually there, able to shudder at the thought of a world of people in torment and burdened by a duty to prevent its existence, to *give reality to* any ethical need for it not to exist.

(ii) No examination of concepts can prove that whatever is ethically required must actually be the case. For a start, ethical requirements might enter into conflict with one another, this guaranteeing that numerous ethical requirements *would not* be fulfilled. Moreover, not even a supremely good situation could be proved to exist just by pointing out that 'having goodness' means 'being something whose existence is to some extent ethically required'. The concepts of *ethically required existence* and of *effectively required existence* are two concepts, not one. So far as mere concepts are concerned, every single ethical requirement might fail to be satisfied.

(iii) None the less, there is no conceptual confusion in the platonic theme that an ethical requirement *by itself* might be responsible for something's existence. Think of what people have often held about divine commands. Divine commands, requirements that various situations were to exist, would be creatively effective, it has often been believed, even if those situations were 'marked out for existence' or 'required' *not in the least in themselves, but only through the divine will*. I can detect no actual contradiction in this, bizarre though many people might think it. All the less do I detect one in the idea that an ethical requiredness necessarily possessed by some possible thing or things – possessed as a matter of eternal platonic fact – was creatively sufficient.

(iv) It could be wrong to keep asking what *gave* such requiredness its creative power, for the platonic theory just is that nothing would give it power in the sense of *standing outside it and making it creatively effective*. It would be the ethical requiredness itself which was creatively effective. Compare, perhaps, the wrongness of asking what *gives* to the colour red its ability to be nearer to purple than to blue. The sheer fact that the creative power *was not logically necessary* would not prove that it could not be necessary in an absolute way. The doctrine that the only absolute necessities are logical necessities, like the necessity of there not being round squares, could seem severely mistaken. It could, for instance, seem necessary in an absolute way that a world of a certain sort would be better than a blank, yet how could a logician possibly demonstrate this? So far as logic was concerned, might not a sceptic be right in thinking that ordinary concepts of good and bad corresponded to mere illusions? Again, it seems not to be mere logic that makes red nearer to purple than to blue.

(v) Suppose you accepted that the creative success of some ethical requirement was at least a logical possibility. There would then be no reason for you to think that its success *would be any more complicated* than its failure. The matter would be eternally fixed in the one way or the other, and neither would be simpler than the other. Neither would be a question of clockwork whirring, engineers or major-generals hatching production or annihilation plans, magicians exerting willpower, etcetera.

(vi) This need not be an attempt to get rid of a divine designer and world-creator. A. C. Ewing, possibly the greatest idealist philosopher of the twentieth century, speculated in chapter 7 of his *Value and Reality* (1973) that the existence of a divine person could be due directly to the ethical requirement for such a person to exist. Any powers had by this person might, I suggest, be explained in a similar fashion. Granted that the divine being was supremely good, and thus unable to will evil things, it might be ethically required that the being be divine not merely through having omniscience, but through being omnipotent too. Saying that the being's existence and powers were in this way explicable – explicable, that is, by reference to the being's own eternal ethical requiredness – would surely be no great insult. If anything, would not the insult lie in fancying instead that the divine being was, and was powerful, for no reason whatever? However, it is not at all clear that belief in God must involve accepting some world-creating person. Western theology includes a long neoplatonic tradition. According to this, God is not a divine person or any other existent. God is instead the creative ground of all being, a ground which is ethical in character. In my terminology, God would in this case be *the creative ethical requiredness of the cosmos*.

Two questions now arise. First, For a cosmos to be dramatically good, what would it have to contain? An omniscient mind, for instance? And second, While some cosmos might be explicable in terms of its creative ethical requiredness, may not ours contain far too much evil?

John Leslie

II

The Problem of Evil would seem much the same whether you believed that God was a supremely good, all-powerful person who permitted evil, or whether you instead used the word 'God' neoplatonically as a name for the fact that the cosmos existed because of its ethical requiredness.

Here are ways in which the problem might be reduced:

(a) Evils might be the results of conflicts between goods. For instance, the good of free decision-making might enter into conflict with the good of acting well *because somebody freely decided to act badly*. Regardless of whether we thought freedom incompatible with obedience to the laws of physics, we could all accept this.

(b) Einstein wrote that the world has 'a four-dimensional existence'. Many take him seriously. People of past ages are not alive today, but this could be closely analogous to the fact that people living in Canada are not living in Britain. Death might then be less of an evil than first appearances suggest.

(c) We might doubt whether our world's elements should be evaluated each in isolation. Perhaps our world is a whole as imagined by Spinoza, a 'monistic' whole. Like the length, the mass and the hardness of a stone, the parts of such a whole would be logically incapable of existing *each in isolation from the others*.

(d) We could insist that 'the cosmos' might mean far more than just the one universe: a single system of causally connected things all obeying the same physical laws. Many cosmologists dislike using the word 'universe' as a synonym for 'absolutely everything'. They speculate that there exist up to infinitely many universes having little or no causal contact with one another, and perhaps obeying different laws.[1] Ours might be far from the best.

(e) Whether or not they were in causal interaction, any number of universes could be included in a single monistic whole, its parts incapable of independent existence. The resulting whole might be infinitely complex, and so could be of infinite value. And perhaps such monistic wholes are themselves infinitely numerous.

Monistic wholes of this kind, in infinite numbers, were pictured in chapter 11 of *Value and Existence,* a neoplatonic book of mine. But may not my picture have been of altogether too shabby a situation? Even making each monistic whole of infinite value might not be sufficient.

[1] I discuss this in *Universes* (Routledge: London and New York, 1989; paperback 1996).

Imagine infinitely many islands each bearing one slightly happy person. This situation could well be infinitely good, yet is there not a clear enough way in which another could be better? Might there not be the same islands with two tremendously happy people on each? Even when quantity is infinite, quality can be important. Now, if Plato is right and The Good is in charge of everything, then why not expect the existence of a divine mind, aware of absolutely all truths or at least of all the ones worth knowing? And why not then complain about my imagined infinity of monistic wholes, each perhaps infinitely complex, that they would better be replaced by infinitely many minds of just that type? Why would anything else exist? Why you and me, and the rest of our universe?

The traditional western picture is of a single omniscient mind. The idea that there could be two or more of them is rejected on several grounds. It is held that God's glory would be reduced if it had any rival. Or it is complained that there cannot be more than one infinity because 'infinite' must mean 'including everything'. Or it is protested that, once there was one divine mind, any other minds would have to be different and inferior since, as the Principle of Identity of Indiscernibles tells us, precise duplicates of anything are logically impossible. Now, my suspicion is that all these objections fail.

However, their failure perhaps would not destroy a platonic or neoplatonic creation story. For you and I could perhaps believe, as Spinoza apparently did, that we and all the things we experienced were simply elements in a mind worth calling 'divine'. Moreover, might there not be infinitely many such minds?

III

It could be judged excessively untraditional to speak of many minds, each 'divine'. In western theology there is only one divinity. Let me therefore fight simply for the idea that there could be infinitely many minds, each knowing everything worth knowing. I myself would then attach the label '*the* divine mind' to just one of these, the one with which I thought my own existence particularly closely linked, much as cosmologists speak of the universe they inhabit as 'the' universe even when believing that there exists many another universe. In the next breath I could talk of 'many divine minds'. No inconsistency there! However, if others preferred to use the words 'divine mind' only of something believed to be unique, then it would be pointless to quarrel with them. My use of the words would simply be different.

But now, how about the argument that multiplying divine minds would reduce the glory of each? This is worth a quarrel, I suggest. Why should being unique be counted as glorious? How could a mind's knowledge be any the less worth having, merely through some other mind having it as well?

Again, why should being infinitely great have to mean 'including everything'? The mathematical idea of infinity, at any rate, allows there to be more than one infinity: the infinity of the odd numbers, for instance, and the infinity of the even numbers as well. Also, people often call a divine mind 'infinitely great' without following Spinoza. The divine mind they believe in is not *absolutely everything*. They think they exist outside it. And finally, if it were objected that two identical existents, each allegedly infinitely great, could readily be surpassed by something which combined the two into a single monistic whole, then my answer would be that No, they could not be combined in this manner, granted that they were identical. *Inside* any monistic whole – defined, remember, as a whole whose components are logically incapable of existing separately – Identity of Indiscernibles is clearly right. For an analogy, consider a stone which has mass, solidity, a length of five inches, *and also* a length of five inches. That is nonsense, is it not? A length of five inches can be had by any one stone only once.

The controversial issue is whether Identity of Indiscernibles remains right when applied to things whose existence is truly separate. If it remains right, then presumably there could be only one mind which was as good as possible, for instance by knowing everything. Any other mind would have to be different and therefore presumably inferior.

Notice that the difference between the supremely good mind and various rivals might be very slight. The supremely good mind might contemplate absolutely all truths, of which there are presumably infinitely many. [Not just truths about some restricted realm of actual things. Truths about all that is either actual or possible.] Or, if not all truths were worth contemplating, it could at least contemplate all that were. Those too would be infinitely many, would they not? Each of an infinity of closely similar minds could then fail to contemplate just one of the truths: a different truth in each case. This would seem to make each such mind only infinitesimally inferior to the very best one.

In point of fact, however, Identity of Indiscernibles would seem to fail when applied to things separate in their existence. Imagine a reality consisting solely of two iron spheres in a space which is otherwise empty. The spheres differ in one trivial respect: the exact position inside each of the iron atom nearest its centre. Imagine also that time is flowing in the way Einstein rejected. When situations 'flow into the past' they are wiped out of existence. The two iron atoms making the spheres different now move, each to the very centre of its sphere. All contrast between the spheres is thereby ended (for in the situation as imagined it makes no sense to call one sphere 'on the left', the other 'on the right'). Does this mean that the spheres cannot continue to be two? That one of them has to vanish, or that there must come to be only one sphere without either of them vanishing? This strikes me as too paradoxical. Identity of Indiscernibles cannot apply here.

If that is right, then a situation consisting simply of infinitely many minds that were identical, minds which knew everything worth knowing, would seem to be a possibility – and, what's more, the very best possibility. So, one might well think, anybody with a creation story inspired by Plato had better argue that you and I could be elements in just such a situation. He or she had better make use of some of Spinoza's ideas.

IV

Ideas defensible even today, but recognisably 'spinozistic', could perhaps run as follows:

(a) There is a divine mind, an eternal, immensely complicated reality which yet manages to be a monistic whole. It is, in other words, fully unified in its existence despite its tremendous complexity. In a perpetual act of contemplation, this mind considers all the intricate details which must be found in a universe obeying the laws which ours does. Now, the mind's contemplation does not consist just in considering *an excellent mental model of* such a universe. How, after all, do physicists describe physical reality? Not with useless phrases such as 'honest-to-goodness stuff', but in terms of its intricate pattern. If successfully picturing every element of a physical world, would not a mind have created – inside itself – a pattern of precisely the sort which physicists describe, and could this not then be a world every bit good enough to count as 'physical'? The actual existence of physical objects, in all their intricacy, *is simply the divine mind's picturing that intricacy in full detail*. Spinoza writes that God has the attributes of thought and of materiality, and that the pattern of ideas is the same as the pattern of things, but I make no claim to be interpreting his difficult words correctly. I think there is no such animal as 'the correct interpretation' of his system, gleaming in its consistency. My suggestion is only that physical reality could reasonably be understood in the way outlined, and that we could call the resulting world-picture 'spinozistic' without being unreasonable.

(b) As well as contemplating all the physical details of inanimate matter, the divine mind thinks about the mental states of each conscious being inhabiting our world. It contemplates 'what it is like', i.e., *what it feels like*, to have these mental states. No doubt they are the states of brains, physical objects with an intricacy which includes not just hugely many connections between elements such as nerve cells, but also all the complexity of individual molecules, atoms, electrons, quarks, superstrings, etcetera. Still, for a brain state to be known to itself in full physical detail would be a miracle. Intelligent brains have to know something about themselves – they have to keep track of their own workings – but a brain's everyday knowledge of itself is knowledge only of some of the activity-patterns inside it, so that the Greeks were no fools when they speculated that conscious life took place in the liver rather than in the head. Now, the divine mind thinks about precisely these activity-patterns, and its thinking about them is the reality of the conscious life of you, me, the Greeks and all the rest of us. It also thinks about all the atoms, electrons, and so forth, which carry the activity-patterns, but in doing so it simply is not thinking about what it feels like to be us.

The activity-patterns are conscious just through being the patterns which they are, unified into mental states in the way in which they are. Their reality, exactly as in the case of the reality of unconscious objects, consists in the divine mind's contemplation of them. The divine mind does not need to do anything extra – anything which we would view as miraculous intervention – in order to make them conscious. However, no mental state would be conscious in a truly satisfactory way if its unity were simply that of individually existing components unified by their complex interactions. As physicists have pointed out, unification of a more thorough kind is found even outside brains. David Bohm wrote that 'on the basis of modern physics, even inanimate matter cannot be fully understood in terms of Descartes's notion that it is nothing but a substance occupying space and constituted of separate objects'; 'the interaction of particles may be thought of as depending on a common pool of information belonging to the system as a whole'.[2] Consider a box containing two photons in the same quantum state. What is the probability that both are in the same half of the box? Were the pho-

[2] Quotations from Bohm's 'A new theory of the relationship of mind and matter', *Philosophical Psychology*, 3, 1990, pp. 271–86.

tons fully separate in their existence, then the answer would be 'One half' – the four possibilities being photon #1 on the left and photon #2 on the right; photon #2 on the left and photon #1 on the right; both photons on the left; and both on the right. The photons, however, are in fact so united in their existence that the first two apparent possibilities are one and the same. As experiments show, the actual probability that the photons are in the same half of the box is therefore *two thirds*. Now, as Bohm and many others have noted,[3] the fusion of systems into wholes which is allowed for by quantum physics has no clear restrictions on its extent. It is therefore very tempting to suppose that in conscious brains the degree of fusion between large numbers of elements is particularly marked, this being the basis of the 'wholeness' which we find when introspecting particular mental states of ours. It is a wholeness which led Descartes to believe that our minds, unlike our bodies, were entities without parts, if by 'parts' one meant things theoretically capable of existing each in isolation.

Let us develop that a little. Although people are right to view introspection with suspicion, its findings must be given their due. When, for example, various objects are all experienced as colour-similar, it is perverse to claim that the colour-experience amounts to nothing more than what could be had by just any machine which could sort soup cans according to their colours. Yes, talk of 'the indescribable what-it's-like-to-experience-a-colour' will fail to help a blind man towards any deep understanding of how it feels to be experiencing many soup cans as of the same colour; the experience does defy full description; but we at least know that it is not just a matter of our minds classifying all the cans in the same one fashion. When we experience various things as all of them red rather than, say, as all making the same sound or all smelling of roses, what is involved here? More, surely, than just knowledge that those things *are being treated by our minds as alike* in some respect, itself differentiated from other respects (auditory or olfactory or whatever) just on the basis of being-treated-as-different! Considerably more, as we can know by introspection. And very similarly, I suggest, we can know by introspection that the unity of the elements forming a simple experience, for instance the experience of two lights flashing on side by side in an otherwise dark room, *is not* a unity of things each having an existence

[3] On pages 101 to 103 of *The End of the World* (Routledge: London and New York, 1996; paperback with new Preface, 1998) I expand this with references to works by Bohm and B. Hiley; R. Penrose; I. N. Marshall; and above all M. Lockwood, *Mind, Brain and the Quantum* (Blackwell: Oxford, 1989).

separate from that of the others. On that kind of point, Descartes was right.

What if he had been wrong? It would follow, I suggest, that human thought would be as lacking in intrinsic worth as the quasi-thinking of what President Eisenhower called 'the military-industrial complex'. The military-industrial complex is a whole which operates much like a mind, I am told. It has a quasi-cunning which pushes it to produce ever more armaments, seemingly regardless of whether the individual humans who compose it are in favour of arms control. But surely its quasi-thinking has no value in itself. The military-industrial complex may have a mental life of some sort, but not one *worth living*. The same would apply to the mental life of a system consisting of men who passed to one another slips of paper each bearing the numbers zero or one, in obedience to a computer program of which each man knew only a tiny fragment. One of the men might, for instance, know nothing beyond the rule 'Pass a zero to the next man when given a zero and a one.' Even if the system as a whole could beat grandmasters at chess or translate Chinese into English or (when supplemented by colour-sensitive television cameras) describe paintings as well as any art expert, its understanding of chess, Chinese, or the beauties of colour would not be understanding of a sort *in itself worth having*. The system's expertise at chess might benefit onlookers by giving them interesting games to watch or it might benefit its human components who were rewarded whenever it was victorious, but no additional benefits would be had *by the system itself*. Now, suppose that conscious minds were just (as I think they are) conscious brains. Suppose also (which I do not think, and which quantum physics can encourage me not to think) that activity-patterns in those brains were in turn always composed merely of separately existing elements: nerve-cell firings, perhaps. It would follow that, no matter how complex the causal connections between those elements, consciousness would have zero intrinsic worth.

One might well add that it is only because mental states can be more than just complex groupings of separately existing elements that the region of one's mind which experiences various things and then formulates reports on them, in a language such as English and with the aid of wide background knowledge, can be a region unified in the right way to know that one's experience of two flashes of light as both red is not something such as could be had by just any machine able to sort soup cans into red, green and blue ones. The region's unity gives it a grasp of what some people try to deny, which is that the strictly qualitative distinction between red as experienced, green as experienced, and blue as experienced, simply could not be reflected by any mere *structure* of zeros and ones developing inside any machine thanks to computational rules that allowed it to process other zeros and ones coming from colour-sensitive electronic devices. It could not be reflected, either, by the mere structure of an entire system of soup cans plus colour-sensitive devices plus computational manipulation of zeros and ones.

(c) How could anything, for instance a human's conscious state at a given moment, or a divine mind contemplating an entire universe, be complex and yet also a monistic whole, *just a single existent*? Spinoza's central insight is that there is nothing too problematic here. The concept at stake is admittedly technical. It is not the concept used by the philosopher who talks of an object both as 'an existent, a tree' and also as a 'a collection of many existents such as branches and twigs'. Still, there is no great difficulty in defining it. A single existent, in our technical sense, is something which is logically capable of existing independently, but which has no parts similarly capable. Furthermore, there is no absurdity in believing that a single existent, so defined, could have complexly interrelated elements *which might easily be mistaken for* elements existing independently. Its complexity could be much more striking than any complexity we see in the colour purple when we view it as combining a red 'part' with a blue 'part'. It could have parts which might very much appear to exist each on its own, although in fact that would not be so. In fact they would be only abstractions, in a sense rather like the one in which the reddishness and the bluishness of purple are 'only abstractions'. This of course is not to say that they would lack reality. Purple really is reddish, and really is bluish.

It might here be useful to remember the case of the photons in the box, each at first glance a fully separate entity but in fact united in their existence. Perhaps, however, the unit formed by the two photons would not be capable of existing all on its own. For Spinoza, the sole thing able to exist on its own is a divine mind that includes all actual existence.

Even if our universe includes no parts able to exist each in isolation from others, it remains true, I suggest, that worthwhile understanding of Chinese or of games of chess or of beautiful paintings, and worthwhile consciousness in general, depends on unification of a more thoroughgoing sort than could be found in the so-called mental life of the military-industrial complex or in any system of people passing slips of paper to one another in accordance with a computer program of which they each understood almost nothing. Within the greater unity of the universe there must be regions, for instance inside human brains, which are particularly closely unified.

These regions can be complicated in the way required for them to be regions of worthwhile consciousness, while at the same time their elements are fused together very much as the photons in the box are fused together.

(d) Although 'God-intoxicated', Spinoza was not drunk enough to reject the plainest facts. While fancying that nothing but the divine mind of which he wrote could exist independently, he presented this mind as having many parts which might easily appear capable of such a feat. He called them 'modes' of the divine mind, believing that individual humans were among them. He made no effort to deny that humans typically think of themselves as each with a fully separate existence.

The right way of developing this, I suggest, is to picture divine knowledge as including *areas of comparative ignorance*. The divine mind could not know just what it felt like to be a particular bat, say, unless having inside its thinking a region of bat-thoughts, a region which was not simultaneously one of thoughts about Freudian psychology or Shakespeare or quantum electrodynamics. But it is not just bats that are ignorant of various things. Divine knowledge could not include knowledge of precisely how it felt to be each particular human unless it included regions each plunged in ignorance of immensely many things. From Spinoza's doctrine that you and I are modes of God's thinking, it in no way follows that we know how many planets there are in the universe or how many kinds of flower became extinct last year, or even what our friends really think of us.

Admittedly, we might want to say that *in addition to* the regions of divine thinking which were comparatively ignorant there was a region whose awareness of what it was like to be each particular bat, what it was like to be each particular human, and so forth, was an awareness of much the kind imagined by people who believe in telepathy. If telepathy really worked, then could I not 'telephathise' your pain in all its details – so that I too suffered from it – while at the same time knowing that it was your pain originally, and without losing my full awareness of being me? Similarly, might not the divine thinking include an overview of human and animal consciousness in all its details, together with full awareness of being divine? Might it not even be possible for such an overview to encompass all truths whatsoever, in something like what humans would call 'a single glance'? I would not presume to deny this. But it would be absurd for you and me to say that we personally had this sort of overview. Within the divine knowledge, there would have to be areas of knowing how it felt to be particular humans, particular bats, particular horses, etcetera, *without* simultaneously knowing all truths whatsoever.

We might well want to add that any divine mind which knew what it was like to be, say, fearing for one's life, or preparing to murder a man for his wallet, or being unable to multiply seven by eleven, *only 'telepathically'*, i.e., without any genuine fear, wickedness or mathematical incompetence, would not know *precisely how it felt* to be fearful, wicked or mathematically incompetent.

(e) Spinoza viewed the divine mind as unchanging. Aristotle gave what could seem a strong argument in favour of this: namely, that any changes in perfect divine thinking could only be for the worse. Such an argument might appear faulty if it were believed that there existed, as well as the divine mind, a world whose alterations could usefully be tracked by that mind, but spinozists like me will say that there is no such world. How, then, can we avoid rejecting the seemingly obvious occurrence of change?

The solution is to recognise that 'change' could mean either of two things.[4] First, it could mean change of the sort Einstein denied: absolute change. A reality which underwent absolute change would initially, *in its entirety*, be describable in a certain way, *and then later*, once again in its entirety, would fit some quite different description. As was recognised by the philosopher J. M. E. McTaggart, the man-in-the-street's view about the nature of time is that the words *'then later'* remove any contradiction from this. It would not be like calling a cow 'entirely brown and also entirely white'. Well, I agree with the man in the street about that. Yet I also accept Einstein's view that reality-in-its-entirety never changes. Although I say that, as a matter of what is logically possible, reality-in-its-entirety might be something changing, my belief is that it actually is not. Still, *that changes to it were logically possible* would seem reason enough for declaring that time of a sort was flowing – the time in which it might without logical contradiction suffer change, although as a matter of fact no change takes place.

That our world suffers change could, on the other hand, be accepted by Einsteinians so long as the word 'change' took a second sense. That change occurred would now mean merely that some cross-sections of reality-in-its-entirety were different from other cross-sections. Imagine a universe developing in the absolute way that Einstein denied, but that is accepted by the man in the street (as is proved, I think, by how people typically feel pity for the dead, no matter how long and happy the lives which they had once been living). Imagine a demon making copies of such a universe's successive states and then gluing the copies together along a fourth

[4] I am here using ideas from 'The Value of Time', *American Philosophical Quarterly*, April 1976, pp. 109–121.

dimension. The glued-together whole would be like the reality Einstein believed in. Now, given the right understanding of these words, there would be nothing wrong in saying that this reality 'included changes': acorns becoming oaks, for instance. The acorns would change into oaks along the fourth dimension, rather as a road starts off narrow in Berlin and changes into something broad by the time it hits Paris.

It would, I suggest, be utterly question-begging to argue that the reality in which Einstein believed included no room for our experiences of dizzying progress, the joys of the unexpected, the feeling of being always confined to the present moment, forgetfulness, and so on. Certainly we experience changes to our successive states of mind, but all those changes are there in the Einsteinian picture. True, they are not there in the way imagined by the man in the street. But they are there all the same, as genuine instances of change, when the word 'change' takes the second of the two senses I offered. It must not be thought, however, that everybody who trusts Einstein's mathematical equations has to picture time's progress in the way Einstein did. Think of how the knots and flowing lines in successive cross-sections of a tree trunk remain describable by the same equations regardless of whether you keep the trunk intact, chop it into slices, or glue such slices together again.

All these points can readily be adapted to a spinozistic world-picture. A divine mind can be described as eternally without change, and yet as including the changing experiences of you and me. So long as the words 'changing' and 'without change' are handled properly, there is no contradiction.

Please let nobody protest that divine thoughts, if eternally unchanging, *would soon change* to being boring! Again, let nobody protest that if the patterns of our world are merely those of eternal divine thinking, then none of us 'can really do anything; it's instead always God who does everything, and he's done it already'. This would be almost as question-begging as saying that if Spinoza is right about what you and I are, then you and I 'don't really exist, for only God does'. Or that computers 'never really beat anyone at chess; it's only their programmers who beat people'.

(f) Spinoza's treatment of the world's evils can seem very defective. In a letter, he compares all evils to blindness, then commenting that blindness is a mere absence of the good of sight. This could seem to lump evil situations together with holes in buckets. 'The reality is the buckets,' we might want to say, 'while the holes are just local absences of bucket'. But when we think of such things as acute miseries, cannot we see that they are not just absences of joy?

On a kindlier reading of him, Spinoza's point could instead be that miseries, while every bit as real as joys, have no negative intrinsic value. Neither a miserable state of mind nor anything else is such that its existence *just by itself* would be worse than a blank, a situation empty of all existents. We should try to avoid misery, but only because it and its accompaniments are worse than what we might have instead.

Some people view this as obviously fantastic. I suggest, however, that nothing can be obvious in this area – not even the point that various things really do have intrinsic value, which is something many clever philosophers seem to me to deny. Still, the belief that intrinsic value is a reality *yet is never negative* might be thought altogether too implausible. May not this be ruinous to Spinoza's general way of thinking?

It could perhaps be replied that the idea of intrinsic value here being used, an idea developed by G. E. Moore, meshes only rather poorly with Spinoza's monism. To Spinoza's way of thinking, the world's parts never could – not even as a matter of what is logically possible – exist 'just by themselves' so that it could then be asked whether they were better or worse than blanks. Yet even so, Spinoza might remain in grave difficulties. Even if no part of the world could possibly exist in isolation, might not this feat be performed by various things *really very much like* various parts of the world? And could it not be thought essential, if we are to make any progress in ethics, to evaluate this or that in isolation, distinguishing the 'intrinsic value' had by some situation in itself from whatever 'instrumental value' it possessed through producing various effects? How otherwise could we discuss, say, the morality of operations which cause pain but save lives?

Perhaps the best strategy for spinozists like me is as follows. By all means let us throw doubt on the idea that there exist things which, were they to exist all alone, would be worse than blanks. But let us also ask people whether they truly believe that a divine mind contemplating a world obeying the physical laws which our world obeys *would be better for being ignorant* of many of its details. Would the divine knowledge be finest if it were confined to things such as Mozart's joyful experience of composing great music – with big gaps with respect to such other affairs as what-it's-like-to-be-Hitler-with-a-splitting-headache? Surely the answer is rather far from obvious.

V

Particularly if we read his *Short Treatise on God, Man and his Wellbeing,* it is easy enough to argue that Spinoza's creation story is platonic or neoplatonic, his God-alias-The-Universe ('Deus sive Natura') existing because of its ethical requiredness rather than through any dryly logical necessity. There are ways, however, in which his world might be thought very inferior to what platonists should expect.

Remember, for a start, that there are (if my arguments were right) no good reasons for a platonist to stop with just a single divine mind. An infinite number of such minds would seem logically available, and very much better. Platonists should feel entitled and even forced to believe in all of them instead of doing what Spinoza did, which was to reject all but one of them.

Next, there is the difficulty that Spinoza's divine being, although allegedly 'absolutely infinite', would seem to know much too little. Spinoza's *Ethics* seems to take it for granted that there is only the one universe, ruled throughout by the same one set of fundamental laws. Why does not Spinoza's God contemplate hugely many universes, or even infinitely many, each at least marginally different from every other?

Furthermore, why does Spinoza's God never contemplate things which are not ordered into universes? Why no contemplation of all possible games of chess, and of every possible move in every possible game that is finer than chess? And of everything which could possibly be proved mathematically, and so on? How could it be better for a divine mind to be unaware of all that? Yet the *Ethics* gives no indication that God thinks about more than the things actually contained in our universe.

It might be argued, also, that Spinoza should have viewed humans (and why not other animals too?) as fully immortal. For him, there is nothing readily describable as 'life after death'; well, why not? When his God has, so to speak, thought through a person's life on Earth, reaching the conclusion that natural laws are at a certain stage dictating that the life shall cease, does he take the obvious option of considering how the life might continue onwards *if the laws broke down at that stage*? No, Spinoza's God simply 'switches off the life' like the scientist who, after managing to create an intelligent, fully conscious, blissfully happy computer, then thinks himself perfectly entitled to cut off its electricity supply. Yet why would it not be better for God to contemplate how the life could keep developing if miracles were allowed?

Why, that is to say, should not a person's consciousness continue after that person's earthly death, perhaps gaining greater and greater appreciation of the wonders included in the divine knowledge, as many religious people hope? In Spinoza's eyes, the person's consciousness would itself be just an element in divine thinking, but it seems to me very uncertain that this would be a good excuse for a 'switching off'. If our imaginary scientist replicated the workings of an intelligent, fully conscious, blissfully happy computer inside his own head, by thinking of them in full detail, would he then have a moral right to terminate them by stopping thinking about them?

These are questions too difficult for this brief paper. I raise them chiefly to show how extraordinarily rich reality-in-its-entirety might be if the ground of its existence lay in a platonic creation principle.

Let me end, though, with the comment that the divine mind might indeed be better if it failed to contemplate a great many truths. Would it really be finer through thinking about all possible pains, frightful disappointments, stupid jokes, rotten poetry or things which monkeys at typewriters might type? I rather doubt it. Moreover, what if spinozists like me thought that the divine mind contemplated all logically possible ways in which worlds, all exactly like ours right up to this present moment, could behave at later moments? It would seem to follow that inductive reasoning – reasoning which uses the world's past behaviour as a guide to the future – would become unavailable to us. Now, inductive reasoning is something which no one should willingly abandon.[5]

---

[5] For more on various themes of this paper, see 'Efforts to explain all existence', *Mind*, April 1978, pp. 181–94; *Value and Existence* (Oxford: Blackwell, 1979); 'The World's Necessary Existence', *International Journal for Philosophy of Religion*, Winter 1980, pp. 207–24; 'Mackie on Neoplatonism's "Replacement for God"', *Religious Studies*, September 1986, pp. 325–42; and 'A Neoplatonist's Pantheism', *The Monist*, April 1997, pp. 218–31.

Enchantment

ROGER FELLOWS

Oscar Wilde remarked in *The Picture of Dorian Gray* that, 'It is only the shallow people who do not judge by appearances.' Over three centuries of natural science show that, at least as far as the study of the natural world is concerned, Wilde's epigram is itself shallow. Weber used the term 'disenchantment' to mean the elimination of magic from the modern scientific world view: the intellectual rationalisation of the world embodied in modern science has made it impossible to believe in magic or an invisible God or gods, without a 'sacrifice of the intellect'.

There is a marvellous description of what it is like to contemplate the world from an enchanted perspective in Hesiod's *Theogony*:

> Verily, first of all did Chaos come into being, and then broad-bosomed Gaia, a firm seat of all things for ever, and misty Tartarus in a recess of broad-swayed earth, and Eros who is first among immortal gods and subdues in their breasts the mind and thoughtful council of all gods and all men. Out of Chaos, Erebos and black night come into being; and from Night, again, come Aither and Day, whom she conceived and bore after mingling in love with Erebos. And Earth first of all brought forth starry sky equal to herself to cover her completely round about to be a firm seat for the blessed gods for ever.[1]

No one nowadays would regard this poetical cosmogony as a rival theory to scientific accounts of the origin of the Universe. But this form of disenchantment is really secondary to the main form which goes as follows. We live in a scientific world. Yet an intrinsic feature of this world is that it disenchants the world of appearance, value and meaning. For instance, we are all agreed that we have colour-experiences; and science teaches us that objects have the power to produce these colour-experiences in virtue of a certain micro-physical structure. The question then arises whether colours are mind-dependent or mind-independent. If the former, then objects are not coloured; if the latter, then it is the colour of objects which causes our colour experiences.

Galileo famously embraced the doctrine that colours and other secondary qualities are unreal, and his view has been a fairly con-

[1] Hesiod, *Theogony* 116 in G. S. Kirk and J. E. Raven, *The PreSocratic Philosophers* (Cambridge University Press, 1966), p. 24.

stant feature of philosophy and science since then. Galileo had this to say:

> ... as soon as I conceive a piece of matter or corporeal substance, of conceiving that in its own nature it is bounded and figured in such-and-such a figure, that in relation to others it is large or small, that it is in this or that place, in this or that time, that it is in motion or remains at rest, that it touches or does not touch another body, that it is single, few or many; in short by no imagination can a body be separated from such conditions: but that it must be white or red ... I do not perceive my mind forced to recognise it necessarily accompanied by such conditions; so if the senses were not the escorts, perhaps the reason or the imagination by itself could never have arrived at them.[2]

Galileo explains his meaning further by pointing out that, if someone tickles us with a feather, we are not disposed to attribute a tickling-faculty to the feather; rather, we suppose that the affection is in us. The feather has a disposition to cause in us a tickling, just as the red pillar box has a disposition to cause in me the experience of seeing it redly. Here, in a nutshell, we have what it is about science, and perhaps naturalism in general, that disenchants the world. If colours do not exist in the world then, for example, aesthetic values cannot be in the world either.

One might be inclined to quibble about Galileo's feather-example. It might be said, for instance, that when I am tickled with a feather, the resulting sensation seems to be in me in the same way that pain is an internal experience. On the other hand when I look at the pillar box, the property red appears to be an external and stable feature of the box. However, it is clear that this appeal to the phenomenological differences between tickling- and colour-experiences is insufficient to blunt the force of Galileo's contention about colour and other secondary qualities.

What is interesting though, is that Galileo never, as far as I know, draws one consequence of his mathematical metaphysics. Galileo says that reality is constituted of a system of quantities, that is, properties or processes with which a number or numbers may be associated. There are primitive quantities, like distance and time; and derived quantities, which are defined in terms of the primitive ones: these include scalar quantities such as length, weight and speed, and vectorial ones such as velocity. Notice that there is, so far,

[2] Galileo Galilei, 'Crew and de Salvio translation', *Dialogues and Mathematical Demonstrations Concerning Two New Sciences* (New York, 1914), p. 40.

nothing here which disenchants the world. The quantitative laws of physics expressible with these quantities, such as the law of falling bodies, refine and sharpen aspects of our experience without being inconsistent with it. (A follower of Aristotle would not agree!) We get the threat of disenchantment by adding the thesis of atomism: the claim that, in addition to the foregoing, reality consists of *invisible* particles called 'atoms'. (Since the time of Galileo science has, of course, immensely complicated the micro-structure of the world.)

The problem that Galileo does not confront is this: since reality consists solely of atoms and quantifiable properties and relations, what account are we to give of ourselves within this picture? Galileo operates with the intuitive conception of the world as consisting of things *within*, and things *without,* the mind. Colours occupy the realm of inner space. But the distinction between inner and outer cannot be maintained coherently if Galileo's account of the world is correct. That is a way of putting a worry which haunts many contemporary philosophers. Objectification requires, as Nagel for one has argued, that reality is viewed from nowhere.[3] But for, for example, objects to *appear to me* redly, there needs to exist a first-person perspective upon the world, that is, a subjective viewpoint. Can we say, seeking to stay in the Galilean framework, that there is no first-person perspective upon the world, that there only appears to be; and that objects, in particular, do not appear to me to be red, they only appear to appear to be red?

I want to stress that I am not treating these remarks as a *reductio* of Galileo's view. They do seem to me, however, to raise a difficulty. Russell famously remarked that naive realism leads to physics, and that physics, if true shows that naive realism is false, and that therefore naive realism is false.[4] To this we have to add that, in particular, if naive realism is false, so apparently is our intuitive conception of ourselves as beings with a first-person perspective on the world. I shall look later on at one attempt to cope with the problem within a physicalist framework, by appeal to the concept of supervenience.

But if Galileo did not grapple with this difficulty, Descartes did. His *Meditations*[5] is a profoundly subtle attempt, starting out from the standpoint of radical doubt, to persuade us of the truth, *inter alia*, of the Galilean distinction between primary and secondary qualities. Descartes retains (as he thinks) the first-person perspec-

[3] T. Nagel, *The View from Nowhere* (Oxford University Press, 1996).

[4] B. Russell, *An Inquiry into Meaning and Truth* (London: Allen & Unwin Ltd, 1948), p. 15.

[5] Rene Descartes, John Cottingham translation, *Meditations on First Philosophy* (Cambridge University Press, 1986).

tive upon the world by removing mind from nature altogether. In his view, we are the possessors of extensionless minds in which the secondary qualities are found a home; there is no conflict between science and mind, between appearance and reality, because mind and matter belong to different, co-existing but non-conflicting worlds. Facts about our embodiment are responsible for our having false or confused perceptual beliefs, such as the belief that the pillar box *is* red. Descartes says:

> when we say that we perceive colours, this is really the same as saying that we perceive something in the objects whose nature we do not know, but which produces in us a certain very clear and vivid sensation which we call the sensation of colour .... If we suppose we perceive colours in objects we do not know what it is that we are calling a colour, and we cannot find any intelligible resemblance between the colour we suppose to be in objects and that which we experience in our sensation.[6]

But this leads us to ask: what would it be for the Cartesian mind, even if we could make sense of it, to see the world as it really is, without having confused or false perceptual beliefs?

Descartes thought that angels were incorporeal beings which, like ourselves, have causal intercourse with the material world. He was pressed to explain how then, if at all, a man differs from an angel. His answer was that:

> if an angel were in a human body, he would not have sensations as we do, but would simply be intellectually aware of the motions which are caused by external objects, and in this way differ from a real man.[7]

Objects, then, are colourless in themselves. They are not invisible to us because they dispose us to take them to be coloured. I shall return to the dispositional theory of colour below, but first I want to examine two strategies for re-enchanting the world. The first denies that there is any problem in the first place, while the second accepts that there is a problem, and tries to resolve it. Finally I shall, unoriginally, make some remarks about the dispositional view of colour (which is Galileo's), and then offer the 'simple view', which is that objects *are* coloured, and that this is why we acquire perceptual beliefs that objects are coloured.

Gilbert Ryle in a series of related lectures[8] confronted the prob-

---

[6] Rene Descartes, *Principles*, in J. Cottingham, *A Descartes Dictionary*, (Oxford: Blackwell, 1993), Part 1, art. 70, p. 36.

[7] Ibid., p. 13.

lem between the austere naturalism of modern physical science and the everyday world. Ryle argues that when we hear that there is a conflict between the world of science and the everyday world, there is the risk of a purely verbal muddle. We can talk of the world of stamp-collecting or the world of politics, but there is no clash between these worlds and the world of science. Here 'world' is just being used as a collective noun to group together all matters which relate to stamp-collecting or politics, respectively. In this sense, says Ryle, it is innocuous to speak of the world of the physicist, for 'world' here does not mean 'the universe' or 'reality'. All of this is true, but I believe that it does not run very deep: it is because the domain of physics, the domain of the fundamental properties of matter, seems to have an ontological priority over other domains, that disenchantment apparently threatens. If matter did not exist, then stamp-collecting and politics could not exist; but the converse is not true.

Ryle also gives an extended analogy to try to show that the truths of physical theory do not drive out the truths of everyday life. An undergraduate member of a college is allowed to inspect the college accounts. (Although Ryle was writing in 1953, anyone teaching in a contemporary university will be quite at home with this reference to accounting procedures.) The auditor tells this individual that the accounts give a complete picture of life in the college: nothing is left out. They show, for instance, the tuition fees that students pay, and the costs incurred by the acquisition of new library books. It occurs to the undergraduate that, although the cost of the book *The Concept of Mind,* which he read in the previous term, is recorded in the accounts, the contents of the book are not. Which is the real book, the one recorded in the accounts, or the one read by the undergraduate? Clearly, as Ryle says, this is a spurious question. There is only one book, which is available to the student, and whose price is recorded in the college accounts. Ryle suggests that the book in the library is part of the everyday world; and that the book-keeping entry, which tells the undergraduate about the book in the language of double-entry notation, is analogous to what the physicist might tell the undergraduate about the book.

Ryle says that he does not want to push the analogy beyond a certain point, but only this far:

> I am not arguing that a scientific theory is in all or many respects like a balance – sheet, but only that it is like a balance sheet in one important respect namely that the formulae of the one and the

---

[8] G. Ryle, *Dilemmas* (Cambridge University Press, 1964).

financial entries of the other are constitutionally speechless about
certain sorts of matters,...

... What is true or false of book-bills is not true or false of books,
or vice versa, and yet the fact that one statement is true of the
book-bills itself requires that there are the other quite different
statements which are true of the books. The corresponding thing
holds in the other field. A bit of the theory of ultimate particles
has no place in it for a description or misdescription of chairs and
tables, and a description of chairs and tables has no place in it for
a description or misdescription of ultimate particles. A statement
that is true *or* false of the one is *neither* true *nor* false of the other.
It cannot therefore be a rival of the other.[9]

Comforting as one may find Ryle's genial humanism, which is redo-
lent of Susan Stebbing's attack on Eddington's two – tables, it is
insufficient to blunt the worry about, for example, the relations
between colours and micro-physical processes. The main worry is
that Ryle, in common with some other Oxford philosophers of his
generation, confines himself to claims about what we may or may
not say about things, without entering into metaphysical issues
about explanation and reduction. And Ryle's approach has difficulties of its own: suppose I say that a red sunset is a certain scattering
of photons by particles in the atmosphere. Then I have described a
slice of the everyday world in terms of 'a bit of the theory of ultimate particles'. Ryle says that this statement is neither true nor
false. (I suspect that he may have believed it to be a category mistake.) Here is an easy way of engendering truth-value gaps. We
noted earlier that the kinematic concepts of classical mechanics,
perhaps supplemented by the dynamical concept of mass, can be
made to square with the everyday world, of which they can be seen
as refinements. The formulae which quantify qualitative perceptions of the world may therefore be thought of as akin to book-
keeping entries, but even to this extent the analogy is a doubtful one.
Book-keeping entries and scientific formulae are both formal: however, book-keeping entries are not law-like, whereas, for example,
the formula $d = 1/2gt^2$, Galileo's law of falling bodies, enables one to
make a potentially infinite number of predictions when combined
with suitable boundary conditions. I conclude that Ryle's attempt to
resist disenchantment is unsatisfactory.

I want to turn now to another attempt to resist the disenchantment of the world, with respect to colour in particular. Recall the
problem: objects are not really coloured; they just appear to be so;

[9] Ibid., 78–9.

colours are 'in us'. So sunsets, paintings and the blush on the countenance of the beloved, are not in nature, but are mental projections by ourselves on to a colourless world. The attempt to avoid disenchantment which I shall now consider, appeals to the concept of *supervenience*. The philosopher John Post[10] and others believe that this concept enables us to live in an enchanted scientific world. Supervenience is a relation which is said to hold between *distinct* domains, for instance, the domain of the mental and the domain of the physical, or the domain of microphysics and the domain of middle-sized objects. The notion is one of token identity. (I have just been castigating Ryle for putting physics and the everyday world into entirely disjoint domains, and I also worry whether the idea, that there exists a mental domain and a physical domain such that we can examine the relations which may or may not obtain between them, is a coherent one. For instance, should a smile be assigned to the domain of the physical or the mental? I shall ignore this worry here, and merely note that, unless I am mistaken, supervenience does seem to share the *Cartesian* requirement of assigning every property, predicate, event, or whatever, into one of two distinct domains.)

Supervenience is famously associated with the work of Donald Davidson who, in his programmatic paper *Mental Events*,[11] argued for a non-reductive materialism. In particular, he argued for a token-identity thesis: mental events (for example, the event of my perceiving the Tower of London) are identical with certain physical events, that is, neurophysiological goings-on in the brain. Davidson specifies that the relation between mental events and physical events is one of supervenience. This specifically allows for the possibility that two people may have different physical states but be mentally identical (that is, mental type indistinguishable). If two people, situations or worlds, are physically identical, then they will be mentally identical. It follows that the physical determines the mental, but not necessarily vice versa.

Since Davidson's paper, the idea of supervenience has spawned a huge philosophical literature,[12] and what I shall say here is very basic. Many philosophers who have discussed the topic have thought that this notion of supervenience is too weak to do what is

---

[10] J. F. Post, 'On Reenchanting the World', *Research in Philosophy and Technology*, 10, (1990), pp. 243–79.

[11] D. Davidson, 'Mental Events' in I. Foster and J. Swanson, *Experience and Theory* (Amhurst: University of Massachusetts Press, 1970), 79–01.

[12] A good place to start is perhaps with the Spindel Conference: 'The Concept of Supervenience in Contemporary Philosophy', in Terence Horgan, ed., *The Southern Journal of Philosophy*, 22, Supplement (1984).

required, which is to provide a non-reductive materialism. Consider the following definition: *A domain A weakly supervenes on a domain B if necessarily for any x and y if x and y share all their properties in B then x and y share all their properties in A*. That is, indiscernability with respect to B entails indiscernability with respect to A. However it is argued that this is too weak to capture the idea that the physical determines the mental, since it is only in this world that B-indiscernability entails A-indiscernability. In other possible worlds it would be possible (that is, consistent with the above definition) for physical indiscernability to be accompanied by mental differences.

To remedy this, the definition of supervenience is amended to read: A domain A strongly supervenes on a domain B just in case, necessarily, for each x and each property F in A, if x has F, then there is a property G in B such that x has G, and necessarily if any y has G, it has F. The problem with this strengthening of supervenience is that it now looks as though we come perilously close to reinstating reduction between the mental and the physical. This is because we may be able to specify (at least in theory) all the relevant physical predicates (properties) and then we would be able to join them together in a mammoth antecedent in a law-like chain linking the mental and the physical. However, assuming that this worry can be dealt with, how does supervenience re-enchant the world with respect to colour? Because to say that an object is red is to say that it would be red to any normal observer in such-and-such conditions. This relation between the observer and the object (strongly) supervenes on the physical, including the neurophysical processes in the observer's head, and the microphysical states of the object's surface. But the red look of the object is not reducible either to goings-on in the brain or to microphysical processes in the object.

How satisfactory is this account? We have seen that supervenience is a token-identity theory. Peter Geach has this to say:

the reason I should offer for rejecting the view that a given state of mind is identical with a given state of the brain is not the weakness of the argument in its favour, but simply that I find it not coherently graspable. Some of the central state materialists think they have given a strict account of what they mean when they say 'identical' just by prefixing the adverb 'strictly' to 'identical', but they deceive themselves. Imagine some philosopher who tried to revive Pythagoreanism. Suppose he were to say, as the Pythagoreans did, that the virtue of justice is the number four. 'How do you mean "is"' I might ask. 'I mean,' says the

Pythagorean, 'that justice is none other than the number four: they are strictly identical'. Do I now understand this thesis any better? Certainly not. And I am equally at a loss if a central state materialist assures me that some cerebral disturbance of mine simply is strictly identical with my sudden recollection that I must go to the bank.[13]

No committed physicalist would, I suspect, be swayed by this argument, but it is salutary to be reminded that, often, technical concepts in philosophy have obscure foundations. Davidson, I might add, does attempt to provide the condition of identity for mental and physical events,[14] but his critics have argued that his account is tacitly circular.

More seriously, John Heil has recently argued[15] that supervenience as normally characterised is a purely modal notion: when it obtains in a particular case it does so by virtue of some other relation, for example, instances of B are causally sufficient for instances of A. Heil says that supervenience-claims need to be judged by substantive features of *this* world if they are to be ontologically revealing. I think that this is right.

The realist view of colour is that things being coloured explains our taking them to be that way; whereas the dispositionalist attributes the fact that objects appear to us to be coloured as due to objects having a disposition, under normal conditions, to appear that way. Since dispositions require a categorial base, the base in question is the imperceptible microstructure. I wish to defend the former view, but I first want to mention some criticisms of the dispositional view made by Colin McGinn.[16] McGinn says that the Dispositional theory has merits in that it copes with the subjectivity and relativity of colour-ascriptions, while allowing that it is

[13] P. T. Geach, *Truth, Love and Immortality* (London: Hutchinson, 1979), pp. 113–14.

[14] Davidson argues that events are particulars and says that event E is identical with event E[1] just in case E and E[1] have the same causes and the same effects. Critics have argued that this account of event identity is tacitly circular since the cause–effect relation is defined over event pairs. Davidson has responded by arguing that his account involves no *formal* circularity. Davidson's positive account is in D. Davidson, 'Events as Particulars', *Nous,* 4 (1970), pp. 25–32.

[15] J. Heil, 'Supervenience Deconstructed', *European Journal of Philosophy,* 6(2) (1998), pp. 146–55.

[16] C. McGinn, 'Another Look at Color', *The Journal of Philosophy,* 43(11) (November 1996), pp. 537–53.

external objects which are coloured. I disagree with this. First, whether colour-ascriptions are mental projections on to objects is the point at issue. Second, the good bishop made much of the perceptual relativity of the primary properties, downgrading bodies, as Kant put it, to mere illusion. Third, it is just not true, as McGinn later seems to acknowledge, that the dispositional theory allows that colours are properties of objects detached from the observer (for example, 'Red' is not a monadic predicate)

McGinn argues that colour-properties do not look like dispositions to produce colour-experiences (how would they look if they did?!) Also, dispositions are not perceptible properties of things in the way that colours are, or seem to be. As McGinn says, you can observe the manifestations of dispositions, and under certain circumstances (with the aid of an electron microscope, say), you might even see the categorial base; but you do not see the property, for example, of being disposed to dissolve. This has to be inferred. This seems to me to be an acute criticism. Also, McGinn says that the dispositional theory misrepresents the phenomenology of colour-perception: to see an object as red is for us to see it as having a simple monadic property; whereas the dispositional theory requires that the relation between observer and object is at least dyadic. He says that being seen as red is not like x being seen as to the left of y. I am not sure that this is a good criticism of the dispositional view. For one thing, not every dyadic relation between objects is a perceptible one: for instance,' x occurred one hundred years earlier than y'. For another, on this account, one of the things which stands in the relation is the observer. Why should it be supposed that the observer would detect that he is standing, as it were, in a two-termed relation? The perception that one object is to the left of another is actually a *three*-place relation between two objects and an observer.

I will now argue for the view that objects do have colours, not withstanding all that physics has to tell us. The view I wish to support, as I said above, is the view that colours are those properties of objects which cause or dispose us to think that they are red; that objects would still be red if there were no human beings. The dispositional view requires that, in the absence of sentience, the universe would be wholly devoid of colour. I will assume a realist view of physics, for if one assumed that the micro-physical properties of matter, photons, electrons and the like, were merely problem-solving heuristic devices – the position taken by the instrumentalist – then there would be no reason to feel any unease about the reality of colour.

The first point I want to make is this: many philosophers and scientists have been impressed by the different patterns of causation involved in colour.[17] They have inferred from this plurality of causes that objects are not intrinsically coloured. For instance, the blueness of the sky is due to the scattering of white light by small particles; and what makes sapphire blue is different from makes blue tits blue. In short, there is not one single molecular structure that makes all blue things blue. But although there is no mono-causal account of what is involved in colour-perception, it is hard to see why this fact by itself entails the subjectivity of colour-perception. Two people can both share the belief that Prague is a beautiful city but whereas one glanced at photographs in a book in England, the other wandered around the actual city.

Wilfred Sellars[18] objects to the mind-independence of colour by appeal to the following principle:

> If an object is in a strict sense a system of objects, then every property of the object must consist in the fact that its constituents have such and such qualities and stand in such and such relations or, roughly every property of a system of objects consists of properties of, and relations between, its constituents.

Clearly, the ultimate constituents of things are not coloured: it would be vacuous to explain why things are red by appeal to their consisting of red particles, so whatever it is to explain why things are coloured, cannot appeal to colour. But, as Quinton has pointed out, to view a thing as red is to perceive that every perceptible part is red, not that every conceivable part is red.[19] To say that the redness of the pillar box is composed of a surface micro-structure of such and such a kind is just to offer an explanation of the pillar box having the property of redness. But this is not to *define* the colour red in terms of the primary properties of the surface. We acquired the ability to operate with the language of colour-expressions prior to having any scientific knowledge.

There is a doctrine, famously associated with the philosopher Saul Kripke, according to which certain common nouns, such as *water*, *snow*, and *heat*, can stand in identity relations with expressions which denote whatever is their essence.[20] So, for instance, we may say that snow is identical with H_2O. Adherence to this doctrine

---

[17] A crisp expression of this worry can be found in L. Goldstein, *The Philosopher's Habitat* (London: Routledge, 1990), pp. 185–86.

[18] W. Sellars, 'Philosophy and the Scientific Image of Man', in *Frontiers of Science and Philosophy* (London: Allen & Unwin Ltd, 1964), p. 63.

[19] A. Quinton, *The Nature of Things* (London: Routledge & Kegan Paul, 1973), p. 204.

[20] S. Kripke, *Naming and Necessity* (Oxford: Basil Blackwell 1980).

would appear to yield Sellers' conclusion in certain cases. The argument would run as follows: 'You admit that H_2O is not coloured, but since snow is identical with H_2O it must follow that snow is not coloured either.' However, it is highly doubtful that 'Snow is H_2O' is an identity statement, since, if it is, then so presumably is the statement that steam is identical with H_2O. It now follows that snow is identical with steam. A more plausible view is that in all such cases we are not dealing with the 'is' of identity, but with the 'is' of composition. The compositional 'is' is plainly non-symmetrical, and we cannot infer the colourlessness of, for example, snow from the colourlessness of H_2O. Kripke's doctrines were concerned with natural kind or substance terms, but the present line of thought readily extends to properties such as the property of being red (although we noted earlier that there is no simple formula on offer to constitute the essence of any colour).

It remains to touch on a final objection to the mind-independence of colour. Some philosophers believe that, because our colour-detection system is contingent, we can conceive that it might have been other than in fact it is: in which case, our colour perceptions might have been very different. There are two cases here. The first is that, if our sensory apparatus had been different, then we might notice certain colour-features of objects which we do not actually notice, and not notice features which we actually notice. At most this yields the conclusion that colour-perception is selective, not that colours are subjective. The other case is the case of the inverted spectrum: what the Martian sees as blue, we see as red, and vice versa. I will make only one brief point about this supposed eventuality, considered here as an empirical, not a logical, possibility. It is overwhelmingly unlikely that the inverted spectrum possibility could be confined to the switching of the perception of a pair of colours. So we must suppose a massive or total disagreement in colour-perception. But now the difficulty is to give a coherent account of how we could determine differences between Martian and Human colour-perception *prior* to the construction of (say) an English–Martian translation manual. And if we have succeeded in constructing such a manual, then surely we have determined that a certain Martian expression more or less means what, for example, 'red' means in English.

It might be objected here that a certain Martian term has the same extension as the English term 'red', but the martian and the human perceptions are utterly and consistently distinct; and that this possibility must threaten colour-objectivity. I do not deny that this is a logical or metaphysical possibility, but only that it is empirically implausible. There are many logical and metaphysical possibilities which do not keep me awake at night. My thought is that what explains the experience of colour is colour, and that what explains colour is the surface micro-structure of objects. Colour-predicates are not fixed directly by the micro-structure of the surface. Since, in general, the explanation-relation is non-transitive, it will not follow that the micro-structure *explains* the experience of colour. I have already agreed that if the Martian system of colour-detection were very different from our own, this might lead them to notice surface-features of objects to which we are blind.

To sum up my view: micro-structures explain colour; colour explains colour-perception; but it doesn't follow from that that micro-structures explain colour-perception.

In this paper, I have tried to save the world from being disenchanted in the case of colour. There may be this dissatisfaction with my remarks: I have not explained how explaining colour in terms of micro-physical processes, and explaining colour-perception in terms of colour- properties causing those perceptions, relate to each other. I do not have an answer to this worry, but, rather unoriginally, I can offer the following analogy. We can explain, for example, why Mary wanted to go to London in terms of her beliefs and desires. Also we believe, at least in principle, that her desire to go to London is accompanied by a chain of neural processes in her brain. Mary's beliefs and desires are answerable to certain rationality principles and constraints. The neural processes in her head are neither rational or irrational: they operate at a different explanatory level. We think that there is a relation between explanation in terms of beliefs and desires, and explanations couched in the language of the brain sciences, but it is not easy to characterise. It is no easier to characterise the explanatory difference between explaining colour-perception in terms of colour, and explaining colour in terms of micro-physical processes.

But colour-elimination or -reduction is not the only source of disenchantment. For instance, Roger Scruton has written movingly of the attempt to place human sexual desire on to a 'scientific' footing.[21] I will conclude by making some all-too-brief remarks about the relation between the workings of the human brain and the idea of personhood. Our idea of personhood involves the thought of a creature with the capacity for language, love, an ability to join with others of its kind in institutions such as the law and the university, and so on. The dominant form of philosophical materialism is token-materialism. As an *ontological* thesis, it carries no explanatory implications: but, in the hands of cognitive- and brain-scientists, it does. For instance, some cognitive scientists believe that the Socratic injunction to know thyself is best undertaken by treating

[21] R. Scruton, *Sexual Desire* (London: George Weidenfeld, 1986), pp. 180–212.

the brain as the functional equivalent of a digital computer, and then trying to determine those computer programmes instantiated in the brain. This is the so-called 'top–down' approach. Others hope that a more direct investigation of neural processes in the brain will lead to an upward understanding of the capacities of persons. It would be dishonest of me not to say that these few remarks do not begin to do justice to a vast and often technical field.

Disenchantment threatens when workers in philosophy and the brain-sciences suppose that the downfall of Cartesian dualism entails that persons can be understood solely in terms of brain-processes allied perhaps to computer programs. The scientific evidence shows that the mind – and, more generally, personhood – depends upon the workings of the brain and other organs; just as it shows that colour depends upon micro-physical processes. But this does not show that we can explain ourselves solely by, as it were, looking within. I side with what I take to be Wittgenstein's view here: we can explain personhood, and all that goes with it, only in terms of our social practices and forms of life.[22] I don't understand what it is for a person to give me a loving glance by attending to neurophysiological processes or twitchings of facial muscles; and it would be equally absurd to try to understand what it is for Atherton to hit a six in cricket by looking at details of his anatomy.

Actually, some might think the cricket example unfair: they might argue that hitting a six is an illustration of a social practice which is essentially relational, whereas having a thought is a non-relational property of a person. Wittgenstein would dissent from this view. And, although I would agree that brain-processes have parts, I find it hard to get hold of the idea that thoughts do as well.[23] We can, of course, do an enormous amount of hand-waving here. For instance, we can propose as a hypothesis, that the structure of, for instance, Mary's singular thought that Vienna is a city, is isomorphic to the sentence, 'Vienna is a city', and that this sentence (considered as a syntactic object) is isomorphic with a process in her brain. But this hypothesis cannot explain the thought, since language is community-based, whereas brain-states are not.

I have tried in this paper to defend the objectivity of colour, and I have also made some all-too-brief remarks about personhood. I shall end with a vaguely Kantian point: a world which includes colour and the existence of a class of persons who relate to each other are both required in order to form a comprehensive picture of reality.

[22] L. Wittgenstein, *Philosophical Investigations* (Oxford: Blackwell, 1953).

[23] See W. D. Hart, 'The Anatomy of Thought', *Mind*, 42, (1983), pp. 264–9.

'Beyond reality': Plato's Good revisited

DAVID EVANS

In our post-modern cultural climate we are often told that reality is value-free. Indeed sometimes it is even said to be fact-free. Yet almost all philosophers have been deeply concerned with matters of value, in addition to their other main pre-occupation: that is the nature of truth and our knowledge of it. The question therefore arises: why should these two – good and truth – be so powerfully connected? And why should this business of value continue to exert the hold on philosophers that it evidently does?

Questions like these relate to many aspects of intellectual history, theory of culture and society, and philosophical analysis itself. My own preferred method of approach is to try to locate some particular figure in the history and some element in the timeless theorising which, by their union, can illuminate the whole complex issue. If I apply that method to the present case, then the obvious candidates for inspection seem to be Plato and Goodness. Plato assigned to value a central and fundamental position in his analysis of reality and our knowledge of it. Good is the basic value concept; it is tempting to reduce all other values – such as pleasure or happiness or duty or moral obligation – to this fundamental mark of value. Although we may not understand what it may mean, we feel sure that this concept holds the key to the nature of value; and although we may not understand what *he* means, we willingly invoke Plato as a guide in the search.

Plato's ruminations on the Good have had their ups and downs in the rough and tumble of philosophical posterity. The reception has by no means been uniformly favourable. Plato's successor, Speusippus, gave up the metaphysical primacy of the concept; and his pupil, Aristotle, attacked him.[1] Neoplatonists found deep inspiration in Plato's conception of the fundamental value principle as also providing the ontological basis of things.[2] In our time this thought has been strongly advanced by Iris Murdoch, with her

---

[1] Speusippus, frr. 34–5 (Lang); Aristotle *EN* A6. See Harold Cherniss, *The Riddle of the Early Academy* (New York: Russell & Russell, 1944), pp. 33–43.

[2] Plotinus, *Enneads* I7.

105

insistence on the metaphysical significance of value – a significance which she very explicitly derives from Plato.[3]

A major reaction to the Platonic tendency was promoted by the protagonists of Enlightenment, Hume and Kant. In their different ways they argued for a very strong separation between matters of scientific fact and issues of value.[4] This divorce permeates their account both of the nature of things and of our psychological and epistemic resources for accessing the facts – or rather, as they would have it, these two realms of fact. The influence of these ideas has remained very powerful in philosophy, right up to the present moment. We are all aware of the challenge posed to an attempt to derive 'ought' from, 'is'. Some philosophers are tempted to try this task, as witnessed by the interest in socio-biological and neo-Darwinian projects in ethics. But there is no lack of colleagues to urge caution on such enterprises.

If Plato were with us now, he would surely reply that the challenge thus formulated gets things the wrong way round. The proper method is to derive 'is' from 'ought' – fact from value. That is the strategy which is promised by saying that the Good is 'the cause of knowledge and truth (508e3–4) ... and also of being and reality to other things, while itself not reality but passing beyond reality in dignity and might (509b7–10)'. These words and ideas have been largely ignored in the otherwise fecund commentary on Plato in the past fifty years.[5] So in my talk today I want to expand Plato's remarks on the Good and show their relevance to contemporary philosophical concerns. If what I say has any merit, there will be the bonus of returning a neglected part of Plato's philosophy to a more central position.

I

The remarks about the Good which I quoted from Plato just now come towards the start of a forty-page section of *Republic* where he

[3] I. Murdoch, *The Sovereignty of Good* (London: Routledge & Kegan Paul, 1970). Another contemporary philosopher who has explored these ideas in more sober, analytical vein is Michael Morris, *The Good and the True* (Oxford: Clarendon Press, 1992).

[4] I. Kant, *Critique of Pure Reason,* A542–57/B570–85; David Hume, *Enquiry concerning the Principles of Morals,* Appendix 1.

[5] There is a brief discussion in T. H. Irwin, *Plato's Ethics* (Oxford University Press, 1995), pp. 272–3. Between my Royal Institute lecture and this publication, I saw Julia Annas, *Plato's Ethics: Old and New* (Ithaca & London: Cornell University Press, 1999). Like Irwin and most other modern commentators, Annas does not derive moral enlightenment from the discussion of The Good in *Republic,* 5–7. I shall review her book in *Philosophical Books* (forthcoming).

develops his thoughts about the role which knowledge of the Good should play in creating and maintaining the best individual and communal life. The leading idea is that goodness is a single principle which underpins the whole of reality and the proper understanding of it. Every other thing depends on this principle for its nature; and thus the Good is the basis of the reality, both piecemeal and collectively, of everything else. Equally an understanding of any reality can only be securely based when it is grounded on an awareness of the Good. The ontology and the epistemology are intimately interrelated. Because everything forms a connected whole, the highest form of rational investigation is universal in scope and foundational in method. Plato has good reasons in the earlier tradition for calling this science 'dialectic', since that method was distinguished by its utter open-endedness regarding scope of subject-matter and outcome in the theses that can be sustained.

Some of what is said in this part of Plato's text may suggest a coherentist vision, according to which the basic reason for casting the net of investigation as wide as possible is the following. Each thing is – or, at least, may be – related to any other thing. So the soundest method is an inclusive one: extend, rather than retract or even maintain, the topics which should be under scrutiny! Carried to a logical, but still prudent extreme, this prescription would require that in order to know anything, one must know every other thing and, therefore, everything. That is certainly one interpretation of the Platonic prescription that the master-science of dialectic should be 'synoptic'.[6] But I think that it is not the only interpretation; there is a better one.

The correct version is surely foundationalist. Plato is not simply saying that everything is connected with everything else in a mutually reinforcing way, with goodness running through the system as a very frequently found theme. He goes further: it is because the nature and reality of each thing depends on goodness, that the Good is not just one principle but the sole and fundamental basis on which anything can be understood.

I think that the best way to assess the significance of these Platonic claims and – more ambitiously – to assay their truth, is by starting with their critics. The earliest and most obviously influential of these is Aristotle, but also important (although less noticed because less explicit) are Hume and Kant. Both kinds of critics accuse Plato of eliding crucial distinctions, of over-simplifying things.

I can best introduce this point by asking you to consider the following sentence:

[6] *Republic*, 537c

It is not good to be a good thief.

This sentence seems clear in meaning and, I would hope, also true. Thieving can be done better or worse; some thieves are very good at it. There are good thieves; these thieves are good. But it is not good to be like that at all. Thieving is bad, and so are all thieves, including the good ones.

Let us consider the way the word 'good' – and the concept of goodness – is deployed in the two places in the specimen sentence. Superficially we may seem to have a contradiction: someone – the thief – is asserted to be good but also not to be good. But it is easy to feel that the apparent contradiction can be defused by invoking ambiguity. For followers of Hume and Kant the ambiguity concerns the concept of goodness itself. We need to distinguish instrumental or functional goodness from moral goodness. Someone who is good at thieving, carries out that activity well. For these critics, as we shall see, Plato's monolithic and over-arching concept of Good misses the distinctive moral sense of the notion which we capture when we call the whole activity, however well done, bad.

Aristotle's fundamental objection focuses not so much on the notion of goodness as on the other concept with which it can be coupled. He argues that far from being a semantic atom with meaning that is independent of its surrounding context, the word 'good' varies in meaning in accordance with that context. The range of variation in its meaning certainly corresponds to the ten-fold distinction of categories, which Aristotle also uses to diagnose ambiguity in such key philosophical terms as 'being' and 'change'. But the complexity is greater than that; and what is particularly important is the distinction which Aristotle draws between the word 'good' used to characterise an end and a means to some end.

So here we have two lines of objection to the Platonic conception; and they have been immensely influential in discrediting that conception in the minds of many philosophers in many eras, not least in our own time. For convenience I shall refer to them as the 'Kantian', and the 'Aristotelian' objections; and different though they are, their compound effect is the same. Plato cannot be correct in making goodness a foundational principle, since the analyses of its complexity and ambiguity reveal that it is no single principle at all. Perhaps, following appropriate disambiguation, some specialised part of the concept might emerge as a significant principle; that is certainly what Kant thought about the will. But such a result does not succeed in making the case that will vindicate Plato and his vision.

I shall try to undermine the Kantian and Aristotelian reasons for saying that Plato is mistaken; and I shall be delighted if, in doing this, I can afford some reinforcement to the philosophical importance of his conception of the Good.

II

The Kantian draws a sharp distinction between one kind of value and others. Roughly – and without being paid-up followers of Kant – we can say that aesthetic, prudential and instrumental values are distinct from moral value and subordinate to it. A person may be a good abstract artist, say, or airline pilot or deep-sea fisherman. Although it is not obvious that it is bad to engage in these activities, as in the case of thieving, neither is it obvious that it is good to do so; the activities are essentially neutral, even though it is certainly possible to engage in them well. Some further test needs to be applied to adjudicate whether the person who is so engaged does, in fact, act well. Moral value, by contrast, is self-validating. 'Nothing is good without qualification save a good will', Kant declared. That famous formulation leads one to judge that there may well be certain other things for which a different mode of valuation is possible and even necessary.

Now the way is clear to undertake the task of separating moral value from other kinds of value. The work of Kant lends legitimacy to this project; and a further reason why it may seem an attractive strategy, is that it allows us to explore the value of works of creative imagination in a way that does not depend on judging their moral value. Such an intellectual facility would seem well worth having. We can enter the galleries and workshops as aesthetes or whatever; in any case we do not have to be moralists! In similar vein various exponents of prudential value could detach themselves from the service of morality. What would count in the relevant value-assessment is the success of some significant element – a person, a project or an action – in achieving a well-defined result.

This line of thought has received explicit expression in one highly influential area – business ethics. Here we find arguments, which are strongly urged and well known, for the validity of the concept of the 'good in business'.[7] This is more restricted than the concept of the 'good in human life' and, most importantly for our analysis, it is not dependent on it. So according to this particular conception of business ethics, there is a gap between asking whether something is

[7] Milton Friedman, *Capitalism and Freedom* (University of Chicago Press, 1962), pp. 133–6. See also Albert Z. Carr, 'Is business bluffing ethical?', *Harvard Business Review,* 46 (1968), pp. 143–53.

good in the business context and whether it is morally good; and once we allow such a gap, it can easily come to seem unbridgeable. We have two distinct universes of value.

In business ethics we actually possess such a Friedmanite programme; it exists, even though it is controversial. There is no explicit parallel form of 'anti-ethics' (if I may so call it) in the discussions of ethics as it applies to medicine and healthcare. None the less there are signs that such an approach may be waiting to emerge. While the health-motive is doubtless more obviously ethical than the profit-motive, so that it is easier to treat health than to treat wealth as an end in itself, from the point of view of morality neither is an unqualified good even though both are certainly goods. So it could well come to be that we will receive a Friedmanite (perhaps it should be called a Singerian[8]) proposal to detach medical ethics from general ethics, so that the latter should not have any power in principle to check or counter the concerns of the former.

I have rehearsed this idea, both as it is actually found in current business ethics and as it might be extended into medical ethics, in order to harness its unattractive and, I believe, unpersuasive quality. Health is too central and core a value for it to he detachable, in the way I have just described, from fundamental value; and so also, I would argue, is a concern with wealth and economic well-being. Attempts by immoralist professionals to surround their activities with sandbags will fail. Morality and its values should then rush back into these areas from which we have just tried to stem the tide. Not only in matters of health but also in questions of wealth, questions about what we should do stand, fundamentally, outside the perimeter and parameters of the specific context in which they are raised.

III

So much for Kant; and now for Aristotle! As I said before, Aristotle's diagnosis of complexity and ambiguity in the idea of good, centres on the concept that accompanies it rather than on goodness itself. The general idea is that to call something 'good' is basically unintelligible until the statement is completed by the

[8] This semi-serious attribution is suggested by Peter Singer and Karen Dawson 'IVF Technology and the Argument from Potential', in Peter Singer *et al.* (eds) *Embryo Experimentation* (Cambridge University Press, 1990), p. 88: 1 'The new reproductive technology makes it necessary to think again about how our established views about the potential of the human embryo should be applied to the embryo in the laboratory.'

semantic input of the 'thing' in respect of which it is said to be good either explicitly or by implication.[9]

Aristotle's position in the possible spectrum that is opened up by these considerations is less extreme than others that can be constructed. Remember our earlier description of the good thief who is not good. Such a person is, let us imagine, a good thief and also a good footballer, but a bad father, a bad leader-writer and a bad person. So as far as that goes, he might be supposed to consist of two good and three bad parts; and on one interpretation he would be more bad than good, by a 60/40 margin, and therefore bad rather than good.

But that is not Aristotle's way. He views certain concepts as having a weighting that can more than balance the others. Thus in the example just given, being a bad person would count much more for overall badness than being good at football and leader-writing, let alone thieving; and badness as a father could plausibly outweigh the other three citations of merit. But in fact talk of 'weight' gives the wrong idea. Aristotle is not a calculator but rather an essentialist. Because the subject of these predicates is a person essentially and the other things only accidentally, it is good rather than bad. It is good at what it is; and even if it were bad in all the other respects and not just some of them, that would not affect the issue.

So Aristotle can offer a construction of our sentence 'It is not good to be a good thief' which makes it intelligible but does not commit him to an absolutist conception of goodness. The surface reading of the sentence is misleading; for it suggests, wrongly, that 'good' in its first occurrence is not elliptical and stands in no need of complementation. Still the complementary predicate ('person' in this case) can remain tacit because, in Aristotle's view, it serves to define the nature of the very subject that, under whichever of its aspects, is being evaluated.

Aristotle urges this analysis as a corrective to Plato's strategy for postulating a form of goodness that transcends specialised forms corresponding to each skill, facet of character or focus of interest. Plato's proposal, he says, makes for a concept which is too general and therefore vacuous.[10] The *human good* represents a concept with sufficient content to be applied to the complex detail of the world – but also one that is general enough to prevent the reduction of a rich and complex substance to a sum of aspects and features. On the basis of this analysis Aristotle goes on to make full use of the con-

[9] *Nichomachean Ethics*, A6, 1096a, 19–34. The idea has been revived in modern discussion by Peter Geach, 'Good and Evil', reprinted in Philippa Foot (ed.), *Theories of Ethics* (Oxford University Press, 1967), pp. 64–73.

[10] *E.N.* A6, 1096b35–7a14.

cept of Humanity in his detailed account of how it is with the Good
– that is, the human good. We are familiar with the details. A human
person is a combination of intellect and emotional character; and
Aristotle's programme in the *Ethics* follows this division in detail in
order to provide an account of what goodness is which is both general and also substantial.[11]

Is Aristotle right about this? His account of ethics has been more
thoroughly studied than Plato's and more influential. Indeed the
two do not seem to be in serious competition, inasmuch as
Aristotle's work, much more than Plato's, contains a great deal of
detailed commentary on the different aspects of living well and living badly. However there does appear to be at least one salient difference between the philosophers, and that concerns their attitude
to the role played by knowledge of value in human life. Plato's
ethics starts with a presentation of the Socratic paradoxes, and its
later developments in no way repudiate them. Most of Aristotle's
explicit reaction to ideas expressed by Plato consists of critical
examination of these paradoxes. I shall say more about the importance of this contrast later.

The point of immediate relevance is that while no doubt Plato
and Aristotle would be at one in assessing the statement – that it is
not good to be a good thief – as both intelligible and true, their reasons for this are significantly different. As we have just seen,
Aristotle's reason is that thieving fails by the definition of humanity:
good thieves are not good because they are not good human persons,
which is something that any thief essentially is. But Plato's reason
would be the more radical one that being a thief, even a good one, is
simply not good for anything – not good at all.

Let us vary the example somewhat. Not only thieves, but also
such things as plagues, fallacious arguments, depressions (climatic
and psychological), blunders and discords are bad.[12] However good
of their kind and also allowing for exceptional circumstances in
which a particular case of such a thing may not be bad – still it is
bad in general that such things exist or occur at all. Why is this?
There is an anthropocentric interpretation of these judgements,
according to which it is the human interest that underlies the general rejection of plagues and such things as bad. But there is an
alternative view which places the disvalue in a more general context
– indeed in one that is completely general, in a word metaphysical.

[11] See further, R. Kraut, *Aristotle on the Human Good* (Princeton
University Press, 1989), pp. 312–47; F. Sparshott, *Taking Life Seriously*
(University of Toronto Press, 1994), pp. 136–49.
[12] The line of thought suggested here has some affinities with Plato. See
Philebus, 25–6.

I think that this is Plato's way; but that will take more argument. My purpose so far has simply been to show that the reasonable Aristotelian construal of the distinction between absolute and relative value, is not the only one that is compatible with the judgements of common sense in these matters.

IV

So far I have considered the challenges that Kantian and Aristotelian analyses pose to the Platonic claim that goodness is the foundation of all genuine understanding of the reality and intelligibility of everything else. My dialectical strategy requires us first to consider these philosophers' counter-proposals, since that will bring Plato's own positive account into sharper focus. From this review the idea of a form of goodness that resists fragmentation, has become much clearer;[13] and I have tried to show how the threat of fragmentation comes from two directions – from Kantian attempts to specify the concept of goodness, and from Aristotelian refinements in the relation of this concept to others.

Enough of the negative phase of the analysis! Let us now consider Plato's own positive defence of his project. The heart of the defence comes in the three images in *Republic* 6–7 – Sun, Divided Line, and Cave – which present the role of the Good in relation to knowledge and reality; but the less well known surrounds, especially the remarks in the latter part of Book 5 and the earlier part of Book 6 which provide the occasion for the more famous sections, are important too. The main themes which I shall address are the justification for assigning power to philosophers, the content of the philosophical understanding thus justified, and the connection between goodness and reality that is presupposed by such understanding.

The claim that has to be defended in the so-called 'philosophical digression' of *Republic* 5–7, is that to achieve the best political and social system a necessary and sufficient condition is the exercise of control by philosophers. Socratic irony abounds throughout the defence of the claim that philosophers should be rulers, especially as Plato develops the twin theses that philosophers would make the best rulers and that non-philosophers are right to be extremely sceptical, indeed even hostile to this claim. The second part of this

[13] The importance of the *unity* of Good in Plato's conception is well emphasised by N. P. White, *A Companion to Plato's Republic* (Oxford: Blackwell, 1979), pp. 46–9.

complex position relies on the idea that a slight imbalance in the relation between the would-be philosopher's innate endowment of character and his grasp of the nature of value can produce disastrous results. The very qualities that make the philosopher an ideal ruler have the potential for a considerable downside when they are exercised in an unsuitable cognitive environment. This means that ordinary society, which is a non-ideal condition, is right to be suspicious of the very kinds of people who also represent its best chance to become perfect.

For our discussion the interesting point about this argument is that Plato makes a strong divorce between qualities of character and the realisation of goodness. The contrast with Aristotle's association of goodness and character is palpable; and it prepares us for the possibility that Plato's conception of goodness will stand, not just as a primitive first draft, but rather as a genuine philosophical rival to the conceptions which we found in the later Aristotelian and Kantian traditions. As we know, Plato assigned to the Good the functions of unifying reality and the knowledge of it, by standing over these potentially diverse realms as a controlling factor. But what can this mean? For a long time I thought that it was little more than a programmatic aspiration, and that its meaning amounted to no more than the idea that for something to be real is for it to be a good specimen of its kind, and that to know what something is requires knowledge of the specific excellence of such a thing. On this basis Plato champions the idea of a synoptic universal science which mirrors the interconnectedness of reality in a way that the subject-specific studies and skills do not.

But I now shall try to show that there is more substance and support for Plato's metaphysics than this slight gloss provides. The main argument comes in 504–6, where Plato is introducing the master study. His argument that the object of his study is the Good comes in two steps, and it is important to understand the connection between them. First, he defends the claim that nothing is more worth studying than goodness; and then he dismisses two misconceptions of its nature. The positive claim is supported by noting that in all cases of enquiry we are interested in good specimens and also in the value of the particular subject under consideration. That is, whatever else forms the focus of our enquiry, our concern throughout is with goodness – and Plato stresses that the goodness must be genuine. Of course, we may make mistakes in our search; but the concerns which motivate us will not be satisfied by anything less than reality.

The second part of the argument in this passage rejects two plausible interpretations of what knowledge of goodness might consist in – expertise concerning pleasure or concerning knowledge itself. As Plato presents it, these answers clearly fail because they leave the issue under-determined. Knowledge has various objects, and not all of them may be good. The safest way to see off that difficulty is to make goodness the object of the required knowledge; but of course, that way shows the very proposal to be regressive. The same problem arises with the proposal that pleasure is the Good. Since not all pleasures are good, the burden of discrimination falls not on the expert in pleasure but rather on one who knows about goodness. Both proposals share the same defect of trying to transfer the target of the enquiry from goodness to something else, and of failing in this attempt. The particular candidates which Plato puts forward and dismisses either reflect category-analysis into qualities and relatives – or more likely they prompted such analysis.

The two parts of the argument here in *Republic* are connected. In the first part Plato shows that an appeal to the concept of goodness is indispensable if we are to understand anything else. In the second part he rules out the possibility that this concept itself could be explained in terms of some other one. Taken together, these two conditions point to a unitary foundation for all understanding, which is what he will claim the Good to be in the ensuing analogies of Sun, Divided Line, and Cave. Although Plato undertakes to be thoroughly reticent about the subject of his reflections in those sections, one thing that he does is to characterise the Good as 'beyond reality'; and I want now to consider how we are to make sense of this phrase.

The passage from which it is drawn is, as M. M. McCabe says, 'pretty mysterious';[14] and she might well have said the same about the following commentary on it by H. W. B. Joseph:

> The Form of Good then is not one among the other forms, to which being belongs and which are objects of knowledge. From one point of view, reality is exhausted in them. That which is good, and the goodness of it, are the same; for nothing of what is good fails to contribute to that goodness which consists in its being just all that it is. From another point of view, its goodness is something beyond everything contained in our description of what is good; for we describe it by running over its constituent parts, the Forms which are the various objects of our knowledge; and its goodness is none of these.[15]

---

[14] *Republic* 509b; M. M. McCabe, *Plato's Individuals* (Princeton University Press, 1994), p. 72.

[15] H. W. B Joseph, *Knowledge and the Good in Plato's Republic* (Oxford University Press, 1948), pp. 23–4.

Joseph's account suggests that the Good is a super-Form, standing to all of the Forms as each Form stands to the perceptible things which participate in it. Such an interpretation can be supported by Plato's claim that the Good is not part of reality, which he combines with his description of it as beyond reality; but it misrepresents the Good to locate it in a different realm from other Forms. Forms are essential to knowledge; this we know from other works of Plato's besides these passages in Books 6 and 7 of *Republic*. What these particular passages add to this account is that in addition to being directed on Forms, such knowledge must be based on a grasp of one individual among them – the Good.

Because it makes sense to ask, with respect to any kind of thing, under what conditions it is good, we can understand the Platonic claim that every Form is dependent on the Good. But the question is necessarily redundant where goodness itself is concerned; and for this reason the claim that the Form Good is the first principle can, indeed, be stated but not demonstrated.

Earlier I spoke of the metaphysical conception of value: according to this such things as plagues and fallacious arguments are bad, not just because we humans find them irksome and offensive but for intrinsic reasons derived from the nature of reality itself This same conception of value seems to manifest itself in the key move in the ontological argument for the existence of God which makes existence a mark of perfection. Aristotle himself says that it is better to be than not to be;[16] and the thought finds an echo in Leibniz' claim that 'those [possibles] exist that are most perfect'.[17] All of these philosophers bear witness to the insight that value forms part of the fabric of reality; and thus they may make us the more receptive to Plato's idea that reality itself – that each individual real thing and the collective which they form – is conditioned by value.

Socrates thought that all enquiry and all attempts at justification, whether in theoretical or practical matters, must stop with the good. He brought his dialectical powers to reinforce the thought that no claim for value – indeed, no claim for anything – could or should evade our powers of rational scrutiny. Plato, whose habit was to provide conceptual underpinning for Socrates' methodical insights, interpreted Socrates' idea about the autonomy of value as a requirement to separate the Good from all other things and to make it superior to them.

If we hit the fast-forward button on philosophical history, we find an echo of this attitude in the contemporary emphasis on the need

[16] *De Generatione et Corruptione* B10, 336b28–9.

[17] *Textes Inédits*, quoted by R. M. Adams, *Leibniz: Determinist, Idealist, Theist* (New York: Oxford University Press), p. 171.

for 'normativity' in conceptual investigation. What this demand seems to amount to is a request not just for *why* some conceptual item is deployed but also *with what good reason* this is done.

All these reflections provide content, I believe, to the Platonic thesis that the Good is the ground of the reality and intelligibility of everything. They give reasons for regarding a grasp of value as indispensable for the understanding of reality. Still, a cautious philosophical critic may be tempted to see Plato's claim as an excessively audacious generalisation – one which ignores and elides distinctions which subtler analysis should reveal. Remember, then, our earlier examination and rebuttal of two notable attempts to draw just such distinctions. The negative part of our dialectic complements the positive.

V

At the time I was constructing this lecture, one philosopher who was much in my mind was Iris Murdoch. This was not, of course, simply because a major theme of her philosophical work has been the central place that should be assigned to the Good in an adequate grasp of reality; in addition we were all bound to think about her because of the wide publicity given to John Bayley's account of her current condition. So I think it appropriate to end by reminding you of a passage from her essay 'The Sovereignty of Good over Other Concepts':

> A genuine mysteriousness attaches to the idea of goodness and the Good. This is a mystery with several aspects. The indefinability of Good is connected with the unsystematic and inexhaustible variety of the world and the pointlessness of virtue. In this respect there is a special link between the concept of Good and the ideas of Death and Chance. ... A genuine sense of mortality enables us to see virtue as the only thing of worth; and it is impossible to limit and foresee the ways in which it will be required of us.[18]

My comment on this is that the mystery should be demystified. The Good is indeed the sovereign concept, in both the complex of values and the spread of reality. Within values, no other concept can occupy the unifying role which the Good does in relation to the varieties of things that attract and motivate us. Within the realm of things, no other concept than the Good has the range of application,

[18] *The Sovereignty of Good over Other Concepts*, p. 99. Iris Murdoch died on February 8, 1999.

as well as the positive content, that enables it to function as a metaphysical foundation. Plato's thesis that the Good is a single principle supplies him with a defence of this conception against the Aristotelian and Kantian attacks.

Of course there is an alternative, and that is pluralism – pluralism within moral value, within value more generally, and more broadly still, within the scheme of reality. I have presented no argument against this position; but I believe that I am at one with Plato, Aristotle, Hume, Kant, Iris Murdoch, in finding it unacceptable. The conception of Good that is anti-pluralist must be unitarian; and I have tried to show how Plato's proposal must be a leading contender in the field.

Is the esse of intrinsic value percipi?: pleasure, pain and value

T. L. S. SPRIGGE

1. Introductory

In this paper I shall speak sympathetically of a hedonistic theory of intrinsic value which, ignoring any other such theories, I shall simply call the hedonistic theory of value. How far I am finally committed to it will partly appear at the end.

The hedonistic theory of value identifies intrinsic value, that is, positive intrinsic value, with pleasurableness as a quality of certain experiences, or components of experience, and similarly identifies negative intrinsic value or disvalue with painfulness or unpleasurableness as a quality of the same.

I mostly prefer the expression 'pleasurable' to 'pleasant' for that quality possession of which makes an experience a pleasure. This is because 'pleasant' in common usage, often implies a rather tepid degree of that quality. Experiences can, of course, be unpleasurable, unpleasant or painful, that is, pains, in the sense relevant for ethics or value theory without being physically painful.[1]

To be valuable otherwise is to be extrinsically valuable as a means to promoting pleasure or preventing pain or in the case of negative extrinsic value the converse. The sharp separation of intrinsic and extrinsic value is sometimes challenged as ethically unhelpful. If what is meant is that the things and activities which it is most desirable to promote are both intrinsically and extrinsically valuable, I agree, but that does not challenge the distinction between the two ways of being *valuable*.

If we combine this hedonistic theory of intrinsic value with ethical consequentialism we arrive at a hedonistic ethic. This hedonistic ethic will be universalist in the sense that it regards the equivalent pleasures and pains of all sentient individuals as equally important. Hedonistic psychology, in contrast, presents itself most obviously as an egoistic theory.

Hedonistic ethics or value theory is more associated historically with empiricism than idealism. However, many empiricist philoso-

---

[1] The suffix 'able' of course has no normative force such as it has in 'desirable', nor does it imply merely what can be pleasant on analogy with 'visible'.

phers have rejected hedonistic ethics while something not far from it has been advocated by some idealists. I suggest, however, that a case can be made for it both on empiricist and on idealist grounds.

The basic principle of at least *British* idealism has been that to be is to perceive or to be perceived, or alternatively that to be is to be experienced in the sense of either being an experience or a component in an experience. I side with the modification of Berkeley's '*esse* is *percipere* or *percipi*' into 'to be is to be experienced' on the ground that consciousness or experience comes in units which normally divide into a self and a not-self side and that both, and the relation between them, are experienced. If one looks at a painting, the painting as seen belongs to the not-self side of one's experience while one's thoughts about it belong to the self side of one's experience. The painting may be said to be an object of consciousness while one's thoughts about it belong to the self side of one's experience and are modes, but not objects, of consciousness.

Pleasure and pain float between the self side and the object side of experience. So far as they pertain to the object side, when one looks at a painting. they will constitute the painting's beauty or ugliness, so far as they pertain to the self side they will constitute one's more detached appreciation or dislike of it.

So, as I see it, *percipere* and *percipi* come together as different ways of being experienced and the idealist should say simply that to be is to be experienced.

I suggest now that if an idealist applies this identification of *being* with *being experienced* to value he may find it hard not to embrace some form of hedonism. For to say that an experience *feels good* is very little distance away from saying that it is *pleasurable*. So if the *esse* of goodness, in the sense of intrinsic good, consists in being experienced or felt as good, 'goodness', in this sense means virtually the same as 'pleasure'. Similarly to say that an experience *feels bad* is very little distance away from saying that it is *unpleasant*. So if the *esse* of badness in this sense is to be *experienced as bad*, then badness means virtually the same as pain or unpleasure.

Admittedly when pleasure or pain is objectified[2] that is, qualifies an object on the not-self side rather than the self-side of our experience, it is usually inappropriate to say that the object feels good, unless indeed it is something handled in which case 'feel' is being used in a different sense. But though we would not say of a paint-

---

[2] Santayana defined 'beauty' as 'pleasure objectified' in George Santayana, *The Sense of Beauty: Being the Outlines of Aesthetic Theory* (New York: Charles Scribner's Sons, 1896), chapter 1, §11. Santayana, of course, was no idealist.

ing that it feels good, we may well say that it looks good. So here again if the esse of visual goodness, or beauty, is *to be experienced as good*, that is to say, *to look good*, then visual goodness or beauty, for an idealist, becomes a form of pleasure. Similarly with what is perceptually presented through the other senses. Ugliness may likewise be described as objectified pain or unpleasure.

Thus there is a clear logical path from idealism to a hedonistic theory of intrinsic value.

What of the path from empiricism to a hedonistic theory of intrinsic value? Well, as I see it, the fundamental principle of empiricism is Hume's doctrine that an idea must be derived from an impression, or 'constructed' out of what is so. Or something at least very much of the same sort. Now if we ask what the impression is from which we get our idea of the intrinsically good, or the intrinsically bad, I suggest that it is from impressions of pleasure or pain.

When life is really joyous everything seems good. Stale questions about the point of life fade away and the present totality of experience seems justification enough. We exaggerate if we identify the present totality of experience with the world, but that is what we tacitly do in such moments. And this goodness or wonderfulness of the world is its pleasurableness. Similarly with pain and unpleasure. When our consciousness is pervasively unpleasant things as a whole seem simply bad. And this is where we get our idea of the intrinsically bad from.

It is generally believed that pleasure and pain can only occur as qualities of experiences or, as I would add to be more precise, components of experience.[3] Yet some people have believed that things lying quite outside of anyone's experience can be intrinsically good or bad. G. E. Moore's description of the goodness of a beautiful world even in the absence of consciousness is too well know for me to quote.[4] But I am rash enough to suggest that Moore was confused as to what he was conceiving and was really conceiving a beautiful world presenting itself to a consciousness enjoying its beauty.

So my claim is that we get the idea of the intrinsically good, worthwhile, or whatever you like to call it, from the impression of pleasure, but that we confusedly think of it as capable of qualifying things other than experiences or components of experience. Similarly with pain and badness. Come to think of it that is what many of us think about the secondary qualities; indeed, it is what

[3] A painting as presented to vision is a component in an experience, but it would be unnatural to call it an experience, though an idealist sounding language in which everything is called an experience is strangely current (e.g. the millennium-dome experience).

[4] G. E. Moore, *Principia Ethica* (Cambridge University Press, 1954, first published 1903), pp. 83–4.

idealists think about the primary qualities of the physical too. So I think I have made my case that empiricism and idealism both point strongly in the direction of a hedonistic account of intrinsic value.

So much by way of introduction. I shall now present my own case for a hedonistic theory of value.

2. Main argument

2.1 If there are objective values they must possess a feature which in fact nothing possesses except pleasure and pain

If there is such a thing as intrinsic value as an objective property of things it must have a certain feature which it has been thought problematic for any objective property to possess.[5]

And this feature is so much the clue to understanding, the concept of intrinsic value that it would seem not only that it must be met by objective intrinsic value, if there is such a thing, but that anything which meets it must be regarded either as simply identical with intrinsic value or as a species thereof.

The feature in question is that of being necessarily attractive or. so to speak, magnetic for the will. That is, the belief that something conceived as a future possibility would possess this property must have some essential tendency to encourage the desire that it will exist or occur, other things being equal.

The same, *mutatis mutandis*, must be true of intrinsic disvalue, if there is such a thing. That is, the belief that something conceived as a future possibility would possess this property must have some essential tendency to encourage the desire that it will not occur or exist.

It must also be true that the recognition that something which exists or is occurring now has the one or the other of these properties must have some essential tendency to encourage the desire that it will continue, or not continue, to do so.

Desire here must be understood as a mental state which has some intrinsic tendency to produce action which is thought likely to actualise what it is a desire for on the part of an organism in whose mind it occurs.

Or, in the case of what we may call negative desire, it must be

[5] On looking up a point just recently in Moritz Schlick's *The Problems of Ethics* I realised that I have probably been to some considerable extent influenced by him in the development of the suggestions in what follows about pleasure and pain, as values and motivators. See Moritz Schlick, trans. David Rynin, *Problems of Ethics* (New York: Dover Publications, 1962, being the 1939 translation of *Fragen der Ethic* first published 1930).

understood as a mental state which has some intrinsic and *necessary* tendency to produce action which is thought likely to stop the actualisation of that of which it is a desire for the non-existence or non-occurrence.

Here again I am speaking of a necessity of a kind which may be thought deeply problematic.

For certainly, as I mean this specification to be understood, the fact that an organism desires something is not the fact that it tends to act, in the sense of moving about, in a way likely to bring its object about, (or prevent its coming about in the case of negative desire) but something distinct which necessarily tends to cause this.

However, my more immediate concern is to argue that pleasure and pain are species respectively of intrinsic and negative intrinsic value. For they precisely meet the requirement which is thought so distinctively problematic in the very notion of there being such a thing as objective intrinsic value, positive and negative.

But how can pleasure and pain be regarded either as identical with or as a species of objective intrinsic value seeing, that they are essentially subjective phenomena?

Such a question rests on a misunderstanding. An objective fact, in the relevant sense, is a fact such that its affirmation is not simply the expression of an emotional attitude or some other mental phenomenon incapable of being true or false. In short, we are dealing with a matter of objective fact wherever it is genuinely true or false that the fact exists. I shall not spend time on what 'genuinely true or false' means hoping that it is clear enough what I have in mind, however difficult to find a satisfactory analysis.

In this sense it is an objective fact whether a certain experience is pleasurable or unpleasurable, and relatedly whether a particular conscious individual is presently experiencing something pleasurable or painful. It is an objective fact, so we may put it, about a subjective state.

I now contend that pleasure is intrinsically attractive and pain intrinsically unattractive (or better: disattractive) precisely in the sense that to know or believe that some experience which one might bring about would be pleasurable has a necessary tendency to encourage the desire that it should exist or occur, and that to know or believe that some experience would be painful has a necessary tendency to encourage the desire that it should not occur.

Of course, these tendencies may be inhibited by other mental states, most obviously by contrary desires.

Ah, you may be saying, if there is any truth in this at all, it is only when the experience is going to be one's own that its expected pleasurableness or painfulness has any such necessary tendency.

T. L. S. Sprigge

To this I reply as follows. The mere belief that an experience, whether mine or someone else's, would be pleasurable or painful does indeed have some tendency to produce a desire that it should or should not occur, a desire which has the tendency to affect action as described above. However, where the experiences will be those of someone else, the desire tends to be a weak one easily overcome by more egoistic desires. But this is at least partly because beliefs about our own future experience are upon the whole more fully realised. Most of what we call our beliefs go with fairly little real conscious grasp of what it is we believe. My claim about the necessary attractiveness or disattractiveness of pleasure or pain may now be qualified as the claim that this tendency depends upon, and is more powerful, the more we fully realise in consciousness what it is that we are believing, when we are believing that some experience promoted by certain activity on our part would be pleasant or painful.

Much of the time, though in words and in expectations about external behaviour we may acknowledge that another is suffering, or is about to suffer, we do not really take in the reality of this. For such beliefs, like beliefs in general, may be more or less intuitively fulfilled, to use Husserl's terminology.

Let us hear Josiah Royce on the subject and forgive a certain suggestion of the pulpit which some Harvard philosophers then thought appropriate.

> What, then, is our neighbour? ... He is not that face that frowns or smiles at thee, although often thou thinkest of him as only that. ... Thou hast regarded his thought, his feeling, as somehow different in sort from thine. Thou hast said, 'A pain in him is not like a pain in me, but something far easier to bear.' Thou hast made of him a ghost, as the imprudent man makes of his future self a ghost. Even when thou hast feared his scorn, his hate, his contempt, thou hast not fully made him for thee as real as thyself. His laughter at thee hast made thy face feel hot, his frowns and clenched fists have cowed thee, his sneers have made thy throat feel choked. But that was only the social instinct in thee. It was not a full sense of his reality. ... Of thy neighbor thou hast made a thing, no Self at all. ...
>
> Have done with this illusion, and simply try to learn the truth. Pain is pain, joy is joy, everywhere, even as in thee . ... The result of thy insight will be inevitable. Seeing the oneness of this life everywhere, the equal reality of all its moments, thou wilt be ready to treat it all with the reverence that prudence would have thee show to thy own little bit of future life. Lift up thy eyes,

behold that life, and then turn away, and forget as thou canst; but, if, thou hast *known* that, thou hast begun to know thy duty.[6]

So at least part of the reason why we are more concerned about our own pleasures and pains than those of others is that our beliefs about our own experiences are much more fully realised. I am probably not alone in shamefacedly sometimes thinking more intensively of my own next meal, if I am a little bit hungry, than the fate of starving people I see on television.

I shall say a bit more about the contrast there is for us between our own experiences and those of others later. I am only concerned to claim that the hedonic quality of the lives of others, as we think our actions might affect them, have some tendency, and necessarily so, however weak it may be, to influence our behaviour in the direction of improving it, and the more so the more vividly their situation is imagined.

This provides a strong case for saying that pleasure and pain, are either identical with positive and negative intrinsic value, or are species thereof. For they meet the requirement of being intrinsically magnetic, positively or negatively, which I have suggested is so essential to our concept of what objective intrinsic value, positive or negative, if it exists, must be.

In spite of this, pleasure and pain are most sharply distinguished from intrinsic value and disvalue by the philosopher who was most influential in the development of the latter concepts. However, as was implied above, it is my belief, when, as in this respect a Humean, I ask from what impression G. E. Moore got his idea of intrinsic value, that what was really magnetic here was, in fact, pleasure confusedly conceived as present in the absence of consciousness, similarly in the case of the negative magnetism of intrinsic badness or 'vileness'.

So may we go further and say that pleasure and pain are actually identical with intrinsic value, positive and negative? My positive answer rests upon the fact that, as in the case of Moore, so with all others who claim to conceive of intrinsic value (positive or negative) as pertaining to things quite other than pleasure and pain (in all their various forms) and even existing outside all consciousness, when I try imaginatively to identify with their thought I find myself thinking of these things as suffused with just that emotional magnetism (positive or negative) which, as it seems to me, can only really belong to a pleasurable or unpleasurable experience or component thereof.

[6] Josiah Royce, *The Religious Aspect of Philosophy* (Gloucester, Mass: Peter Smith, 1965), pp. 156–62.

T. L. S. Sprigge

2.2 Pleasure and pain as intrinsically prescriptive realities existing in rerum natura

Some philosophers may think that the intrinsic appeal to the will, which we are ascribing to pleasure and pain, does not justify their identification with what we all refer to clearly or confusedly as intrinsic value, positive and negative. For that it must be shown that they are somehow inherently prescriptive in the sense of having a kind of imperatival force which cannot be gainsaid by those who are properly aware of them.

However, to me it seems that there is little difference between the notion of something as thus intrinsically prescriptive and the notion of something to know of which is necessarily to desire its existence or non-existence, continuation or cessation.

As such, even for those not yet persuaded that they are identical with positive and negative value, pleasure and pain pose a formidable challenge to the idea that nature, so to speak, does not offer imperatives of its own which are not some kind of freely adopted human option. So let us consider them simply in this light for a little.

Perhaps the defender of the view that nothing in nature can be intrinsically prescriptive will claim that it is merely a contingent fact that we are attracted by, and desire the existence of, what we expect to be pleasurable, and similarly, *mutatis mutandis*, with pain.

But I do not think that it is *merely contingent* that we desire the occurrence of the one and the non-occurrence of the other. That there is a certain necessity to this, where the pleasure and pain is our own, will be granted by most people quite readily. The further claim, that it is mainly because the experiences of others are only half believed in, that the thought of their pleasure and pains is so much less strongly motivating, may be less readily granted. So let us consider the egoistic concern with our own pleasure and pain first.

Is a species of animal whose tendencies are contra-hedonistic possible? I believe that we find such an idea absurd. It seems obvious that any being capable of pleasure and pain, and capable of anticipating them, will be concerned to get the former and avoid the latter. But if a contra-hedonistic species is impossible then pleasure and pain are intrinsically magnetic, positively or negatively, for all those capable of experiencing and expecting them.

Two alternative responses are possible for those who wish to deny that nature contains anything with this sort of necessary appeal to the will.

(1) The first is that this is a mere trivial analytic truth. For 'pleasure' (the objector will say) is simply being used as a common term for such experiences as a conscious individual as a matter of

contingent fact, likes and seeks, and 'pain' simply as a common term for experiences which such an individual dislikes and tries to avoid.

But this seems simply wrong. If one goes for a long time without serious pain, one can more or less forget its distinctive nature. But then, when it comes, one is reminded only too well of what it is like, that is, of its reality as a distinctive quality of experience. And that one responds by attempting to bring it to an end is a distinct fact, though one with a necessary relation of tendency, to its having this quality.

This is as true of such mental pain, as depression, as it is of physical pain.

Similarly, if one is gloomy over a period one may half forget what pleasure is. But immediately it comes one is orientated towards continuing it, and does so other things being equal.

If a contra-hedonic species is impossible, then, it would seem to be a transparently necessary truth that any being who can experience and conceive them, must desire pleasure and the avoidance of pain. Moreover, since this is not a mere matter of definition it would seem that it is what used to be called a 'synthetic *a priori* truth'.

I speak of the necessity as 'transparent' because I am not concerned with the necessities of which some speak, especially in connection with the laws of nature, which are radically distinguished from the *a priori* knowable.

(2) The alternative strategy for those who are reluctant to admit the existence of real necessities in nature is to insist that it is only because it is so very much the norm in fact, that we are inclined to think it a necessary truth that pleasure and pain, or the prospect of them, have the the effect on us which they do but that this is really something essentially contingent.

Two cases are stressed here, in connection with pain. First, we are reminded of the phenomenon of masochism. Secondly, we are informed of brain operations which produce a state in which pain is recognised as pain, but is not minded. Similar results, it is said, may be achieved through meditative practices.

Regarding masochism, I would argue that what is painful at one level can be pleasurable at another level. I might even appeal to Moore's principle of organic unities here, giving it a hedonistic interpretation which he might have disliked. That is, there may be states of consciousness in which an included pain adds to the pleasure of the whole. In masochism, I urge, for a mixture of reasons, partly physiological and partly more psychologically determined, the response of dislike to something going on within consciousness is wrapped round in, so to speak, a blanket of pleasurableness, this being the more over-all character of the total experience. An attempt to imagine masochistic delights will surely support this.

Regarding the experience of pain which one does not mind we should distinguish here between a character of a physical sensation and the painfulness which usually comes along with it. The person who does not mind his pain is aware of a sensation which he used to find painful but which no longer is painful.

Of course, there is such a thing as Stoic bravery, but the person who withstands torture without imparting the information which would stop it, as much desires that the pain would stop as anyone else but he has an even stronger desire not to betray his cause or his associates, and we are not saying that pleasure and pain are the only things we desire, though I shall shortly be claiming that all desire involves pleasure and pain even when they are not its objects.

What of counter-examples to the attraction of pleasure? May not certain ascetic inclinations actually turn one away from sources of pleasure? Yes, I am sure that this is so. But here the pleasure, for whatever reason, seems somehow sordid, that is, bad in a particular kind of way, and this badness, which is a certain painfulness in which our thought of it bathes it, is more powerful than the expected goodness of it.

2.3 The more basic explanation of why we desire pleasure and avoidance of pain

Our claim then is that there is a certain transparent necessity to our desire for pleasure and for the avoidance of pain. But is this necessity the consequence of the operation of some still more basic necessity? I suggest that it is, for we ought to distinguish between the necessary effects of actual pleasure and pain on our activity and the necessary effects of conceived pleasure and pain in virtue of which we necessarily desire the one and desire the avoidance of the other.

This basic necessity, so I suggest, is that it is of the nature of consciousness to move somehow towards the pleasurable and away from the painful, and – so far at least as its past can influence its future at all[7] – to prompt to activity which in the past has sustained

---

[7] The astute reader may realise that, as a panpsychist (see below) I hesitate as to whether all forms of consciousness allow of any such ability to learn at all. Maybe there is learning in the so-called inanimate world, but maybe, as I suppose science suggests, there is not. But even if not I should suggest that there is some kind of necessary movement towards the pleasurable and away from the painful as they occur and that this is the noumenal grounding of the laws of nature.

or produced pleasurable experience or has terminated, or diminished the intensity of, painful experience.

Also there must be some basic power of calculation on the basis of experience as to what is likely to increase or sustain pleasure or terminate or diminish pain where this is not a matter of the exact repetition of a past situation.

An objection worth a brief comment is that certain obsessive ideas seem to be sustained in consciousness precisely because of their unpleasantness. The answer is surely that there is something in our situation which continually evokes them. And their result is behaviour which consciousness calculates may expel them from our system by presenting the world as one in which their content has no place. Our thought thus dwells on them as something to be expunged from reality.

The views presented here on the influence of pleasure and pain on behaviour might be described as a phenomenological version of the reinforcement theories of psychologists like B. F. Skinner.

When I say that consciousness prompts to activity on this basis I assume that the consciousness is linked up with a brain, or some other guiding machine within the individual whose consciousness it is. I am in no position to theorise as to the nature of this link. What I do urge, however, is that whenever there is a link of a kind which makes a consciousness the consciousness of a particular organism it must be one which allows for this influence.[8]

However, the influence may not be entirely from consciousness to the physical and vice versa. There is activity which is internal to consciousness and here we can take it that a consciousness, as long as it continues at all, will influence its own internal activities in this way.

This is a very dualistic picture of the relation between consciousness and an organism. I am quite prepared for the truth to be rather that consciousness is the felt inner nature of certain brain processes, and that physical theory will find an analogue, perhaps to some extent already has done so, of this necessary tendency of consciousness to prompt to activity which has been hedonically useful in its past.

This is very easy for me to grant since I am in any case a panpsychist who believes that the mental, in the sense of consciousness, is the inner nature of all physical processes. That is, all physical processes are the outer or structural appearances of a system of flows of experience, of more, or much less, personal kinds.[9]

---

[8] I am inclined to say that consciousness can only be causally linked to an organism in a way which allows this tendency to prompt to activity which has been hedonically valuable in the way indicated.

[9] See my *The Vindication of Absolute Idealism* (Edinburgh University Press, 1983), especially chapters 3 and 4.

Therefore it is likely that what we call *our consciousness* is the inner nature of certain processes in the brain. However, I suspect that these physical processes are ones which do not conform entirely to the standard laws of physics.[10]

What I do insist on is that if epiphenomenalism is false, and though I once believed in epiphenomenalism it has come to seem to me very implausible, consciousness – meaning by this not some so far not quite understood physical process identified only by its function – but consciousness, as what we know the true nature of by being instances of it, must have some kind of dynamic of its own which settles the kind of influence it can have on the brain and via that on behaviour, or if it is itself the inner nature of brain process the way it interacts with the inner nature of other brain process, and thus with the remainder of the brain and the organism.

If consciousness develops according to the hedonic principles I have adumbrated, then there must be some way in which this should be taken into account in a more full explanation of human and animal action, which will be based both upon brain research and phenomenological reflection.

How does this basic hedonic principle relate to what we might call the derived hedonic principle that pleasure and pain, conceived as effects of action open to us, are intrinsically attractive or disattractive, which is as much as to say that we tend necessarily to desire pleasure and the avoidance of pain, though of course any particular desire of this sort may be checked by other desires?

It is simply this. These ideas operate like any other components of consciousness in the sense that, to the extent that they are pleasurable, consciousness does what is required to sustain or strengthen them, while if they are unpleasurable consciousness does what is required to remove or weaken them. Now nothing so sustains or enriches an idea of an action which one might do as the doing of that action, and nothing removes an idea of an action so effectively as another action which prevents it. And this is true not only of ideas of actions, but of ideas of states of affairs which one's actions may produce or prevent. Thus pleasant ideas of things to be done or brought about tend to realise themselves, that is to make real that of which they are the ideas, while unpleasant ideas tend to make real that which prevents the occurrence of what they envisage.

And this, in my opinion, is what desires are, namely pleasurable ideas of behaviour on our part, or of its consequences, which pass into action because this is what best sustains belief in their content or, if the ideas are painful, tends best to prevent the actualisation of their content.

[10] Ibid., chapter 4.

However, these pleasant or unpleasant ideas which our embodied consciousness has learnt to sustain or be rid of, by banishing their objects from that real world of which its awareness is compulsory, need not be ideas *of* pleasures or pains. Our goals are a matter of what the ideas are of, not the quality of pleasurableness or painfulness in virtue of which they cause behaviour.

Thus I may be concerned at the despoliation of some beautiful countryside by a new road, and my idea of the badness of such despoliation may be so strong that it passes into activity calculated to hinder its construction. It is because the idea of this despoliation is painful that consciousness prompts behaviour which looks as though it may prevent it. But it is the despoliation which I am trying to prevent, not my own pain or anyone else's.

So our desires consist of self-realising or self-de-realising pleasant or unpleasant ideas of what can be produced or prevented by our behaviour but they need not be ideas *of* pleasure or pain at all. The basic hedonic mechanism of consciousness prompts behaviour which will strengthen our pleasant ideas and weaken our unpleasant ideas, and this will include especially behaviour which will bring about or prevent that of which they are the ideas.

But though, on this view, our goals need not be pleasures or pains, there is a special tendency for pleasure and exemption from pain to become main objects of our concern. This is because, although an idea of a pleasure and a pleasurable idea must be distinguished, it is also true that the more vivid our ideas of pleasure, the more pleasurable they become, and similarly, *mutatis mutandis*. with ideas of the painful.

My views on this matter are associated with the belief that in a fully realised idea of some situation one is attributing to it qualities which are actually there as qualities of the idea itself, though the more normal case is that there is just the most fleeting adumbration of them. In the case of desires the fuller the realisation of the goodness or badness we are attributing to the envisaged situation the more powerful the influence of their own hedonic quality upon us.[11]

So ideas of pleasure and pain are likely, in virtue of their own pleasurableness or painfulness, to be particularly strong prompts to behaviour.

Another perspective on the matter is this. If I am right, our idea of intrinsic goodness is derived from the impression of pleasure actually experienced, and our idea of badness is derived from the impression of painfulness. Thus when we think of something as

[11] A return to the introspective investigation of mental phenomena (such as 'ideas') is certainly called for. Why is it that I at least can imagine sounds so much more adequately than colours?

intrinsically good we are really thinking of it as having this quality of pleasurableness, and when as intrinsically bad this quality of painfulness. But nothing can really have this quality except pleasurable experience, or pleasurable components of' experience, or, in the negative case, painful experience or painful components of experience. So the thought that something unexperienced, or not pleasurable, can really be intrinsically good is always an illusion, and similarly thoughts of things as intrinsically bad.

We can now see that psychological hedonism, of the kind I have been developing, which concerns not the goals of behaviour, but its mental causation by pleasant and unpleasant ideas, can explain why it is that we can genuinely mind how what we do affects the pleasures and pains of others. This is because, in so far as we imagine them with vividness, they, must prompt behaviour which is expected to produce the one and prevent the other.

From this point of view, the problem is rather why, for the most part, we are so selfish rather than why or how we can ever be altruistic. To this there are two aspects. First, it is easy when comparing my attitude to my own comfort and that of others to forget that it is not only *ideas of my own pleasure and pain* which operate upon me, but *pleasures and pains themselves* (I mean pleasures and pains which do not consist in ideas). Thus if I am reluctant to give up my seat on a bus to someone who looks very frail it is my present actual comfort which acts against its disruption as much as my idea of the discomfort of standing up, and when I eat greedily, it is the pleasure of *eating* which makes me continue to do so, perhaps at the cost of greater goods, rather than *ideas of eating*. Thus the pleasures and pains of others can only influence me through my ideas of them while my own pleasures and pains can operate on me non-ideally.

But the other factor, as we saw above when I quoted Josiah Royce, is that we tend not to believe in the reality of the pleasures and pains of others quite as vividly as we believe in the reality of our own.

Natural selection offers an easy explanation of this fact if explanation is needed.

3. The relation of the hedonistic theory of value to the moral ought

3.1 *The* ought

The topic of this series of lectures is value rather than such notions as that of the *ought*, moral or otherwise. But unless there is some tie in with the notion of *ought* a theory of intrinsic value is incomplete.

It will be expected that I hold a hedonistic consequentialist ethic, and that is roughly, true.

However, there is something unfortunate about the word 'consequentialism'. It suggests that it is never what one is doing now but only its subsequent consequences which matter. Moreover, there is some difficulty in distinguishing between the consequences of an act and the act itself. C. I. Lewis thought that the act was the mere more specifically uncharacterisable *oomph* of decision and everything else its consequences.[12] But I believe that this *oomph* is simply the relief from the tension of indecision, and that decisive or spontaneous actions are not thus preceded.

The proper solution is simply to consider the character of the act itself as among its most important consequences. And by the character of the act I mean here the character it has strictly *at its own time*, for if it is characterised in terms of its objective relations to past facts – unless, indeed, these are inherent in its present character – the spirit of consequentialism is lost. And of course for hedonistic ethics the relevant character is its present unique pleasurableness or unpleasurableness.

But even with this explanation, it is all too easy to see consequentialism as failing to do justice to the value of action in its own time. But in many cases, where consequences are slight or largely unpredictable, that is what most matters. An enjoyable country walk is its own justification unless it leads to trouble. I do not know what expression other than 'consequentialism' would meet this point better.

That intrinsic value and disvalue lead to an **OUGHT** follows from their inherent positive or negative magnetism. What one believes one ought to do is that towards doing which one is most drawn by the positive magnetism of some good expected to be its result, or negative magnetism of some evil it is expected to prevent. Since one's being so drawn is a mistake if one misconceives the nature and value of the present character and consequences of the act, it would seem to follow that to be right is to be thus drawn by a true judgement of the same nature.

This yields the most basic sense of 'ought'. But what one more specifically *morally ought* to do is what it would be best that one should be encouraged to do by the approval and disapproval of others, and indeed of oneself, not that is, what they actually approve and disapprove but what they ought to do, in the basic sense.[13] This points, I would argue, not so much to rule utilitarianism as to what

[12] C. I. Lewis, *The Ground and Nature of the Right* (New York: Columbia University Press, 1955), p. 43

[13] Although I did not use the expression there, Part Two of my *The Rational Foundations of Ethics* (London: Routledge and Kegan Paul, 1988) is, in effect, a defence of way-of-life utilitarianism.

may be called 'way of life utilitarianism'. Desirable action is action in the spirit of that way of life which is hedonically the best available for all those engaged in it, or affected by it, and what one is morally obliged to do is that which it is part of the goodness of that way of life that one should be blamed for not doing.

In supporting way-of-life utilitarianism, rather than direct utilitarianism, I distance myself considerably from the cost/benefit approach to moral issues characteristic of, and to some extent derived from, Jeremy Bentham.[14]

3.2 The hedonistic calculus

In virtue of this a hedonistic calculus need not function largely in deciding what I ought to do. However, it does seem that, at some very basic level, some sort of hedonistic calculus must hold. For it is a hedonistic calculation which provides our reason, when we feel the need to reflect on it, for living according to the norms of the way of life we regard as best.

Bentham's hedonistic calculus, with its seven dimensions of pleasure and pain, intensity, duration, probability, proximity, fecundity, purity and extent, was never presented as something which could be used in any mechanical or precise way.[15] Rather it specified an ideal ground for decision making, not fully available to us in practice, to which our grounds of decision making should approximate so far as possible. Even so it would seem that there must, for utilitarianism, be a truth as to what it would be best to do determined by the dimensions which figure in that calculus even if we cannot have more than a reasonable guess at it.[16]

I have three main answers to this.

(1) The utilitarian may argue that what is objectively true is that every first level fact in favour of an action must consist in pleasure promoted or pain prevented and conversely with first level facts against an action. But the second level at which these pleasures and pains are weighted against each other is a matter of how an individual is attracted to the mix of pleasures and pains produced by an act, whether for himself or others, and this is a mat-

---

[14] For example, even when a cost/benefit analysis may favour vivisection, way of life utilitarianism may condemn it as incompatible with the spirit of the best form of life possible for us.

[15] Jeremy Bentham, *An Introduction to the Principles of Morals and Legislation*, chapter IV.

[16] There is a difficulty, however, in the idea that probability figures in ultimate truth rather than in human thought.

ter of personal psychology. What is ruled out are reasons which have nothing essentially to do with pleasure and pain.

(2) The second answer goes further than this and says that with any mix of pleasures and pains distributed between different persons and times there is a truth as to how an adequate synthesising imagination of them all would be attracted more or less to it than some other mix.[17]

(3) A third point worth making is that it is obviously always desirable to go for pleasures which are fecund and nearly pure in Bentham's sense, that is pleasures which are productive of further pleasures and unproductive of pains, and for the avoidance of fecund and pure pains on the other. This is a policy which largely dispenses with the need for a precise hedonistic calculus. And it must be this above all which gives value to a particular way of life.

4. Objections to the hedonistic theory of value

4.1 Pleasure is not one uniform kind of sensation

Let us now consider some of the objections to equating the pleasurable with the positively valuable and the painful with the negatively valuable.

A first objection is to the alleged impoverishment of the notion of value implied in the claim that there is only one good thing in life, a simple sensation of pleasure, and only one bad thing, a simple sensation of pain or distress.

Well, certainly if pleasure were a uniform sensation differing only in intensity and duration, then it would be sad, indeed, to think it the sole good in human life.[18] For then what gives us pleasure would only be a means to an end which it might be better to obtain in some more immediate way. Listening to the music of Bach or listening to the music of Delius, enjoying a vigorous swim in beautiful surroundings or the companionship of a loved one – all these would be just different means to obtaining the one desirable sensation of pleasure.

But this is a quite wrong conception of pleasure. There are all sorts of pleasures, each enjoyable in its own way for those with the capacity and in the mood for it. Each such enjoyable experience has its own distinct sort of pleasurableness, and it is intrinsically impossible that that kind of pleasurableness should come with any other

[17] For more detail see my (*Rational Foundations*), chapter VII.
[18] Much of G. E. Moore's classic critique of J. S. Mill's hedonism turns on this conception of pleasure. See Moore, *Principia Ethica*, §§ 47–8.

sort of experience. Pleasure is a genuine generic universal but its species are infinitely varied.

We must not move from this to saying that pleasure is for each person simply such experiences as he tends to go for, whatever their character may be. We may if we wish, speak of pleasure as enjoyed or liked experience, but this is not altogether helpful. It suggests that pleasurable experience consists in two components, an experience which in itself is hedonically neutral, and then a mental act of liking directed at it. But when we really like things our mind is not thus divided into two components; there is one component an essentially pleasurable experience with its own individual sort of pleasurableness. Much worse, however, than the view that pleasure is experience at which a mental act of liking, is directed is the view that it is simply, what the organism goes for, in an entirely, behavioural sense of 'goes for', for here the whole qualitative nature of pleasure is lost sight of.

In the case of pain too, where by 'pain' is meant not a particular sort of physical sensation, but any unpleasant experience, there is pain or suffering of many different sorts. Physical pain, to take the most obvious example, is a different matter from the grief of bereavement.

But if pleasures and pains are of radically different kinds, can there be even so much of more and less about them as even our way of life utilitarianism must leave standing? The answer is, perhaps, that although they are qualitatively different there is a sense in which one pleasure can be more pleasurable than another, and similarly with pain, and that there are certain ways of living, for each of us, where one's total state of mind is on the whole pleasanter than it would be if one lived otherwise.

4.2 Wicked pleasures

Another objection to hedonism is the widespread belief that wicked pleasures are not just instrumentally bad but intrinsically so. Enjoying hurting someone or relaxing from your work as a concentration camp guard as those condemned to die perform beautiful music, are both pleasures (it may be insisted) which are evil in themselves.

I certainly feel the force of this objection and find it somewhat disturbing. There are two aspects to my answer.

First, since beauty is one of the great goods which a proper hedonism should recognize I ally myself with Francis Hutcheson in holding that character or personality can be beautiful or ugly. The ugliness of the hidden portrait of Dorian Gray was indeed a transformation into visual terms of his ugliness of character.

A character is beautiful, above all, to the extent that it is open to appropriate influence by all that is best and all that is worst in the world. It is good for us that such characters should appeal the most. The pleasures of concentration camp guards can hardly be abstracted from the personality of their subject so far as our reaction to them goes.

As for the pleasures of cruelty, the proper way to reproach those addicted to them, is to persuade them that the sorrows of their victims far outweigh what positive value they have. That way, you admit that there is something good about the sense of power which perhaps is the core of their appeal but insist that there are other ways of enjoying one's power which are not so calamitous for others. But should not cruelty and sadism be impossible on our account? No, for aggression has to some extent been selected for in the development of the species, and, in its extreme forms, makes the signs of suffering on the part of its victim an exciting component in the not-self part of the cruel individual's consciousness, and, this together with the pleasure of power distorts his conception of the reality of what it is like to be the other.[19]

4.3 The experience machine

A third objection to a hedonistic theory of value is that it apparently suggests that the cognitive validity of an experience is irrelevant to its value. And this has the unacceptable implication that someone who enjoys the thought that another person loves them, when in fact the love is a deception which will never be revealed to its apparent object, is in a state which is in itself just as good, just as valuable, as it would be if the love of the other person was real.

What of values encountered in an enduringly illusory world produced by a so-called experience machine? Well, I am near enough to being some kind of phenomenalist to hold that life-long deception here is short on meaning, though the subject *calls* for a fuller discussion, especially of the experience of physical effort.[20]

However, when the deception is as to the feeling of another conscious being the phenomenalist way out is closed, so far as I am concerned. My inclination, however, is to think that actually our experiences so interpenetrate that really what we experience is the relationship between us and another, and that this relationship

[19] See my (*Rational Foundations*), pp. 235–238.

[20] There is certainly a real world which determines facts about what sensations are available, but it is more the availability of the sensations, than the real world causing them, which constitutes the truth of ordinary physical object statements.

necessarily has for each of us a qualitative character which it could not have if really there were no such relationship.

4.4 The ethical a priori

In his 'The Conception of Intrinsic Value' in *Philosophical Studies* G. E. Moore claims that the intrinsic value of something depends on its intrinsic nature but does not belong to its intrinsic nature.[21] Two things could not be exactly alike (have the same intrinsic nature) and the one possess and the other lack intrinsic value to a certain degree, and yet the value is not one of its intrinsic properties. In fact, there is a sense in which a value predicate does not describe what possesses it (see p. 274). (Here Moore seems within an inch of the view that value judgements are something other than statements of fact.) Is anything like this true of pleasurableness on our account? No, for it would seem (as Moore himself mentions) that its pleasurableness does belong to the intrinsic nature of an experience. However, we would bring pleasure very close to Moore's account of intrinsic value if we decided that the pleasurableness of an experience always depends on its other characteristics, so that two experiences could not differ only in their degree of pleasurableness. Now I am rather inclined to believe that this is true. Is it not plausible to say that if hearing a certain piece of music is pleasurable for me and not for you, then the music is organised differently within your experience from mine? And may not something of the same sort be true even of less complex experiences? And what of painfulness? Anyway, the case for identifying pleasure and pain with intrinsic value and disvalue is much stronger if this dependency holds. We may still identify them if it does not, but would have to admit that in realising their identity we also realise that intrinsic value and disvalue do not quite live up to expectations.

However, I am quite happy to recognise a necessity here since, in any case, I hold that that there is much more necessity *in 'rerum natura* than are dreamt of in most post-Humean philosophy.

4.5 Environmental issues, panpsychism and the absolute

The thought that all that matters is pleasurable or unpleasurable experience, even when pleasures and pains are regarded as immensely, various in quality, seems to rob anything non-conscious of any real value. Nothing in nature, apart from the experiences of animals, seems to matter.

[21] G. E. Moore, *Philosophical Studies* (London: Routledge and Kegan Paul Ltd, 1922), chapter VIII.

My views on this matter can only be briefly stated. I believe that there are several different conceptions of the natural or physical world which can be regarded as having varying degrees of truth.

First, there is the world as revealed to our senses, that which constitutes what Husserlians call the life world.

This is basically a construction which we join in making each on the basis of their own perceptual fields. As much of it as is perceived genuinely exists, but what is not perceived of it does not exist, or if it does its status is only that of a permanent possibility of perception. When we are appreciating something beautiful, it is not our sensations which we are appreciating but the object present as a component in our consciousness, and which we believe can be present in the consciousness of others too. Its beauty is that of an object, and that beauty may be regarded as objectified pleasure, to use Santayana's expression again.

Actually calling it *objectified* is misleading, since it suggests it was once subjective. For it was only once primitive infantile consciousness had divided itself into self and not-self that beauty arose as peculiarly a quality of the latter. It would therefore be better to call it *objective* rather than *objectified* pleasure.

The value of beautiful things in the life world is among the greatest of values. This world is only fully actualised when it is perceived, but among the most important things anyone can do is add to the beauties which are there to be actualised. This is what a great artist does.

Moreover, when confronted with great works of art it is we who are under judgement as much as they are. Are we capable of actualising them in our mind in their full wonderfulness?

A thought about music may help here. Few will believe that unheard music, as when one leaves a Hi-Fi playing something lovely in an empty room, is in itself of value. But the great composers have added objects to the world of music which are important in their own right. That is, they can only be actualised in a consciousness, but when actualised they are so with a value which belongs to them and to nothing else.

Moving on from the life world, must there not be a more absolute reality which is the source of those experiences on the basis of which we construct it? The answer must be affirmative, and the most obvious candidate for this role is the world as described by the more fundamental sciences. But is *the world of science* any more an ultimate reality independent of our awareness of it than *the life world*? Only so, I suggest, if we interpret it as the abstract structure of a reality whose inherent nature it as much obscures as reveals.

So what is its inherent nature? I have already indicated my answer above in describing myself as a panpsychist. This is, in brief, because it seems to me that in the end there is no conceivable reality except experience and its modes and objects, from which I infer that the inherent or noumenal reality of nature at large consists in an immensely complex system of interacting streams of experience.

This allows me to hold that there are values in nature other than those realised in the consciousness of men or animals. However, as to what these values are I believe we must remain entirely or almost entirely ignorant. For it is not the values in the hidden ocean of non-animal feeling which we are appreciating when we admire beautiful things or scenes in nature, only the values of the life world which their influence produces for us. It is just possible, however, that some experiences of natural beauty, or of the sublime, do genuinely reflect some inarticulate but genuine participation in this larger life of the universe.

I should perhaps admit that I also believe that all the experiences which make up the stuff of the world are united in one cosmic consciousness and that without this they cannot interact. Doubtless that fact grounds further values which ordinary utilitarianism can with difficulty allow.[22]

Idealism and utilitarianism are usually thought of as belonging to very different schools of thought. But my utilitarianism springs from my attempt to think what value really is, and my idealism springs from my attempt to think what nature really is, and in both cases my views spring from what I regard as the insight that their being is their being experienced. And experienced positive intrinsic value is appropriately called 'pleasure' and experienced negative intrinsic value is appropriately called 'pain', or at least 'unpleasure'. So if my idealism seems to be brought in simply to allow for values which utilitarianism does not normally recognise, then I must insist that both stem from the same essential insight.

It may be that my position would have more appeal if I gave the words 'pleasure' and 'pain' a less central place in my argument and simply contended that value consists in experience which feels good, or objects within consciousness which look or otherwise present themselves as good, and that disvalue consists in what feels bad or looks, or otherwise presents itself, as bad. Such might be an equally correct way of putting my position, but it seems appropriate to keep my language in touch with the utilitarian tradition in which, however eccentrically, my outlook on this matter belongs. I might note that somewhat the same combination of utilitarianism and idealism is present in the ethical thought of process philosophers in the tradition of Whitehead and Hartshorne, though my agreement with them is only partial.[23]

[22] See my (*Vindication*) chapters 5 and 6 or (*Foundations*) chapter X.

[23] For an important discussion of the utilitarian tendency of ethics based on process metaphysics see Clare Palmer, *Environmental Ethics and Process Thinking* (Oxford: Clarendon Press, 1998).

On criticising values

A. W. PRICE

> Most of the change we think we see in life
> Is due to truths being in and out of favor.
> Robert Frost

> Our appreciating what we do need not preclude our supposing
> that there are different values, to which we are perhaps insensitive,
> in the artefacts of remote cultures – as if, when we take the value
> we find in the objects we appreciate to be really there in them, we
> use up all the room the world might afford for aesthetic merit to
> occupy.
> John McDowell

I Evaluation and description

If we cannot agree that evaluations are judgements that both
describe things (ascribing properties to them) and express sentiments, we lack any shared understanding of a common topic. If we
ever come to agree how the describing and expressing relate, we
shall lose a debate. Suppose that evaluation is a mode of description
essentially expressive of sentiment, and that some evaluations can
be known to be true: then there must exist properties of such a kind
that they can be apprehended only from appropriately affective
points of view. Alternatively, it may be that evaluation involves
some element distinct from description, so that, in principle, one
could always accept the descriptive core of an evaluation while distancing oneself from a non-descriptive element that makes it evaluative. We may distinguish the two kinds of view as *lumping,* or
descriptivist-*cum*-expressivist, and *splitting,* or descriptivist-*plus*-
expressivist.[2] Both ascribe to evaluations an expressive aspect as

---

[1] As will transpire, a closer-fitting title would be 'How to comprehend,
confirm, and criticise evaluations'. I take my epigraphs from Frost, 'The
Black Cottage', and McDowell, *Mind, Value, and Reality* (Cambridge,
Mass: Harvard University Press, 1998), p. 114. Jennifer Hornsby and
David Wiggins warned me of a few errors.

[2] Not for the first time, I borrow the terminology of 'lumpers' and
'splitters', in affectionate remembrance, from sermons on the Trinity
given at Balliol by the Revd Frank McCarthy-Willis-Bund.

well as a descriptive content; what is at issue is whether the former is integral to the latter, or detachable from it.

What implications are these views likely to have for the contestability of evaluations (by which I mean their liability to contradiction)? I shall start by suggesting that splitting comes in two contrasted forms that imply opposite extremes: according to one of them, *all* evaluations are especially contestable just because they are evaluations; according to the other, *no* evaluations are so contestable. Both forms, I shall now argue, share an ineliminable defect. I shall then propose a way of lumping devised at once to lack the defect and avoid the extremes.

A familiar, if no longer fashionable, pattern of analysis represents any evaluation as conjunctive in form. Thus, according to prescriptivism, to evaluate an object as being of a certain kind is to do two things: it is to ascribe to it some property identifiable 'purely descriptively' (that is, dispassionately); and it is to commend or censure it for possessing that property. It would appear to follow that any evaluation is inherently contestable, in this sense: any evaluation that an evaluer may make can be contradicted, perhaps eccentrically but without error, by another evaluer. For, even if two speakers agree about the property (simple or complex) relevant to assessing the object as an instance of a certain type, one of them may commend it for possessing that property, while the other censures it. This is one way of splitting.

A different way ascribes to evaluations two separable aspects, but not a conjunctive form. It concedes the existence of value-terms with a distinctive conventional role, but relates this not to their senses (which fix their extension) or their logic, but to their tone or colouring (Frege's *Farbe* in contrast to his *Sinn*). Thus 'loaded' terms are conventionally derogatory or complimentary in a way irrelevant to their applicability. One example, antiquarian and inoffensive to us, might be the Greek term *barbaros,* denigratory of non-Greeks. Its colouring had no bearing on its extension: Persians could not deny it to be true that they were *barbaroi,* even if they resented the expression. It was also irrelevant to its logic: analytically, if Persians were not Greeks, they were *barbaroi.*

Both these ways of splitting invite an objection that is now a commonplace: it may only be from some evaluative point of view that there is any unitary quality common to the objects to which even a single speaker would apply some evaluative predicate. The point is commonly now made metaphorically: it may only be from some such point of view that the extension of the predicate has any *shape.* Even if the point be granted, hope may be placed in a reply: perhaps an evaluative predicate connotes different qualities from context to context of utterance in accordance with the differing communicative intentions of speakers. If we speak of 'family resemblance', the issue may then appear to be fine one: lumpers find a single property held together (like a family) by family resemblances apparent from some evaluative viewpoint; splitters find a series of properties held together (like members of a family) by family resemblances so apparent. But this is no small difference. Where lumpers find a pair of complex sense and property, splitters find a series of pairs of senses and properties. There are two implausible implications. First, the actual content not merely of what speakers *mean,* but of what they *are saying,* will vary from context to context with no unifying meaning. Second, the actual content of what some speaker is saying on a particular occasion will be accessible only *via* an understanding of what he means, rather than vice versa – an unpromising prospect.

Hence it seems better to adopt a view that makes the expressive aspect of an evaluative predicate integral to its sense. Such a view is stated by David Wiggins when he writes that evaluative predicates are 'non-natural predicates with a distinctive sentiment-involving kind of sense'.[3] This conception, and its implications for contestability, are what I wish here to explore. (Let me start with a parenthetical warning: it will become evident that, as I interpret the thesis, *value* is a concept of art; anyone who fails to appreciate this may well find in my view a paradoxical quality that is not, I believe, among its real deficiencies.)

Take the term 'elegant'. It is properly, if not in all cases currently, applied to pieces of music and ceramic, schemes of decoration, literary and epistolary styles, medicines, manners, mentalities and modes of living. No doubt elegance is a family concept, but what is the blood-tie? It is surely a sense of style. Someone who lacked all taste for elegance would lack the concept, and someone who lacked an elegant taste would possess it imperfectly. Mastering the concept is a matter of degree; for there is no clear line to be drawn, and indeed no real distinction to be made, between understanding the concept and internalising a culture, nor between linguistic competence and stylistic sensitivity. Neither is there any separation to be made between aesthetic and other appreciation: to find a woman physically inelegant because she was visibly pregnant would be a perversion of taste and a misapplication of the concept. Few if any of us possess a uniformly good taste, but no one utterly rustic or

---

[3] David Wiggins, 'Ayer's Ethical Theory: Emotivism or Subjectivism?', in *A. J. Ayer: Memorial Essays,* ed. A. Phillips Griffiths (Cambridge University Press, 1991), p. 180.

vulgar would be in a position even to misapply the concept (though he might borrow the term without earning a right to its use). Good taste is not additional to mastery of the concept – a conception that might well invite scepticism or relativism about the standard of taste; rather, grasping the concept involves sharing the standard, implicit, imprecise, and open-ended, that defines its content. One might gain a sense of the concept through a superficial reading of the novels of Jane Austen; but to make the concept one's own one would need to appreciate them, and to appreciate what she appreciated.[4]

II Supervenience, intuition, causation

A distorted view of the situation that generates problems may be evidenced by anxiety about supervenience, and scepticism about grounding. These connect if one takes supervenience to be a relation between two sets or kinds or levels of properties that excludes relations either of reduction (of the higher to the lower) or of entailment (of the higher by the lower). It is an evident truth that two pots of which only one is elegant in shape must differ in their proportions in a neutrally specifiable way: they could not be discriminable aesthetically but not otherwise. (However, it may be hard to pinpoint the relevant differences, and impossible to do so exactly or exhaustively; indeed, if the pots differ considerably, there may be no such thing as the relevant differences between them.) Yet one need not be perplexed about how a pot's elegance of shape relates to its measurements, nor about how one is able to apprehend it. In general, a property is a principle of grouping, defining and giving shape to a set. For an item to possess a property is for it to fall under a concept. Value-terms classify things distinctively within perspectives defined by their own affinities and saliences; they do not create new worlds independent enough of the old world for their dependence upon it to be a deep problem. To borrow some wording from Peter Hacker, the elegance is not something *in addition to* the shape, like some ethereal veneer spread over a molecular carcass;[5] rather, it is a Gestalt-property that the pot possesses not by virtue, but in respect, of its shape. (A pot may well count as elegant *tout court* by virtue of its elegant shape, as a picture would not; but that is different.) As the shape may vary, if only minutely, without any effect upon the manner (let alone the fact) of the elegance, one cannot say that the

---

[4] On Austen's use of 'elegant', cf. K. C. Phillipps, *Jane Austen's English* (London: Andre Deutsch, 1970), pp. 51–3.

[5] Peter Hacker, *Appearance and Reality* (Oxford: Basil Blackwell, 1987), p. 204.

elegance *is* the shape; and to describe the shape geometrically but with the proper imprecision is rather to specify than to capture the elegance.[6] Yet this is not something correlated with the shape that could distract attention from it; rather, the pot shows itself to be elegant in shape from the point of view discriminative of elegance, the *only* point of view from which one can tell whether a thing that might be elegant is elegant or not.[7]

One should not fear that there must be a logical gap between perceiving the pot's proportions, and finding them elegant – which is indeed one way of perceiving them (*seeing* them *as* elegant). Very often the application of a concept is not a piece of inference, and needs no grounds or criteria. A correct answer to the question

[6] We may say that, in a minimal sense definable as one-way necessary co-variance, the pot's elegance 'supervenes' upon its precise proportions in that any variation in the former requires a variation in the latter, though not vice versa. However, it would be odd to say that the elegance obtains 'in virtue of' the precise proportions (which would be a relation not just of co-variance but of dependence) when these can vary minutely without affecting the manner of the elegance, and detectably without affecting the fact of the elegance. It might be better to say that the manner of the pot's elegance obtains in virtue of an approximate shape, and the fact of its elegance in virtue of a very approximate shape – supposing that there *are* such things as more or less approximate shapes; but we would have to bear in mind that the boundaries of those would only be definable by reference to the elegance (as they are recognisable only by experience of it).

[7] Some may still urge a metaphysical reduction that is neither epistemic nor definitional: the sense of a value-term might be a route not to a *sui generis* value-property, but to an essentially open-ended disjunction of properties (where each property was distinguishable non-evaluatively, though the disjunction was only determinable evaluatively). This piece of ontological cleansing invites an objection, and a caveat. The objection is that value-properties commonly come in degrees, but the disjunction does not. The caveat is that, even if every one of the disjuncts is a natural property in the sense of pulling its weight within an empirical science, the disjunction may not be a natural property in that sense. (On 'natural', cf. D. Wiggins, 'A Neglected Position', in J. Haldane and C. Wright (eds), *Reality, Representation, and Projection* (Oxford University Press, 1993), pp. 330–1.) Indeed, the disjunction is idle even as an explanation of particular evaluations (it would be crazy to attempt to spell it out in explaining any of them). One might call it the reflection that the value sheds upon reality neutrally described, and compare the shadow cast by a cloud upon a contoured landscape: the shape of the shadow is fully determined by the occlusion shape of the cloud, the laws of optics, and the lie of the land; a creature may intentionally move into sun or shadow; but the cloud does not map any natural boundaries that could explain either the shadow or anything else.

whether a pot is oval in shape is likely to manifest grasp of the meaning of 'oval' non-inferentially; likewise with 'elegant', since it is a term of taste indicating a Gestalt. Not that it follows that nothing more can be said: it may help to point things out, and make comparisons. One must add that not all values are of a kind: there are criteria of courage if not of elegance; an act may count as courageous by virtue of its disregard of the risks, whose specification may itself be evaluative. So here there are partly different points to be made. (One danger in talk of the supervenience of value upon fact is that it can suggest that all values are on a level, occupying, as it were, the first floor of the house of concepts.) Where one can detach premises and conclusion, the application of a concept may rest analytically on premises from which it is absent. One can give grounds for applying a concept even when there is no question of reading the concept out of the grounds that one gives. What the grounds can show, decisively or defeasibly, is whether the concept applies; *this* must be rich enough to determine what is relevant to its application, but *they* need not be so rich as to be containing the concept already. Thus a narrative, say, of Charles II's escape after the Battle of Worcester may entail that he was brave even though it eschews either applying or citing that level of evaluation.[8]

Possessing a concept is having the ability to tell when it applies; if the concept is aesthetic, this ability rests on sense (that is, sensitivity to sensibilia) as well as sensibility. It is a profound mistake to insist on going deeper, and to demand something more, beyond aesthetico-linguistic competence, to confirm the reality of the concept's instantiation. (The position of this paper is best not called 'realist', for that might suggest that it *is* trying to supply something extra.)[9] Philosophers who have sensed a gulf to be crossed have looked hopefully or dismissively to a conception of knowledge that is either intuitive, or causal; I doubt the pertinence of either appeal. There is surely such a thing as intuition idiomatically so called: common experience or prejudice, apparently confirmed by recent experiment, supposes that, in the personal sphere, women tend to be better at it than men. But this is not a canonical mode of answering certain kinds of question; rather, it is a short cut, or a makeshift,

[8] Thus it is not the case that a value-property is either reducible to natural properties, or never inferrable from them.

[9] No doubt aptly, talk of 'realism' tends to invoke or provoke other 'ism's, notably scientism. Even Paul Valéry can write: 'L'homme froid est par là le mieux adapté à la réalité, laquelle est indifférente. – Les choses n'avancent ni ne retardent, ne regrettent ni n'espèrent'; *Tel Quel* (Paris: Gallimard, 1941), p. 120. It is not clear why, or how, 'things' are to determine their own categories.

in many areas. It would be incoherent to rest the application of a set of predicates on nothing better than intuition, in this sense. (Compare a claim that a certain range of mental states is, in principle, only accessible to telepathy.) Rather, what one person counts in a certain context as intuiting, others must be able to know otherwise and more reliably. In what may be the only sense of the term that is both useful and distinctive, 'intuition' is always secondary and parasitic, never primary or free-standing.[10]

A more recent tendency has been to relate a person's knowledge that p to the counter-factual, 'If it were not the case that p, he would not believe that p.' If this is taken to be a causal relation, it becomes debatable whether values can be objects of knowledge, since they are implausible inputs into any psycho-physical mechanism of the generation of belief. Take a simple case of aesthetic perception: some would say that an appreciation of the beauty of a sunset is to be explained causally, yet not by the beauty, but by the conjunction of a colouring, and a sensibility taken to be responding aesthetically to a neutral stimulus; which may seem to explain the beauty away. However, this line of argument raises two questions. First, if the counter-factual *is* to be causal, should we require that the supposed fact that p feed into a causal mechanism? It is a common presumption, whether *a priori* or *a posteriori*, scientific or scientistic, that causal relations rest ultimately upon causal mechanisms; but the observed relations and the postulated mechanisms should not be confused. The presence of a £2 coin in a pocket can have many effects, of which it is explanatory *precisely so described*, even though being a piece of currency is not a property known to physics or physiology. Equally, nothing that we learn from physics or optics connects with a sensibility to explain the appreciation of the sunset; and its colouring feeds into a causal mechanism no better than its beauty. If we demand to be given a mechanism, we must discard any

---

[10] James Griffin attempts an anodyne usage when he characterises a moral intuition as 'merely a moral sentiment or belief that persons have independently of any moral theory or philosophy that they might adopt'; *Value Judgement* (Oxford: Clarendon Press, 1996), p. 3. However, when he then expresses scepticism about 'piecemeal appeal to intuition', citing R. M. Hare, and writes, 'Intuitions ... are just beliefs', he is surely lapsing into a sense of an epistemic gap to be bridged, apparently by 'theory'. It is true to say that he offers no word of explanation as to why he wants to call non-theoretic moral beliefs 'intuitions' when, apparently, he would not apply the term to non-theoretic identifications of blends of colours or commonplace causes. It is presumably a lesson from Davidson that beliefs of a conceptual category to be 'just beliefs' (until rescued by a theorizing *deus ex machina*) would not even be beliefs.

present hope of a causal understanding.[11] Secondly, *should* we take the counter-factual to be causal? Surely the only thought that it has to capture is that no one can know that p without exercising an ability to tell whether or not p is the case – which suffices to imply that he would not believe that p unless p. Take mathematical knowledge: one can say of a person 'If it were not the case that $91 \div 7 = 13$, he would not believe that $91 \div 7 = 13$' without ascribing a causal power to the truths of arithmetic.[12] May one not equally be able to tell that some value is present in some type or token whether or not its presence is causally explanatory of one's ability? Evidently so, one would think, in cases of general reflection; and not evidently *not* so in cases of particular perception. Take, this time, a moral example: I think of some type of act as cruel; meeting an instance, I perceive it as cruel. Suppose that I am justified: type and token amply satisfy the criteria. Perceiving or imagining such behaviour, I cannot conceive it otherwise, for there is nothing else to think. Is this not cognition that p with or without causal explanation by the fact that p?[13] Such questions bear even on the most straightforward cases of perceptual knowledge. Using my eyes, and applying my concepts, I can surely now see that I am standing in front of a brown wooden lectern. Let us keep open whether the fact of my standing here helps to explain the perception causally. (Certainly the fact does not entail the perception even if the perception entails the fact.) What *is* clear is that we have here either a cognitive relation that is not a causally explanatory one, or a causally explanatory relation that is not a mechanical or optical one. As Robert L. Arrington has remarked, 'The language of moderate-sized dry goods is very different from the language of physics, chemistry, and physiology.'[14] I see the lectern to be a lectern, but it is not *as* a lectern that it reflects light of various wave-lengths into my eyes. If we say that I see it as a lectern because it is a lectern, it is really not clear either that the 'because' *is* causal, or that it *cannot* be.[15] Equally, I conceive clearly

[11] Think also of explanations that cite dispositions. Dispositions are not parts of mechanisms (even when they are grounded in mechanism); and yet they can surely be explanatory in their own way.

[12] Cf. D Wiggins, *Needs, Values, Truth: Essays in the Philosophy of Value*, 3rd edition (Oxford: Clarendon Press, 1998), p. 153, note 17.

[13] One may be tempted to say that there is external causation where there is no mental reflection. But intelligence can work swiftly and implicitly; and thought may open the door to a causal input.

[14] Robert L. Arrington, *Rationalism, Realism, and Relativism* (Ithaca, NY: Cornell University Press, 1989), p. 175.

[15] Note also that the presence of a matt black surface may explain a perception, causally or otherwise, even though it reflects no light. (I owe this point to John Hyman.)

neither reason to deny, nor need to assert, that values may be causally explanatory of evaluations. A claim that they cannot be so is either false, or not fatal to an epistemology of value.

III Concepts thick and thin

Philosophers of a different persuasion have tended to focus on the term 'good', about which R. M. Hare likes to quote the *Oxford English Dictionary:* 'the most generic adjective of commendation'. I have instead paid attention to a term, 'elegant', which stands for what Bernard Williams has called a 'thick concept'. He glosses the notion as follows: '"Thicker" or more specific ethical notions ... seem to express a union of fact and value. The way these notions are applied is determined by what the world is like (for instance, by how someone has behaved), and yet, at the same time, their application usually involves a certain valuation of the situation, of persons or actions.'[16] It is unclear whether he is suggesting that the application of 'good' is not world-guided; and yet he rightly resists separating the two aspects. We might better specify that the thin concepts expressed by 'good' and 'ought' are general but not generic. It may help to read the *OED*'s initial definition of 'good' to the end: 'the most general adjective of commendation, implying the existence in a high, or at least satisfactory, degree of characteristic qualities which are either admirable in themselves or useful for some purpose'.[17] This suggests that it is not the function of 'good' to ascribe a value, even a generic one, just as it is not that of 'ought' to give a reason. Rather, a good F must have, to a high or at least satisfactory degree, the qualities needed or desirable in an F, just as an act that ought to be done is one for which there exist strong or adequate reasons – a resultant feature that is not itself an *extra* reason (unless we wish every reason to generate an infinity of reasons, in the manner of the Third Man Argument). What qualities are to be expected of a good F will be variably determined by the function of an F, and

[16] Bernard Williams, *Ethics and the Limits of Philosophy* (London: Fontana, 1985), p. 129.

[17] Though I find this helpful, its mention of 'commendation' should be accepted as a decent piece of lexicography rather than as an implicit contribution to philosophy; cf. Paul Ziff, *Semantic Analysis* (Ithaca, NY: Cornell University Press, 1960), pp. 228–32. Ziff is also salutary on 'approval'; ibid., pp. 223–7.

the point of view pertinent in context.[18] In certain cases, it may be that none of them is a 'value' in my sense; for perhaps none has to be detected in a way that is, in Wiggins's phrase, 'sentiment-involving'. If there is an art of penmanship, aesthetic values may, in certain contexts, be relevant to a good pen – but hardly to good blotting-paper (whose criteria may not be evaluative in any way).

Once we cease to separate descriptive from evaluative meaning, and start to conceive of descriptive meanings that are sentiment-involving, we must maintain that the involvement of sentiment need not destroy the determinacy of sense to be expected of description. We can be open to persuasion, from case to case, that the application of a value-term may be essentially contested (a phrase of Gallie's, a concept of Plato's), that is, naturally subject to argument and debate, within a wide margin.[19] Yet, as with vagueness generally, if such terms lacked a sense fixing a core, and lighting a margin, of applications, nothing would be said by using them. Trying to apply a term altogether contested would be like trying to play croquet at the Red Queen's with mallets that had a life of their own. Nothing would count as *what one was actually saying*.

IV The scope for criticism

All this may cause one comfort in respect of one's own values, and unease in respect of those of others – at least, of those whom one finds alien. Some may prefer to make aptness for truth a prerogative of evaluations that apply values that we share, or at least respect. Yet one can acknowledge that most evaluations are true without trying,

[18] Cf. J. O. Urmson, *The Emotive Theory of Ethics* (London: Hutchinson, 1968), chapter 9. Does this introduce an element of relativism whereby an ascription of goodness may come out as true or false from different points of view? No, for the relevant point of view, as indicated by the context, already fixes the content of what is being said. A judgement inviting conflicting verdicts from different points of view is to that extent indeterminate – which is not to say that how things show up from a given point of view is always indisputable.

[19] W. B. Gallie, 'Essentially Contested Concepts', *Proceedings of the Aristotelian Society,* 56 (1955/6); Plato, *Euthyphro* 7b6–8a2. Cf. Myles Burnyeat: 'It is typical of a virtue concept that its range should be liable to controversial extension or modification. For to state and defend criteria for collecting manifestations of a virtue is to articulate a way of grouping certain phenomena which exposes something of one's outlook on life in general'; 'Virtues in Action', in G. Vlastos (ed.) *The Philosophy of Socrates* (New York: Doubleday, 1971), p. 212.

impossibly, to accept all the values that they apply. Williams writes about the interpreter of an alien culture, 'We can understand why the observer is barred from saying just what the locals say, and we can also see that he is not barred from recognising that what they say can be true.'[20] I take the recognition to be general and not particular: he could not concede some particular proposition to be true without thinking, if not saying, it himself; but he can have reasons, not all of them *a priori*, for supposing that the locals are not just sounding off, but are applying a set of values that they only sometimes misapply. Yet he may be unable to enter into their culture so as to grasp the sentiment-involving senses that constitute their value-concepts.

However, it extends the scope of understanding that taking on a sentiment is not all or nothing. Evaluations can provide practical reasons, but need not motivate action when possible; and the same can be said even of desires. The primitive sign of wanting is trying to get, and the relation of desire to behavioural manifestation remains internal, and not purely contingent. Desiring is a mode of conceiving a possibility that engenders motivation. And yet, once a system of desires has got going, it takes on a mental life of its own that may become detached from the externalities of action and satisfaction. The paths to enjoyment or enactment may be impeded not just by external obstacles, contrary inclinations, and hard choices, but by irony, inhibition, inertia, habit, boredom – and who can say what? Between desires actively displayed and desires idly entertained stretches a multi-dimensional spectrum. Within the genesis of value, loves and hates acquire a sociolinguistic standing and fixity in the form of evaluations. Whole fields of evaluation may for some blossom in thought without bearing practical fruit. The same is true of propositional states in general: a mind is formed by a mental landscape to whose contents it stands in very various relations of identification, acceptance, recognition, indecision, and rejection. Ambivalence allows a man to occupy a point of view that falls within a perspective defined by a second point of view that he also occupies. This permits a double take that is as essential in life as in the theatre. The dichotomy of sincerity and insincerity is an illusion of moral or romantic ideals of veracity and authenticity that do not fit human actuality (especially, perhaps, in England).[21]

[20] Williams, *Ethics and the Limit of Philosophy*, p. 145.

[21] Let us concede that a lack of commitment can carry a cognitive cost; for it may generally be the case that someone to whom the culture is alien is not good at discriminating or resolving or detecting borderline or debatable or novel instantiations of a value. Yet this is less plausible of someone fully acculturated but also ambivalent. No one may have a keener nose for class differences than an inverted snob.

A. W. Price

An example may make the point that one can acknowledge the truth of evaluations without accepting the values they apply. Once upon a time there was an English ideal of being a gentleman. One finds its content set out nobly by John Henry Newman, and mundanely by Gwen Raverat.[22] From the outside it was an elusive ideal, since it did not proclaim itself, for the reason, Raverat suggests, that its adherents 'felt so deeply about it that they really did not like speaking of it'.[23] It was a standard of implicit comparison that it was vulgar, and so ungentlemanly, to express. Henry James is a witness, as one would expect: 'It may he said that in a thoroughly agreeable style good-breeding is never an aggressive quality, and that a gentleman who keeps reminding you that he is a gentleman is a very ambiguous personage. But Charles de Bernard is gentlemanly by juxtaposition, as it were. He quietly goes his way, and it is only when you compare his gait with his neighbors' that you see how very well he holds himself.'[24] As a concept, the gentlemanly possessed what Mark Platts has called 'semantic depth': it could always be better understood.[25] Newman familiarly wrote, 'It is almost a definition of a gentleman to say he is one who never inflicts pain',[26] and Oscar Wilde (whom Ada Leverson was to call 'the last gentleman in Europe') capped him by adding the word 'unintentionally'. Social change has made the ideal a period piece, with what in the age of the common man are widely seen as unacceptable class connotations. From our point in time, it may be viewed curiously, nostalgically, humorously, critically. Delivered from certain points of view, judgements of the form 'Being a gentleman is a good (bad) way to be (ideal to have)' may be determinate in sense, and even true. But no attitude to the ideal could aptly be expressed by denying, say, that Mr Darcy was a gentleman. This, I suggest, is typical of values that are not one's own: though the outsider will not choose to apply them himself, it is not generally open to him to contradict those whose values they are.

[22] J. H. Newman, *The Idea of a University*, ed. I. T. Ker (Oxford: Clarendon Press, 1976); G. Raverat, *Period Piece* (London: Faber and Faber, 1952).

[23] Raverat, *Period Piece*, p. 217.

[24] *French Writers* (Library of America, 1984), p. 162.

[25] M. Platts, *Ways of Meaning* (London: Routledge & Kegan Paul, 1979), p. 249. If this punctures the pretensions of the 'realism' of which Platts takes semantic depth to be a sign, he might prefer to say that conceptions of the gentlemanly can always become more refined, but without any increase in *understanding*. Then the thesis of realism will transcend that of cognizability in applying only to values that we privilege in some way still to be explained.

[26] Newman, *The Idea of a University*, p. 179.

Of course, this provokes a question: what of values that do or can repel? It should not be inferred, say, that I would have us acknowledge the truth of sadistic evaluations before it be established that there are any such things. Moral monsters may be blind to our values, or respond eccentrically to them. Whether they form a sub-culture with its own values is another question; if they do, it must be a wicked one. We need not suppose that 'That is untrue' is the only criticism of an evaluation with any bite (rather as we need not think that 'That is irrational' is the only criticism of an action that counts); and it not evident that all truths must be accessible from morally acceptable points of view (think of the real affinities and disparities that are apparent only to a malicious sense of humour). We must not be over-evaluative about 'values' in my sense: a 'value', as I use the term, need not be a proper ground of approval or disapproval (whatever fixes that); rather, it unites an open class determined by similarities only visible to sentiment. Relevant here are Allan Gibbard's tribesmen who find it more or less *gopa* to kill an outgroup member in the face of danger.[27] Could we not concede, if we had to (which is as yet quite unclear, but hardly excluded *a priori*), that they may be alert to a property of actions, uncapturable in naturalistic terms, to which it is morally better to be blind? Compare also the Greek virtue-term *sôphrosynê,* of which Myles Burnyeat has written that it 'is untranslatable, because the phenomena it grouped together for Greek culture do not form a whole to our outlook'.[28] Must it be false that *sôphrosynê* characterized Charmides if Greek culture shows up badly in that respect? How badly? In what ways, and from what points of view?

I am committing myself to the strong distinction that Wiggins has drawn between an evaluation and a practical judgement (which I think entails that nothing can be both),[29] and confirming it by a weak one between even a correct evaluation and a practical reason (to the effect that one need not be the other). An interpreter must be free to grant the truth of an evaluation without accepting or approving it as a practical reason bearing on the question, whose answer is a practical judgement, 'What is to be done?'[30] Resting

[27] A. Gibbard, 'Morality and Thick Concepts', *Proceedings of the Aristotelian Society,* Supplementary Volume 66 (1992), pp. 267–8.

[28] M. Burnyeat, 'Virtues in Action', p. 216.

[29] Cf. Wiggins, *Needs, Values, Truth,* pp. 95–6.

[30] Thus, on this view, I may detect *a value* as showing up from some evaluative (that is, 'sentiment-involving') point of view that I can occupy imaginatively, and yet recognise no related practical reasons. Yet we might say that *I value* a thing only if it speaks positively to a sentiment that I take to heart. This would seem a matter for stipulation.

insecurely on relevant evaluations, practical judgements stand to truth altogether more questionably. Of difficulties that arise in maintaining the distinction, let me attend briskly to just one (which was drawn to my attention by my former pupil Peter Taplin). Practical judgements may have to be made case by case because of an incommensurability generated by the plurality of values. I quote from Wiggins: 'Where [the objects of concern] A and B are incommensurable ... there is no (however complicated or conditionalised) correct, unitary, projectible, explanatory and/or potentially predictive account to be had of how A and B trade off against one another in some reasonable agent's choices or actions, or within the formation of his springs of action.'[31] Evaluations, by contrast, appear to be projectible: if there were such a thing as a theory of cruelty, Wiggins says elsewhere, 'it would have to be such as to entail a potentially counterfactual claim that this or that kind of object or situation would, in the absence of error by subjects, bring down upon itself this or that kind of reaction from subjects'.[32] Yet it may be objected that moral evaluations often involve situational comparisons between values. Take courage, for instance: surely an act only counts as courageous if the end is worthy of the risks; and then there may seem to be little room between finding a prospective act courageous (a moral evaluation), and finding it right (a practical judgement). However, while a courageous act requires a respectable end (and a necessary or noble one if the risks be grave), it need not be best or wise or even permissible in the circumstances. Thus we do not count it as courageous to rob a bank (at least out of criminality), though it take nerves of steel;[33] and yet we can acknowledge the courage of a reluctant witness who commits contempt of court in order to respect a confidence, without endorsing or even licensing disregard of the law. The practical question 'Is this courageous act actually to be done?' is sensitive to context, even for those who practise courage, in a way that may preclude an answer entailed by generalities, however complicated or conditionalised, whereas the evaluative question 'Is this act courageous?' is not. So it remains the case that evalua-

---

[31] Wiggins, *Needs, Values, Truth,* p. 370.

[32] ibid., p. 158.

[33] Cf. Plutarch, *Moralia* 208c: 'When some criminal was submitting calmly to torture, Agesilaus remarked, "What an thoroughly wicked man he is to apply endurance and fortitude to evil and shameful ends!"' What makes this citable as a 'Spartan Saying' is that it turns the screw: the fortitude of a villain is not only not a virtue – it is a further vice.

tions stop short of practical judgements, and are less problematically capable of truth than they.[34]

Yet I do not wish to cheapen truth by buying it too cheaply. Local misgivings may arise where global scepticism is out of place. Values are not atomic, but take on an identity within fields of value; equally, the sensibility that is sensitive to some value must be sensitive to other things too. Critical reflection may reveal that certain conceptions of values, and uses of value-terms, are unsustainable since they yield an incoherent pattern of description and response. An example can be found in Thomas Hardy's saga of 'a pure woman' (as he subtitled his novel), *Tess of the D'Urbervilles*.[35] Tess had been seduced as a young woman by Alec D'Urberville, passively on her part, as Hardy presents it, and without any real responsibility. When she later confesses this on her wedding night to Angel Clare (supposing that he had already received a note from her about all these things), he deserts her – and sets the tragedy in train. In finding Tess unchaste, Angel Clare was losing hold of the point of the attribution of unchastity. He was using a value-term in a sense that lost contact with any value that one could keep in focus. In intending but failing to invoke a value, he was not thinking a truth (as he came in the end to see). This well illustrates the devaluation to which values are liable: a superficial mark of unchastity (sexual relations outside wedlock) is raised to the rank of a sufficient condition, with the effect that what was once a value becomes a bare circumstance masquerading as one, to which (as in cases of sentimentality) clings a now unapt emotion.

Of course, Hardy intends this to tell not just against a fictitious character of his own invention, but against an ossification of morality, as he saw it, within his own culture. Such criticism *is* possible, and I do not wish to appear to have excluded it. Yet how am I to escape a charge that, on the present account, any use of a value-term generates truths once it has become projectible? There are two lines of reply. One generalises what had to be said about Tess's 'unchastity'. Uses of a value-term that lose contact with any sentiment that

---

[34] The problem may be briefly stated as follows. 'This act is courageous' may be true, on my view, in virtue of the sense of 'courageous'; yet 'This act is to be done' can hardly be made true by the sense of 'to be done'. Of course, one can specify, say, 'morally to be done' (if that *is* sufficiently determinate). But then the judgement is no longer inherently practical: if 'morally' is a qualifier and not an intensifier, 'This act is morally to be done, but I will not do it' is neither admirable nor necessarily acratic.

[35] Cf. D. Wiggins, 'Reply to Roger Crisp', in S. Lovibond and S. G. Williams (eds) *Essays for David Wiggins: Identity, Truth and Value* (Oxford: Blackwell, 1996), pp. 263–4.

makes sense within a wider mentality fail to invoke any value. Once this becomes evident, as with what Hare calls 'inverted-comma' uses, the term may take on a different sense that makes possible a different truth; but, halfway between living value and disenchanted fact, truth is lost. Of course, it is contestable when this has occurred. (Hardy, tired of the heat of the kitchen, was soon to retire from writing novels.) An earlier character, most accessible now in Eugène Vinaver's annotations to Malory, is the Arthurian knight Sir Dinadan, whom Vinaver rather fancifully calls 'l'un des premiers révolutionnaires du moyen age chevaleresque'.[36] He knows the price but not the value of chivalry, and so drifts through the Tristan story as a 'wandering knight who every day goes seeking for the meaning of the world, but cannot find it.'[37] A typical exchange is with a knight he meets who challenges him to joust. Dinadan finds this greeting less than courteous ('courtois'), and engages him in eristic. Is the challenge out of love or hate? If love, it is a love detached from friendship, and Dinadan would prefer enmity. The challenge is withdrawn.[38] Dinadan is exploiting a possible tension within the knightly ideal of courtesy which permits him to reclassify the practice of jousting instead of shaking hands as a piece of barbarism. Hence he can reject as uncourteous conventional conduct that loses the point of courtesy as he commonsensically conceives it. Right or wrong, jesting or in earnest, he makes sense.

The other line of reply raises an issue not less intricate than intriguing. If every conception of a value yields a sense of a value-term determining an extension, we risk achieving immunity from substantive disagreement by splintering a moral language into a set of moral dialects. A sentence from Stendhal's *Lucien Leuwen* may serve as a text: 'Ces usages sont comme les cruautés du moyen age, qui n'étaient pas cruautés de leur temps, et ne sont devenues telles que par les progrès de l'humanité.'[39] Stendhal did not need to look back so far: in his *Chroniques Italiennes,* he narrates the execution for parricide of Giacomo Cenci (and of his sister Beatrice), but suppresses details that are 'trop atroces'.[40] We may well be reluctant to

[36] *Le Roman de Tristan et Iseut dans l'Oeuvre de Thomas Malory* (Paris: Librairie Ancienne Honoré Champion, 1925), p. 137.

[37] 'Je suis un chevalier errant qui chascun jor voiz aventures querant et le sens du monde, mes point n'en puis trouver'; *The Works of Sir Thomas Malory,* ed. E. Vinaver, 2nd edition (3 vols.; Oxford: Clarendon Press, 1967), p. 1494.

[38] ibid., p. 1491.

[39] Stendhal, *Romans et Nouvelles* (2 vols.; Paris: Gallimard, 1952), vol. I, p. 1200.

[40] ibid., vol. II, p. 707.

arbitrate that breaking a parricide on the wheel, though 'cruel' in a modern sense, was not 'cruel' (or 'crudele') in a sixteenth-century one. And yet, where senses are sentiment-involving, how can a marked change in sentiment fail to cause a change in sense that has that kind of implication? Perhaps we may say that we have different interpretations of a single sense, rather than a set of different though overlapping senses, if one of them is privileged, and so may be *right*. In the case of the Cenci, we must not privilege ourselves just because we are ourselves, nor because of the asymmetry whereby we can imagine that we are addressing and suppose that we are correcting the Romans of the *cinquecento*, while *they* could not pretend to be addressing and correcting *us*. We need reason to believe two things: first, that we owe our view to 'les progrès de l'humanité' and not to squeamishness (for, if cruelty is simply what one's stomach cannot take, 'cruel' is no more objective than 'nauseating');[41] second, and relatedly, that our mentality (if not chronology) so relates to theirs that we could intelligibly *persuade* them to apply 'cruel' as we do. In this instance we would hope, by appealing to agreed types and tokens of cruelty and of other values of theirs, to make them alive to the anomalousness of their penal views.

A final observation. Though I have distinguished the truth of an evaluation from the existence of a practical reason, we may acknowledge that what commonly gives point to pressing for the reconception of a value is a concession-*cum*-contention that the value can reliably supply reasons for and against practices if and only if it is reconceived. Hence the present issue ties in aptly with the debate about internal *versus* external reasons.[42] What I have just suggested about contested evaluations reflects what might reasonably be said about disputed reasons. In neither case need we deny any real disagreement, or despair of a common grasp of truth, so long as rational agreement is an intelligible aspiration. Here, as there, I think that we should have a generous notion of persuasion that permits it to work, as necessary, through actual experience as well as argument and imagination. In the case of reasons, I am hopeful that this may achieve, what is always to be desired, a dissolution of the debate; but now I can only mark the connection.

To conclude. It is not a proper aspiration of philosophy to make

[41] Stendhal's habitual irony makes him ambivalent: where his Italian original describes the crowd's sudden emotion when they realised that Giacomo's younger brother Bernardo was reprieved, he noted, 'On voit bien comment chez un peuple esclave de la sensation présente, la pitié serait pour le coupable qui va souffrir'; ibid., vol. II, p. 1456.

[42] Cf. Bernard Williams, 'Internal and External Reasons', in *Moral Luck* (Cambridge University Press, 1981).

a difference, nor even to say things that take us by surprise. One may wonder whether moral philosophers do not tend to be revisionary in part for the reason that it demands less attention and patience to advance a novelty than to address an actuality; most aestheticians, happily, have more regard for the past, that neglected constituency. At its best, theory articulates. Philosophers who think to correct common views that they do not understand theoretically by theoretical inventions of their own are not testing like by like; and theorists who hope to ground the superiority of one set of values to another upon first principles are likely to distort their own values by devising foundations that are out of place.[43] Yet I have no desire to claim that evaluative knowledge is more attainable than is verified in the actual course of evaluative thinking. And nothing guarantees that that is always in good condition. Alas, in certain fields theory has already introduced contamination; let us keep our own hands clean of that. I end by adapting something said by Denis Donoghue: undermining a man's moral or aesthetic sensibility is not the work of a gentleman.

---

[43] It turns my earlier quarrel with him into a quibble that neither of these points is an objection to the role that Griffin still hopes to find for theory.

Should we pass the buck?

JONATHAN DANCY

My topic is the relation between the right and the good. I introduce it by relating some aspects of the debate between various British intuitionists in the first half of the present century.

I

In *Principia Ethica* (1903) G. E. Moore claimed that to be right is to be productive of the greatest good. He wrote 'This use of "right", as denoting what is good as a means, whether or not it be also good as an end, is indeed the use to which I shall confine the word' (p. 18). By the time he wrote his *Ethics* (1912, e.g. p. 6) he seems to have weakened his position, and offers conduciveness to the good not as a definition of 'right' but as an account of the one and only property that makes acts right. Even if it be the only right-making property, conduciveness to the good will not be identical with the rightness that it makes.

One might ask why Moore changed his view, and an obvious answer is that he came to see that the notorious Open Question Argument, by which he strove to establish that goodness is not identical with any good-making feature, can be used equally well to show the same thing of rightness. If it is an open question whether goodness is conduciveness to happiness, it is equally an open question whether rightness is conduciveness to goodness. And if, as Moore claimed in the first case, its being an open question shows that the answer to it is no, the same applies in the second case.

W. D. Ross details all these matters with further references, and with his customary clarity, in the early pages of his *The Right and the Good* (1930, pp. 8–11). Though he argues that Moore's second view is a vast improvement on his first, Ross's own position is quite different. Rightness and goodness are utterly distinct; indeed, no one thing can be both right and good. Goodness, for Ross, is a property of motives and outcomes, and rightness is a property of acts. An act can be intrinsically right or wrong, but never intrinsically good or bad. Acts can be instrumentally good, or conducive to good; but Ross announces, surely correctly, that instrumental value is not a form of value at all. So it turns out that acts can have no value at all. Motives, by contrast, can be intrinsically good or bad but never right or wrong. On this picture the very idea that one might define

159

the right in terms of the good is quite peculiar. Also peculiar is the idea that the only way that an action could get to be right is by having the best consequences.

H. W. B. Joseph's response to this in his *Some Problems in Ethics* (1931) was that Ross's position was absurd. 'Why', he asked, 'ought I to do that, the doing which has no value (though my being moved to do it by the consciousness that I ought, has), and which being done causes nothing to be which has value? Is not duty in such a case irrational?' (p. 26). Rightness, for Joseph, must be in some way dependent on goodness. He pursued this idea by claiming that the word 'right' is ambiguous. In one sense it means 'obligatory', and Joseph writes (p. 61) that 'obligatoriness is not a character of actions. There is no ought-to-be-done-ness, or ought-to-be-for-borne-ness. To say that an act is obligatory means that the doing it is obligatory on me.' In the other sense, 'rightness is a form of goodness, to the realising of which the actions belong; and it is the thought of goodness which moves us when we do an action from a sense of obligation' (p. 104). In this way Joseph rejects Ross's claim that rightness and goodness are utterly distinct.

In his second book *The Foundation of Ethics* (1939) Ross's position becomes more complex. He has already argued that there are two uses of 'good', attributive and predicative. The attributive use is at issue when we speak of a good liar or a good knife. The predicative use is the one that is of importance for ethics, and it is found when we speak of a good man, or claim that virtue, knowledge and pleasure are good. Ross claims that when we say that the pleasure of others is good, we mean that it is a proper object of satisfaction. This is a 'definition' of this use of 'good'. When we speak of a man, or of a motive, as being morally good, however, we mean something else, something that cannot be defined but only paraphrased (p. 283). The paraphrase is that the good, in this use of 'good', is a proper object of approval, worthy of approval or admiration.

Why is this not a definition? Because Ross is still sticking to his original view that goodness, in *this* sense, is an intrinsic property of objects, not a relation. If being good in this sense were being worthy of approval or admiration, it would be a relation. But it is not; this sort of goodness is the property that in approving or admiring we take the object approved or admired to have. For to approve is to think good, and 'admiration is not a mere emotion; it is an emotion accompanied by the thought that that which is admired is good' (pp. 278–9).

It is worth pausing to note what Ross means by a relation here. It is not what we would ordinarily mean, because we would ordinarily think that for a relation to obtain, there must be at least two relata and both must, in the relevant sense, exist. But in suggesting (even if only to reject the idea) that goodness might be a relation, Ross is clearly not thinking of relations in this way. For something can be worthy of approval even if no approval and no approver is forthcoming.[1] Further, though Ross thinks that goodness in this sense is not a relation, that is not his reason for rejecting the claim that goodness is identical with being worthy of admiration and approval. Ross's real point is that the goodness that we take the object to have cannot be identical with its being worthy of our so taking it, because it must be that in the object that makes our so taking it an appropriate or fitting response.

It would have been possible to avoid this result if we had been more catholic in our choice of attitudes or responses that the good action is worthy to elicit. In his *The Definition of Good* (1947), A. C. Ewing defines the good as that which ought to be the object of a pro-attitude (pp. 148–9). He attributes the term 'pro-attitude' to Ross, and continues '"pro-attitude" is intended to cover any favourable attitude to something. It covers, for instance, choice, desire, liking, pursuit, approval, admiration. ... When something is intrinsically good, it is (other things being equal) something that on its own account we ought to welcome, rejoice in if it exists, seek to produce if it does not exist. We ought to approve its attainment, count its loss a deprivation, hope for and not dread its coming if this is likely, avoid what hinders its production, etc.' (p. 149).

By stressing the broad variety of attitudes that may count as pro-attitudes, Ewing seems to avoid Ross's only argument that we cannot define the good (in the relevant predicative sense) as what is worthy of a certain response. Ewing seems, that is, to be in a position to say that goodness is not a distinct evaluative and intrinsic property in objects, one whose presence we can discern and to which we do or at least should respond with approval and admiration. The goodness of the object just is the relational fact that we should respond to it with approval, admiration or other pro-attitude. The evaluative 'good' has been defined in terms of the deontic 'should'. And with this result, the intuitionists reversed Moore's position, the position with which I started this brief history. Moore defined the right, that which we ought to do or should do, in terms of the good. Ewing defined the good in terms of how we should respond.

This is the end of my brief historical introduction. At the point we have reached (the late 1940s) the intuitionists' broadly cogni-

---

[1] It is just possible that Ross thinks of the relevant relation as 'being worthy of *our* approval', which would bring him back into line on this point.

tivist approach to ethics was eclipsed by the onrush of non-cognitivism. Fifty years passed before these sorts of issues could again be debated with any sense of seriousness.

Fifty years on, Thomas Scanlon writes as follows in his *What We Owe to Each Other* (1999, pp. 95–7):

> To value something is to take oneself to have reasons for holding certain positive attitudes toward it and for acting in certain ways in regard to it. ... To say that something is valu*able* is to say that others also have reason to value it, as you do. ... this account ... takes goodness and value to be ... the purely formal, higher-order properties of having some lower-order properties that provide reasons of the relevant kind. [It holds] that it is not goodness or value itself that provides reasons but rather other properties that do so. For this reason I call it a buck-passing account.

My question is whether we should in this way seek to pass the buck. Should we take it that to be valuable is to have features that give us reasons, in the way that Scanlon suggests?

II

I start with some comments on the buck-passing view as expressed above by Scanlon. First, I think there must be a slip in the way that Scanlon tries to capture the buck-passing account of taking something to be valuable. It cannot be right to say that to take something to be valuable is to take it that others also have reason to value it, as you do. For in valuing it we do not take ourselves to have reasons to value it; at least, not on the buck-passing view. On that view, to value it is to take oneself to have reasons of certain other sorts. The quotation I gave above does not reveal this, but Scanlon does detail these sorts of reason. He talks of reasons for admiring, respecting, preserving and protecting; of reasons to be guided by the goals or standards that the value involves; of reasons for promoting; and of reasons to act in certain ways. To value something is to take oneself to have reasons of these sorts, reasons that are given one by features of the object (or perhaps more broadly of the situation) which act as ground for the reasons and, in doing so, as ground for the value. But when we value the object we are not taking ourselves to have reason to value it, exactly. So when we come to think of the valu*able*, rather than just of the valued, we should surely be thinking of others as having the same reasons as we do, reasons to admire, protect, promote, etc.

With that slip corrected, Scanlon's view is very similar to Ewing's. Scanlon's is expressed in terms of reasons while Ewing spoke of how we ought to respond. But a definition of value in terms of reasons is very similar to one in terms of oughts, especially when we notice that Ewing was speaking of *prima facie* oughts, and Scanlon is speaking of what one might call contributory reasons. Crucially, the notion of what one ought to do is a deontic notion, as I take that of a reason to be, and the notion of a value is evaluative; Ewing and Scanlon combine to give a deontic definition of the evaluative, and this is what is at once attractive and worrying about their position.

What I mean by this is that we should not forget the position they are trying to undermine. We might think that there are just two families of normative concepts. The first family is the evaluative family. Here we are dealing with the good and the bad, the noble, the fine and the evil. Second is the deontic family. Here we are dealing with the right and the wrong, shoulds, oughts and musts, obligations, requirements and prohibitions. Ross took the view that these two families are utterly different. His picture of the normative realm is therefore far more complex than is that of Ewing or of Scanlon – or of Moore, of course, at the other end. Complexity has its advantages and its disadvantages, as we will see. But we may be permitted to hope that the Ewing/Scanlon view, the buck-passing view, has not only the advantages of simplicity. If we are to accept it, there must be more to be said in its favour than just that.

And of course there is. At least, there is if Scanlon is to be believed. He argues for the buck-passing view by arguing against two alternative positions, supposing that if they fail the buck-passing view will emerge as the sole remaining contender. Unfortunately, I will now suggest, he does not consider every available alternative. So his argument by remainder ends up looking a bit weak.

The opposing views, according to Scanlon, are (1) 'the teleological view' and (2) 'the view that value is a property the presence of which grounds or explains reasons'. Interestingly, these two views look very much like the earlier and the later views of Moore. In Moore's terms, the 'teleological view' is the view that rightness is to be defined in terms of value rather than the other way around. The second view is the view that value is the right-making property, though not identical with rightness. Expressed in terms of the relation between values and reasons, rather than between value and rightness, the teleological view will be that reasons are to be defined in terms of some relation to value, and the second view will be that goodness is a (or the) reason-giving property. Now I accept that both of these views are wrong. We abandon the teleological view because we suppose that we cannot define reasons in terms of

163

values, whatever the proper account of the relation between reasons and values turn out to be. We abandon the second view because we recognise immediately that the badness of a toothache, for example, does not add a further reason to the reasons for going to the dentist that are already given by the nature of the toothache, its painfulness. As we might put it, the badness of the toothache exists in virtue of certain features, features which give us reason to act in certain ways; the badness of the ache adds nothing to the reasons given us by those lower-level features. In short, value adds no reasons to those generated by the ground for that value.

Does it follow from this that to be of value is just to have reason-giving features? I do not see that it does. Two further views remain unrefuted. The first is Ross's view, expressed in terms of the relation between reasons and value rather than in terms of the relation between rightness and goodness. Values and reasons are just utterly different, and neither can be defined in terms of the other. This was clear, for Ross, because the things that are duties have no value at all, and the things that have value cannot be duties. There is indeed a link between values and reasons, since where there is intrinsic value we *always* have a reason. Ross, after all, thought that 'one of our main duties is to produce as much that is good as possible' (1939, p. 257). The prospect of value always gives us a reason, then, and this is something that needs to be explained if values are as different from reasons as Ross thought they were from duties. But Ross incurs this explanatory debt by adopting a picture for which he thought there were perfectly good independent reasons.

The second view that remains is one that, without committing itself to any vast difference between values and reasons, supposes none the less that the evaluative is distinct from the deontic, even if both sorts of properties result from the same ground. If they result from the same ground, one and the same object can have both evaluative and deontic properties; it can be good, and can be something that we have sufficient reason to do. This final view incurs the same explanatory debt as Ross's did, if it is combined with the claim that a ground for value is always (or even therefore) a ground for reasons as well.

Here then is a map of the five possibilities I have mentioned, where r = reasons, v = value and g = ground, and the relation '$\rightarrow$' is the grounding relation:

1. Early Moore (teleological view): $g \rightarrow v = r$ (reasons defined in terms of value)
2. Later Moore: $g \rightarrow v \rightarrow r$ (reasons grounded in but not defined in terms of value; value adds to the reasons given by the ground)

3. Ross: $g_1 \rightarrow v$, $g_2 \rightarrow r$ (i.e. the ground for reasons differs from the ground for value)

4. Buck-passing View: $g \rightarrow r$
   $\uparrow$
   v (i.e. being of value is having features that ground reasons)

5. Last View: $g \rightarrow v$, $g \rightarrow r$ (reasons and values are distinct but may have the same ground).

My only point here is that one does not establish the buck-passing view by refuting the two views of Moore. If that is right, and fair criticism of Scanlon, the main argument in favour of the buck-passing view will be its theoretical neatness. This neatness largely consists in the fact that it does not require us to say why it is that wherever there is value in the offing, there are at least some reasons. Ross' view is vulnerable to this requirement, as is the Last View.

At this stage, I need to introduce a different topic, attitudes to which will help us to decide between the buck-passing view and its alternatives. This topic is the relation between ground, rightness and reasons.

Remember that we agreed with Scanlon that the badness of the pain cannot add to the reasons generated by the features that make the pain bad (i.e. effectively, by the way it feels). Now are we to say the same sort of thing about rightness and wrongness? Are we to suppose, that is, that though goodness and badness cannot add to the reasons coming up from below, rightness and wrongness can? Should we suppose that the thin properties (or relations) are in general incapable of adding to the reasons thrown up from below? It is perhaps a bit surprising that Scanlon's answer to this question is no. According to Scanlon, the wrongness of an action can add to the reasons not to do it, though the badness of the action cannot. There are the reasons given us by the features that make it wrong, and then there are further reasons given us by the fact that it is wrong, or by its wrongness.

Even if, considering the matter simply in structural terms, we would probably expect all the thin properties to behave as reason-givers in much the same sort of way, that expectation could be overturned by a closer investigation of what actually happens. Derek Parfit considers the relation between two claims:

(1) This act violates standards of conduct that we all have very strong reasons to regard as important and to follow.

(2) This act gives the agent reasons to feel guilty and gives others reasons for indignation and resentment.

Jonathan Dancy

Suppose now that (1) specifies what it is for an act to be wrong. Parfit continues 'if our violating such standards would give us a reason to feel guilty, and would give others reasons to be indignant or resentful towards us, these facts do seem to give us further reasons not to act in this way'.[2]

If Parfit is right, the picture of the relation between ground, wrongness and reasons is like this:

$$g \rightarrow w \rightarrow r$$

While if the alternative view is right, it is more like:

$$g \rightarrow r = w$$

This is because those who think that the wrongness of an action cannot add to the reasons against doing it that are thrown up from below, are motivated by a certain conception of what wrongness and rightness are. We might call this the 'verdictive conception'.[3] In deciding whether an action is right, we are trying to determine how the balance of reasons lies. Our conclusion may be that there is more reason (or more reason of a certain sort, perhaps) to do it than not to do it, and we express this by saying that it is therefore the right thing to do. The rightness-judgement is verdictive; it expresses our verdict on the question how the reasons lie. It is incoherent, in this light, to suppose that the rightness can *add* to the reasons on which judgement is passed, thus, as one might say, increasing the sense in which, or the degree to which, it is true. And the same is true of wrongness. So when I expressed the 'alternative view' above as I did, I meant by this to show how that view understands wrongness-judgements as expressing, or capturing, how things are at the level of reasons. And I supposed that if this is correct, the wrongness of the action cannot itself add to the reasons that it captures.

We might think of this as a buck-passing view about rightness and wrongness. Scanlon wrote that his view 'is called the "buck-passing view" because it takes the normative force of a claim that something is good or valuable to be inherited from that of the reasons which it asserts to be present'. To claim that something is good is to claim, according to the buck-passing view, that it has features that give us (*pro tanto*) reasons to take certain attitudes to it. Similarly, we might say, to claim that an action is right is to claim that it has features that give us overall reason to do it. This is a buck-passing view because it holds that the normative force of a

---

[2] This quotation is taken by permission from a draft of Parfit's forthcoming *Rediscovering Reasons*.

[3] I take this name from Philip Stratton-Lake's forthcoming *Kant, Duty, and Moral Worth*, chapter 3.

claim that something is right or wrong is inherited from that of the reasons which it asserts to be present. So for Scanlon to adopt what I called the 'alternative view' about the relations between rightness and reasons would, one would have thought, have been for him to be a consistent buck-passer.

Think now about the arguments that Parfit produced in support of the non-buck-passing conception of rightness and wrongness. They amounted to the claim that if the wrongness of our action would give us a reason to feel guilty, and would give others reasons to be indignant or resentful towards us, these facts give us further reasons not to act in this way.

Should these arguments persuade us not to be consistent buck-passers? I doubt it. The same arguments seem to apply to badness. Suppose that my acts are bad as well as wrong. I would say that the badness of my behaviour gives me reason to feel ashamed, and gives others reasons to take certain attitudes towards me. Won't those facts then give me further reasons not to behave in those ways, if this is what happens in the case of wrongness as Parfit suggests?

Alternatively, we could look again at the suggestion that if the wrongness of our action would give us a reason to feel guilty, and would give others reasons to be indignant or resentful towards us, these facts give us further reasons not to act in this way. It would be possible to hold that the wrongness of our action does not *give* us reason to feel guilty. What it does is to show that if our action is wrong, we have reasons to feel guilty, and others have reason to feel indignant or resentful towards us. It does not show that the wrongness of our action adds to those reasons.

Be this as it may, we have now come across three possible overall views. The first is Scanlon's and Parfit's. They are buck-passers about the good, but not about the right. I have been suggesting the possibility of a more consistent buck-passing view, which passes both bucks. But I have also aired the possibility of a view that passes the rightness buck but not the goodness buck. This is because I have yet to be convinced of the buck-passing view for goodness. In the final section of this paper I try to say why.

III

The points I raise here are not supposed to constitute a refutation of the buck-passing view for goodness. (I will call this just the 'buck-passing view' from now on, forgetting any problems there may be about passing the rightness buck.) They are supposed only to raise doubts. I try to raise doubts by pointing to significant areas of debate in meta-ethics which the buck-passing view would automatically resolve. My suggestion is that this is probably not the right way to resolve these issues, and that they would be better resolved by argument than by a sort of peremptory definition. Of course, if the buck-passing view were true, the issues would indeed be resolved, and that would be the end of the matter. But remember that the only effective argument we have seen for the buck-passing view is that it offers a pleasing theoretical neatness. I like neatness, but I do not like to see apparently significant issues resolved by a definition whose only recommendation is that of neatness.

The first point here involves the contrast between consequentialism and deontology. The buck-passing view threatens to resolve this debate in favour of consequentialism. Deontologists have suggested in one way or another that there are duties, and so reasons, that are not value-involving. An action can be one's duty even though doing it has no value and its being done generates nothing of value. Standard examples here are of trivial duties. Suppose that I promise my children that I will tie my right shoelaces before my left shoelaces on alternate days of the week if they will do their homework without fuss. One can imagine arguing that though I ought to tie my right shoelaces before my left shoelaces today, since I did the opposite yesterday, my doing so has no value of any form. The buck-passing view rules this out in advance. To have value is to have reason-giving features, we are told, and since this is an identity statement it goes both ways. So to have reason-giving features is to be of value. So the deontological view expressed above is ruled out in advance of any significant debate.[4]

We might try to recover the issue we thought we had, by recasting the debate between consequentialism and deontology as a dispute about whether actions are made right solely by the value of their consequences, or whether they cannot also be made right by their intrinsic value.[5] This debate is still alive, even if the buck-passing view is true, for on both sides of the issue there is the sort of

[4] Derek Parfit has suggested to me that one could avoid the thought that the buck-passing view, being an identity claim, goes both ways by distinguishing two sorts of reasons – or, probably better, by distinguishing two sorts of things that reasons can be reasons to 'do'. I suggested above that the buck-passing view is pretty catholic about the sorts of reasons it is talking about, talking of reasons for admiring, respecting, preserving and protecting; of reasons to be guided by the goals or standards that the value involves; or reasons for promoting; and of reasons to act in certain ways. If some of these sorts of reason are involved in value, as we might put it, and others are not, the identity between having reason-giving features and being valuable will fail. I agree that this is so, but my present view is that there is no effective way of carving the reasons up appropriately.

[5] Philip Stratton-Lake suggested this to me.

relation between reasons and value that the buck-passing view can allow. But there would still be one position on this issue that is ruled out in advance, namely that of Ross (and also that of Prichard, one might say). For Ross would not accept that actions that are right are made right by their intrinsic value, or by the features that give them that value. As I briefly pointed out at the beginning of this paper, his view was that no duty has value of any sort, and that nothing that has value is a duty. And he had independent philosophical reasons for the two parts of this view. Can it be right to say that we know his view to be false because of the attractions of the buck-passing view, when those only amount to theoretical neatness?

There is a further point of the same sort, which concerns the notion of agent–relative value. There were in fact two reasons for the initial deontological view that reasons are not essentially related to any sort of value. The first I alluded to above, namely the possibility of valueless but still right acts. The second is a worry about maximising. Suppose that we allow that every right action has some sort of value, just in virtue of being right. It should then turn out that we have reason not to do the action ourselves if we can thereby enable two other agents to do actions of similar value. And this is at odds with the basic deontological picture of duties. This picture is built on a distinction between two sorts of rule. To take an example that I think I owe to Philippa Foot: there is the rule 'do not shout' and there is the rule 'see to it that as little shouting as possible takes place'. The first of these is a deontological rule; it is addressed to the agent, saying, as it were 'don't shout – this means you' or 'don't be a shouter'; and we break that rule if we shout. The second rule is quite different. We do not necessarily break this rule by shouting; indeed, we would possibly only be able to keep the rule by shouting, as when we need to shout in order to shut everyone else up. In this sense, deontological rules are not maximising rules. You should not shout even if, by shouting, you can minimise the incidence of shouting. A maximising rule is not the sort of rule that deontologists take themselves to be talking about. But if we introduce a link between reasons and values, we undermine this deontological picture of rules (obviously, and especially, of moral rules). For we reintroduce the possibility that the value at issue in keeping the rule is best served by breaking it.

There is, however, a possible way out of this difficulty. It involves the introduction of agent–relative value. If the sort of value that doing one's duty has is agent–relative value, it might be possible to shatter the maximising picture even though one has retained a general connection between reasons and value of the buck-passing sort. Now I don't want here to go into the details of how this might be done, if indeed it can be done at all. My point at this juncture is going to be merely that, if we are to try to prevent the adoption of the buck-passing view from undermining a significant aspect of deontology by introducing a conception of agent–relative value, this is a considerable theoretical cost, and it is a cost, once again, that we have committed ourselves to paying just for the sake of theoretical neatness. What is more, many people doubt the coherence of the notion of agent–relative value in the first place. If the buck-passing view can only be sustained by introducing a piece of dubious philosophy, it is looking much less attractive.

I turn now to a completely different source of disquiet about the buck-passing view. There is a history to this too. For Ross held that goodness is an intrinsic property, while rightness is a relation. Rightness is the relation of being fitting to the situation (1939, p. 52), while goodness is a property of motives and that is not a relation at all. Moral goodness, in particular, is a monadic property of 'acts of will, desires, and emotions, and finally relatively permanent modifications of character even when these are not being exercised' (1939, p. 292). Had such goodness been able to be defined as whatever is worthy of admiration and approval, it might have been seen as a relation (though, as discussed earlier, this might not be quite what we would now mean by a 'relation'). But we saw that Ross refused to allow this 'definition', though he did not reject it as a paraphrase.

I don't mean here to appeal to the detailed argumentation by which Ross defends his position. I don't even mean to defend his view that goodness, at least moral goodness, is not a relation at all. The real point, I think, is one about the polyadicity of rightness and of goodness – and this is a point that translates into thoughts about the polyadicity of reasons. Let us allow, without asking why for the moment, that rightness is a many-place relation. The point will then be that even if goodness is also a many-place relation, it has fewer places than rightness does and fewer than reasons do. Now if this is true, it cannot be correct to define goodness as the presence of reason-giving features. For the presence of reason-giving features will have more places in it, so to speak, than the goodness has.

The reason for supposing that goodness is less polyadic than reasons is that reasons belong to, are for, individuals. There are no reasons hanging around waiting for someone to have them. If the situation generates a reason for action, it must allot that reason to someone. (I don't mean to suggest that this is always or often difficult.) But goodness is not like this. Something can be good or bad without specification of an agent. The desolation or destitution of someone is bad even if there is nobody around to do anything about it, nobody who has any opportunity to do anything about it, and so nobody who can be said to have a reason to do something about it. Someone's destitution, then, has features that *would* ground reasons for any agent suitably situated, but it does not follow that those features already ground reasons. And if it does not, we can be sure that to have value or disvalue is not itself to have reason-giving features.

One might reply that there are surely reasons for the destitute person, created by his destitution. In that case, a better example might be the lonely and sudden death of someone without friends or relatives, far from any possible help. We could say that this is bad, even if there is nobody who has reasons to grieve or indeed reasons of any other sort.

Derek Parfit suggested to me in conversation that there may be a weaker form of the buck-passing view that is consistent with the original motivation but which is less vulnerable to this sort of worry about polyadicity. This weaker form understands having value, not as having reason-giving features, but as having features that are potentially reason-giving. To have potentially reason-giving features is a less polyadic matter than to have actually reason-giving features, since something could be of the former sort without our needing to specify any particular individual for whom the reasons are reasons (since the reasons don't yet exist). This manoeuvre seems sound, so far as that goes, but it raises worries of another sort. For it seems far too easy to have features that are potentially reason-giving – that would, in certain circumstances, give us reasons. Something that has no value at all might well have features that would, in certain circumstances, ground reasons. So this weakening of the buck-passing view seems to me to enfeeble it.

The failure of these replies seems to me to establish that goodness and reasons do not have the same degree of polyadicity. Is that result consistent with the buck-passing view? I doubt it. To have features that ground reasons, where reasons are polyadic to degree n, is, I suggest, necessarily itself a property that is polyadic to degree n. Just having those reason-grounding features is, of course, not necessarily polyadic at all. But that is irrelevant. Being in pain may be the reason-grounding property, without itself being other than monadic. But that this feature is reason-giving must itself share the polyadicity of the reasons given, since it is a feature that can only be instantiated when the various empty spaces in the specification of the reason have all been filled up.

IV

My overall conclusion, then, is, that the buck-passing view needs more defence than it has so far received. The buck-passing view I am talking of is, of course, the view that to be good, or valuable, is to have features that give us reasons of certain sorts. The discussion above tended to favour the other buck-passing view, the view that for an action to be right is for it to have features that give us overall reasons (perhaps of a certain sort) in favour of doing it. If we yield to this pressure, neither we nor Scanlon will be consistent buck-passers. We will pass only the rightness buck, and he passes only the goodness buck. And a challenge might here be mounted in favour of consistent buck-passing.

In reply to that challenge, the appropriate response is to point out that rightness and reasons are concepts of the same normative family, the deontic family. It is not, therefore, so surprising if there are the sorts of links between them that are involved if we pass the rightness buck. There would be no worries about polyadicity, for instance, for all the deontic concepts seem to be polyadic to the same degree. Equally, the deontologists may feel that goodness does not always generate reasons, or, more probably, that reasons do not always pass via goodness. The maximising worries that support this sort of thought have nothing to say against passing the rightness buck. So I think that, although it would be prettier if we could pass both bucks, and that there is an initial attraction in the cry 'both bucks or neither!', the terrain is not flat enough to allow us to do this.

Refusing to pass the goodness buck does nothing to reinstate something that we all think mistaken, the thought that the value of an object adds to the reasons that come from below, the reasons given us by the features that generate the value. This thought is a mistake, but that does nothing to support Scanlon's buck-passing view. Nor can we defend that view by asking 'how can there be value without reasons?' (the opposite of Joseph's question how there can be reasons without value). This question is irrelevant. The question before us has been whether to be valuable *is* to have reason-giving properties, not whether all valuable things are ones that have features that give us reasons to treat them in one way rather than another. The latter is not disputed. But to allow that anything with value will have reason-giving features is not to accept the buck-passing view. These things may go regularly, constantly or even invariably together without being identical.

Suppose, however, that they do go invariably together. Or suppose that to be valuable is to have what we might call 'potentially reason-giving features', ones set up to give reasons for any suitable agent, should there be one. These thoughts create a link between values, between being valuable, that is, and reasons. And we still need to find a way of explaining this link. My final remark is the admission that on this score the buck-passing view has an advantage, though not, I think, a final one. All reductive views, after all, give peremptory answers to questions about interconnections between the 'two' features that they reduce to one, and those peremptory answers are often, as here, unsatisfying.[6]

References

Ewing, A. C. (1947) *The Definition of Good* (London: Macmillan).
Joseph, H. W. B. (1931) *Some Problems in Ethics* (Oxford: Clarendon Press).
Moore, G. E. (1903) *Principia Ethica* (Cambridge University Press).
Moore, G. E. (1912) *Ethics* (Cambridge University Press).
Ross, Sir W. D. (1930) *The Right and the Good* (Oxford: Clarendon Press).
Ross, Sir W. D. (1939) *Foundations of Ethics* (Oxford: Clarendon Press).
Scanlon, T. M. (1999) *What We Owe to Each Other* (Cambridge, Mass.: Harvard University Press).

[6] Many thanks to Derek Parfit and to Philip Stratton-Lake for many discussions of these topics and helpful criticism and suggestions.

'The right and the good' and W. D. Ross's criticism of consequentialism

DAVID WIGGINS

> *There is but one unconditional commandment, which is that we should seek incessantly, with fear and trembling, so to vote and so to act as to bring about the very largest total universe of good we can see.*
>
> William James, in The Will to Believe

> *The ardor of undisciplined benevolence seduces us into malignity and whenever our hearts are warm and our objects great and excellent, intolerance is the sin that does most easily beset us.*

> *I rather think that the distant prospect, to which [Robespierre] was travelling appeared to him grand and beautiful; but that he fixed his eye on it with such intense earnestness as to neglect the foulness of the road.*
>
> Samuel Taylor Coleridge, on Robespierre,
Conciones ad Populum, 1795

1 The theme announced for these lectures is the philosophy of value. It may seem that moral philosophy, along with aesthetics, the philosophy of art, the philosophy of environment ... ought to be a proper part of the philosophy of value. I have chosen mottoes to illustrate the dangers of that supposition.

The supposition that the whole of ethics can be subsumed within the philosophy of value has a long history. It is older than the familiar confrontations – Coleridge versus Bentham and Paley, Whewell versus Mill, Sidgwick, James ... Ross versus Moore, Bernard Williams versus J. J. C. Smart, Philippa Foot versus Samuel Scheffler. (We may find traces of the supposition in Leibniz, for instance.) It marks one of the places in human thinking where philosophy, so far from dissipating ordinary confusion, has aided and abetted it. Or so I claim. This confusion has now gone so far, I think, that we shall never fully escape it until we pay careful attention not only to the issue but to the history of some of the extended disputations to which it has given rise in philosophy. On this occasion, the historical episode I shall commend to your attention is Sir David Ross's critique of G. E. Moore.

David Wiggins

Ross's *The Right and the Good* was published by Oxford University Press in 1930. The style of the book is dense. The mode of argument is close and sometimes tortuous. Even with one foot in the grave, I could not be sure I was reading it with the precision it deserves. But *The Right and the Good* is above all a work of intellectual excitement, an excitement long since forgotten that nevertheless anticipates some of our present day preoccupations. The first two chapters, on which I propose to concentrate my whole discussion here, represent one notable document in the development of the case against the position we now call (after G. E. M. Anscombe) moral consequentialism. Even though not quite everything went right in Ross's conduct of this case, we need to study that case if we are to improve upon it.

2 By 'moral consequentialism' (let me explain) I mean not the view that consequences matter – for absolutely nobody denies that consequences matter – but the view that the rightness or wrongness of an act can be defined in terms of the merit or the demerit of the consequences of doing the act. Or I mean the view that the rightness or wrongness of doing a particular act at a particular time can be grounded exhaustively in considerations of all the consequences of doing the act (including any consequences there will be of others doing things relevantly similar to this thing) without further and separate regard to what the act itself is. Thus moral deliberation between alternative acts is seen by consequentialists as a process of ranking alternatives by reference to that which would result from the doing of each available alternative. Thus consequentialism celebrates the subordination of moral questions to the philosophy of value. In other words, it celebrates the subordination of the right to the good.

Salient among the consequentialists who were considered by Ross was G. E. Moore. I think that Ross saw Moore's account of morality as the culmination of all earlier attempts to base rightness on productivity of some sort of result. Moore had claimed in *Principia Ethica* that 'right' meant 'productive of the greatest good'. In a passage that Ross quoted at page 9 of *The Right and The Good*, Moore had claimed:

> our duty, therefore, can be defined as that action which will cause more good to exist in the Universe than any possible alternative. And what is 'right' or 'morally permissible' only differs from this as what will *not* cause *less* good than any possible alternatives.

In his later book, *Ethics*, Moore adjusted this claim a little (as Ross remarks). Instead of offering an analysis of the word's meaning (or

176

of its sense, as one might now say), Moore saw himself as offering productivity of maximum intrinsic good as 'the reason why an action is right, when it is right'.

One could spend time here on the nature of this shift – the shift, as I should say, from the elaboration of sense to the further explication of reference. One could dwell too upon Ross's reading of Moore's doctrines of definition. But our chief concern must be the general nature of consequentialism and the nature of Moore's 'agathistic (or ideal) utilitarianism'. In this particular form of consequentialism, much emphasis is placed upon the irreducibility of good – and/or upon its irreducibility *a fortiori* to anything that is part of the subject matter of the natural sciences or psychology (cf. *Principia Ethica*, p. 40). But, once he is safe within the realm of the ethical, and settles down to frame his own agathistic doctrine, Moore no longer scrutinises every substantive definition or putative analysis by use of the open-question argument. One might expect that Moore would have been alert to the suggestion that an act might produce the greatest possible amount of intrinsic good yet still not be right. But in practice, when he discusses 'right' in chapter 1, section 17, and chapter 5, section 89, there is no echo of the open-question argument, potent though it would have been to alert Moore to the entirely question-begging character of his argument for the equivalence that Ross quotes.

So perhaps the situation is as simple as this. According to agathistic or ideal consequentialism, a right act is one the doing of which maximises intrinsic goodness or produces no less intrinsic goodness than the doing of any other.[1] And it is the doubtfulness of this putative equivalence, the doubtfulness of what Broad called of Moore's 'ethical neutralism',[2] which seems to have been the chief spur to Ross's writing of *The Right and the Good*.

3 How does Ross argue against the equivalence? First he says that there is a presumption that in 'right act' the word 'right' means the same as 'morally ought to be done'. In that case, the word 'right' has a quite different application from 'morally good'. For the words 'morally good' fit into the frame '*x* is a [morally good] man', where-

---

[1] Ross seconds this weakening of 'right'. 'It may sometimes happen that there is a set of two or more acts, one or other of which ought to be done by me rather than any act not belonging to the set. In such a case any act of this set is right, but none is my duty; my duty is to do "one or other" of them.' (p. 3). He acknowledges an element of stipulation in this finding.

[2] For the expression 'ethical neutralism', as used of Moore, see C. D. Broad in *The Philosophy of G. E. Moore*, (ed.) P. Schilp, (Evantston and Chicago 1942), especially pp. 43 and 51.

as the words 'morally ought to be done' do not fit into it. Here, however, with some presentiment perhaps of the danger of committing a cancelling-out fallacy,[3] Ross acknowledges that

> someone might say that while 'morally good' has a wider application than 'right', in that it can be applied to agents as well as to acts, yet when applied to acts they mean the same thing.

Against this, Ross records his agreement with the view that the only acts that are morally good are those that proceed from a good motive. But if so (he concludes), and if the Kantian principle that 'ought' implies 'can' excludes our being required always to act from a good motive, then neither the rightness nor the obligatoriness of an act can be the same as its moral goodness. Our duty is to do certain things, not to do them from the sense of duty. And then, in a further clarification, anticipating something that has been stressed more recently by Richard Cartwright[4] and Jennifer Hornsby,[5] Ross writes that clearness would be gained if we used 'act' of the thing done, and 'action' of the doing of it. The latter, the doing of the act, can then be that which is from good motives. [Cp. p. 156]. This excellent ruling, not always in fact observed by Ross – but I shall try to stick to it myself and sometimes I shall even correct Ross quotations accordingly – clears the way for Ross to say:

> 'right' and 'wrong' refer entirely to the thing done, 'morally good' and 'morally bad' entirely to the motive from which it is done. A firm grasp of this distinction will do much to remove some of the perplexities of our moral thought. [7]

Ross's ruling also smooths the road to his announcement of his own opinion that notions such as that of right are 'ultimate and irreducible' [11], not analysable that is by deployment of any other moral philosophical or sociological notions; and his further opinion that:

> the rightness *prima facie* of certain types of act is self evident ... to minds that have reached a certain degree of maturity; and, for minds to reach the necessary degree of maturity, the development that takes place from generation to generation is as much needed as that which takes place from infancy to adult life. [12]

[3] See P. T. Geach, *Reference & Generality* (Ithaca: Cornell University Press, 1968), p. 61.

[4] See Richard Cartwright's essay 'Propositions', reprinted in his *Philosophical Essays* (Cambridge, Mass., 1987).

[5] See Jennifer Hornsby 'Which physical events are mental events' PAS 81 (1980–81); her review of Davidson at *Ratio*, 24,(1) (1982), 88–9; and *Simple Mindedness* (Harvard 1997), v. index, s.v. 'actions'.

It is to such minds as these that chapter 2 of *The Right and the Good* will be addressed. In that chapter, Ross sets forth his argument against the claim that productivity of the maximum good is what makes right actions right.

4 After certain preliminaries, Ross reminds us that, when someone fulfils a promise because he believes he ought, he thinks more of the past than of the future: 'What makes him think it right to act in a certain way is the fact that he has promised to do so – that and, usually, nothing more' [17]. The only thing that Ross thinks would lend credibility to the other view, the productivity of good view, is an exceptional case in which the prospective disastrousness of doing the thing we promised to do prompts us to judge it not right. But Ross thinks the productivity view furnishes a worse explanation of that exception than the fact that there are other duties we have beside that of keeping promises, e.g. the duty to have regard for the distress of others (not least perhaps those to whom the promise was given). Ross says that ideal utilitarians seem to have fallen into the erroneous supposition that 'the only morally significant relation in which my neighbours stand to me is that of being possible beneficiaries of my action' [19].

> They do stand in this relation to me, and this relation is morally significant. But they may stand in the relation of promisee to promiser, of creditor to debtor, of wife to husband, of child to parent, of friend to friend, of fellow countryman to fellow countryman, and the like; and each of these relations is the foundation of a *prima facie* duty. [19].

After some discussion of the nature of the *prima facie* (a matter to which I shall return shortly), Ross offers the following provisional division of duties:

1 Duties resting on previous acts of my own either (a) promises or implied promises, entailing duties of fidelity, or (b) wrongful acts, entailing duties of reparation.
2 Duties deriving from the acts of others, such as duties of gratitude (or, as one might say with greater generality, of reciprocity).
3 Duties of distributive justice.
4 Duties of beneficence.
5 Duties of self-improvement.
6 Duties of care not to injure others or non-maleficence, rightly perceived by Ross as not reducible to duties of type (4) or beneficence. ('Even when we have come to recognise the duty of beneficence, it appears to me that the duty of non-maleficence

is recognised as a distinct one, and as *prima facie* more binding. We should not in general consider it justifiable to kill one person in order to keep another alive, or to steal from one in order to give alms to another' [p. 22].)

In sum then 'the essential defect of the "ideal utilitarian" theory is that it ignores, or at least does not do full justice to, the highly personal character of duty'.

The last claim resonates with things that Bernard Williams and Peter Winch and others have been insisting upon in other ways over the last three decades. Ross may not exactly mean by these words all and only that which Williams or Winch would want to mean if they used them. Ross does mean at least this, however: Most of the duties this or that person has are duties that arise (*inter alia*) from his or her historic situation (comprising *inter alia* what he or she has done or received, what responsibilities he or she has incurred), and these duties are duties in relation to other persons in *their* historic situations similarly historically and specifically characterised. This is not of course to say that Ross disallows other sorts of duties. Conspicuously, he insists on the duty of non-maleficence to no matter whom (type (6)), and he insists on beneficence (type (4)) (where there is unfinished business about recipients).[6] But the ideal utilitarians' or consequentialists' great mistake, according to Ross, is to want to assimilate *all* other duties to the paradigm of duties of the type (4). Other duties are simply not intelligible when they are conceived in accordance with that paradigm:

> If the only duty is to produce the maximum of good, the question who is to have the good – whether it is myself or my benefactor, or a person to whom I have made a promise to confer that good on him, or a mere fellow man to whom I stand in no such special relation – should make no difference to my having a duty to produce that good. But we are all in fact sure that it makes a vast difference. [22].

In sum, nobody who pays the slightest attention to the moral ideas by which we do in fact live can find the consequentialist definition of 'right' credible.

5 I have not yet recapitulated everything Ross says that needs to be discussed in this connection (about *prima facie*-ness, for instance). But this is the moment to survey the strengths of Ross's own defences against the ideal or agathistic consequentialism that he chiefly set out to combat. Ideal consequentialism, if it fails, is all

---

[6] The supposed neutrality of these two duties is not exactly the same.

the more interesting for failing, *despite* respecting so scrupulously as it does the autonomy of the ethical. Precisely perhaps because of its recognition of the distinctiveness of the ethical, however, Ross himself is not so proof against its charms as one might have expected.

The issue comes to the fore sooner than Ross might wish, and with effects not intended by Ross, when he says, à propos of the duty of beneficence, that it is 'self-evident' that we have a duty to produce as much good as we can. See *The Right and the Good* [25] (echoed on this point by the *Foundations of Ethics* [FE 313 *et passim*]). The idea of producing as much good as possible, which is foundational in some other systematisations of moral thinking, first arises in the scheme of Ross, who is opposed to an equivalence between productivity of good and the grounds of rightness, only in connection with his account of the simple duty of beneficence, or type (4). That might seem to insulate Ross from this duty's having any larger effects. As the book proceeds, however, type (4) duty seems to grow in scale and importance and it becomes more and more doubtful how beneficence as Ross conceives of it can ever be confined within the space Ross originally assigned to it.

There is good and there is intrinsically good. With regard to the second, it emerges that, according to Ross, there are three main things that are intrinsically good, 'virtue, knowledge and, with certain limitations, pleasure'. But then, he says:

> since a given virtuous disposition, for instance, is equally good whether it is realised in myself or in another, it seems to be my duty to bring it [the virtuous disposition] into existence, whether in myself or in another. [24]

There are several passages to this effect in *The Right and The Good* and *The Foundation of Ethics*. The definition of the intrinsically good is given in *The Right and The Good* as follows: (p. 68) 'the intrinsically good is best defined as that which is good apart from any of the results it produces.' [cp. 115].

6 So, having separated the right and the good, Ross then ratifies certain connections between them. Sixty or seventy years further on, some of these connections put one on to one's guard. The recipe for perplexity here is no longer novel – either theoretically or practically.

Let us suppose that ethnic non-quarrelsomeness is a moral virtue. And let us suppose that in the Balkans somewhere some reflective, self-conscious person, a patriot of some sort, possessing both determination and armed power, deliberates as follows:

181

The only way out of the present situation is to bring into being communities which do not see themselves as ethnically divided and in which the issue of ethnicity can be allowed to go to sleep. That is the essential prerequisite of their becoming communities in which questions of race can be discounted and the positive virtues can eventually be cultivated of ethnic non-quarrelsomeness and non-factiousness. That is for the long run. But now, in the real world of 1997, the only way in which even the first step can be achieved is at cost of a certain minimum of rearrangement, even at cost of measures of partition or of ethnic cleansing, as some call it. And that, alas, is what must happen now ... I can see no alternative.

Suppose that this deliberation is markedly *more thorough* (at least) and takes into account *more facts, political* and *historical*, than any other deliberation that looks steadfastly for some way out of some present impasse; and suppose, as it seems Ross supposes, that the duty of benevolence requires that we should produce as much intrinsic good as possible. Then agents who have this thought must inevitably face the altogether insidious question of how many objects of virtuous concern it is right for them to sacrifice in order to fulfil their duty to promote some larger and more widespread future virtue, the virtue of ethnic non-quarrelsomeness or non-factiousness which they see open-endedly continuing into the distant future within less troubled communities.[7] Indeed, if there really is a *prima facie* duty to maximise good, then agents who have the

[7] If the example just given does not carry conviction, apply the recipe again and find another one. The example does however stand in need of clarification, as Professor C. B. Ricks has made me see. The patriot's idea (let me explain) is not that some cloistered virtue of racial non-quarrelsomeness can exist wherever everyone is of the same race (or everyone sees everyone else in this way). The patriot's idea is that, in the short term future of certain torn communities, the question of race must be put therapeutically to sleep, so that in the longer term, among new generations to come, ordinary questions that will arise of race and racial difference can be managed more calmly and reasonably. Compare the advice of an allergy specialist that, for a considerable period, the patient should withdraw from all contact with an irritating agent to which he has become hypersensitive – *before* resuming ordinary life on a better regime. The patriot's idea is not confused, or even simple minded. But the magnitude of the distant prize and the consequentialist framework in which the patriot has chosen to deliberately distract his attention from the true nature of that which he is preparing to countenance. Or so I contend. Whatever prospect his idea holds out for human peace and virtue stretching into an open-ended future, it will give cover in the present to other and much more disquieting intentions.

thoughts just expounded must prepare to answer the question of what could ever *release* them from the positive alleged duty to maximise future virtue – by this or any other effective method.

How can things have gone wrong so quickly for Ross, to whom we look as the non-consequentialist par excellence and to whom we look to play the role of the arch enemy of such reasonings? Ross himself calls producing as much good as possible a 'general obligation' [27]. That seems ill-advised. Worse, all he gives us with which to counter this general obligation are the things that he calls special obligations. So it begins to appear that, having initially denied that there should be any presumption at all in favour of an equivalence between productivity of good and that which makes right acts right,[8] Ross has somehow given back the whole initiative to the ideal consequentialist. Isn't Ross in danger of falling backwards into the position, which he needed to avoid, of being forced to insist upon the various special types of obligations as *exceptions* to some 'general obligation', the agathistic and general obligation whose existence he explicitly allows to be 'manifest'? Surely G. E. Moore must have bewitched him?

7 Dismayed and disappointed by this, anti-consequentialists can turn over again all the evidence to be found in *The Right and The Good* about whether the doctrine that gives this trouble says exactly what Ross meant. Have I perhaps got him wrong? There are further clues I have not deployed (I shall use one or two of them later) especially at pp. 58, 63, 105 and 154. Or else we can turn to the parallel, perhaps more hopeful, stretch of argument to be found in Ross's Gifford lectures, published in 1939 as *The Foundation of Ethics*.

In the *Foundation of Ethics*, Ross writes [FE 69] that Moore says that he finds it self-evident that being optimific is always a ground

[8] Cp. *Foundations of Ethics*, page 319. 'If we are right in holding that the general nature of things that are obligatory is that they are activities of self-exertion, what can we say about their particular character? Perhaps the most widely current view on this question is that the special character of all acts that are right, and that which makes them right, is that they are acts of setting oneself to produce a maximum of what is good. This seems to me far from being, as it is often supposed to be, self-evident, and to be in fact a great oversimplification of the ground of rightness. There is no more reason, after all, to suppose that there is one single reason which makes all acts right that are right than there is for supposing (what I fancy no one who considers the matter will suppose) that there is a single reason which makes all things good that *are* good. And in fact there are several branches of duty which apparently cannot be grounded on the productivity of the greatest good ... fulfilling promises.'

of rightness. But Ross says that he himself can find no self-evidence about it. Not only that. Ross raises several difficulties. (1) Increasing the population with people just happy enough not to be better off dead would increase the total of happiness: but that wouldn't make it right to increase the population thus. (2) Suppose an extra dose of happiness is to be introduced into the world. It ought to be indifferent on the consequentialist view how it is distributed. But it is not really indifferent. Then, after another argument (3) which I omit, Ross points out in an argument (4) that 'we think the principle "do evil to no one" more pressing than the principle "do good to everyone" except when the evil is very substantially outweighed by the good. This consideration seems to be perfectly clear' [FE 75]. Ross mentions these and other points. And something very important indeed seems to lurk here. But then, instead of ferreting it out further, he messes about trying to construct the utilitarian answer to each point. Rather than see him do that, one might have hoped that Ross would try to apply these points (1), (2), (4), and make them work for him, especially point (1), in order to reinforce the claim that it was *never self-evident at all* (that it was always an illusion that it was self-evident) that simply being optimific was (as such) *even a candidate* to coincide with grounds of rightness – even a candidate to coincide with one of the grounds of rightness. I think that it is obvious that that is what he ought to have tried to do (consider the title of the book *The Right and the Good*). Instead of that, however, Ross allows an impression to grow up that his chief concern is only to carve off from everything else one special and distinct realm of obligation, viz. that constituted by the five other types *prima facie* duty already set out in *The Right and The Good*. It comes as no surprise then when we find Ross, a hundred and eleven pages later, debating the problem that he describes in almost consequentialist terms as that of 'balancing duties of special obligation against the duty of maximising [intrinsic?] goods' (see [FE xii], [FE 185]) or 'of producing the maximum good.'

Yet not quite all is lost. The thing that saves Ross from collapsing into a consequentialist – if you call that saving him – is his remembering in Foundations of Ethics to insist on this: that

> where a special *prima facie* duty exists, as well as the general prima facie duty of producing the maximum good, our final judgement about our duty depend not [my italics] on a comparison of goods, but on comparison of *prima facie* duties ... We study the situation in detail till the morally significant features of it become clear to us. [FE 186]

So it appears that, if Ross were confronted with the Balkan example I have mentioned or he were asked whether there is the slightest *prima facie* obligation on anyone for population to be increased in order that nett happiness be (however barely) increased, then he would have to aver that he confidently expected that such *prima facie* duties to produce maximum good would be swamped (albeit not qualified, for he has no way to qualify them in the form in which they present themselves to deliberation) by all the other *prima facie* duties we should need to review when we sought to discover 'which of the [acts]⁹ open to one [it] would be objectively right [to do], [the doing of which] would discharge in the fullest possible measure the various claims or *prima facie* duties that are involved in the situation.'

8 I shall return to the thing that I lament in this compromise. But now I need to paint in some of the rest of the picture. It is at this sort of point in his scheme, where *prima facie* duties need to be balanced against one another, that Ross is apt to have recourse to the celebrated Aristotelian *aperçu*

> *En tei aisthesei he krisis* [RG 42], [compare Aristotle NE 1109ᵇ²³, 1126ᵇ⁴].

Ross quotes this tag several times. It means that the judgement lies in perception. But Ross is apt to say it allusively. Because it is necessary in the new condition of moral philosophy for it to be expanded unallusively, I will attempt that straightway, enlarging at the same time upon Ross's conception of the conflict between *prima facie* duties. When that is done, we can return to the supposed *prima facie* duty to produce the greatest intrinsic good.

To claim as Ross does, that 'the judgement lies in perception' implies first that there does not need to be one general principle by which any or every conflict of duties may, in whatever context, be arbitrated. It implies that it is no more sensible to expect to find one principle of this sort than it is to search for some general ground or explication for all judgements of rightness. Nevertheless, just as one may expect that, for each judgement of rightness, there will be *some* ground or explication, so one might expect that, for every context in which a conflict of *prima facie* duties arises,¹⁰ moral perception will find some recognisably convincing consideration by which to arbitrate the conflict. Such a particular finding will be local to context,

---

⁹ Ross writes 'actions', forgetting (as so often) the excellent preliminaries set out in chapter 1 of *The Right and Good*, already here rehearsed, concerning acts and actions.

¹⁰ Or 'for every non-tragic context in which a conflict of *prima facie* duties arises', one might prefer Ross to say, though he does not.

highly specific, and almost devoid of generality. Indeed the Aristotelian tag, when it is read in the larger setting of Aristotle's view of practical reason, suggests that the arbitratory finding must itself be the creature of the context.[11] Of course, if one were able to disentangle the finding of perception *completely* from the context – if, by means of a conditional, one could write enough of the context into the finding itself, for instance – then that would be the transposition of the finding into something specific, universal and explicitly codifiable in a self-sufficient sentence of the form 'It is always right, when ... to do the act _ _ _ .' But in practice, when they are understood literally, all such claims prove to be incorrect. Or that is the plausible contention conveyed by *en tei aisthesei he krisis*. The practical knowledge or understanding that produces the decisive consideration, *alias* 'the finding of perception', never needs, *as a condition of its adequacy*, to have the wherewith to write explicitly into its finding for the context the whole of the thing that is relevant in the context.[12] Why suppose that, whenever there is something it is one's duty to do, it *must* be possible to find a universally true sentence of the form 'It is right when . . . to do the act _ _ _ '? Why suppose that it is a readily remediable accident that we don't in practice expect there to be many unqualified and unrestrictedly true sentences in the form 'It is *always* right, when ... to do the act _ _ _ '?[13] (Contrast simple prohibitions and all the other

[11] To say that much, however, is not of course to deny that such a consideration will commit those who accept it to something universal. For on a proper understanding of the distinctness of generality and universality, the consideration could be utterly specific and still point towards something unqualifiedly universal. It is useful, here and everywhere, to make use of R. M. Hare's distinction in *Freedom and Reason* (Oxford, 1963), chapter 3, between the general/specific distinction and the universal/particular distinction. See also R. M. Hare, *Moral Thinking* (Oxford, 1981), 41.

[12] Cp. Nic. Ethics 1143[b]. Nb. especially the *anapodektoi phaseis ton presbuteron*. If you do not believe me when I say this on Ross' behalf, then you should take note of the fact that, typically, the premises of a practical syllogism that expresses ordinary practical insight into a given context are neither numerous nor long. A practical syllogism only needs premises that are adequate for its context. That is what makes the practical syllogism finite, manageable *and serviceable*. Why should it count against our claim to have practical knowledge if we are unable to rewrite the premises of our moral reasoning in a form that makes such reasoning self-sufficient and independent of context?

[13] I formulate the schema in this way in order to respect the point that there may be true universal prohibitions. Note here that there is not a doing of the act of refraining from φ-ing (an action of refraining from φ-ing) wherever someone does not φ.

forms of speech which bear on practice and encapsulate moral wisdom, but do not purport to tell you what *positively and determinately* to do under all circumstances.)

All right. So much for one reason for saying '*en tei aisthesei he krisis*'. But one who places Ross's kind of reliance upon the Aristotelian *aperçu* now needs to be prepared to address a question that Ross does not mention. From whence, if not from a general formula, does practical perception draw its sundry context-specific findings, maxims, arbitrations, unproven declarations or *anapodeiktoi phaseis* (NE 1143b) and the rest? And what organises these things? Ross never says – perhaps because he assumed that his readers would know Aristotle. I think Ross never expected *anyone* to find his view at all mysterious. What then was he taking for granted?

If we insert something Ross must have been assuming his readers might supply, then the answer to the question is that these perceptions are the perceptions of practically wise people ('mature minds'). Such people can judge of such constantly evolving, essentially contestable matters and judge them in the light of their contextually adjustable conceptions of the human good – the good of human beings living well in the society of other human beings who are living well in that society. Anyone who has some grasp of that sort of ideal or *skopos* has some sense not only of the *hoti*, the that, but also of the *dioti*, the why or wherefore, of action in accordance with virtue. Such a one will exercise irreducibly practical knowledge in search of (in context) practicable specifications of happiness or *eudaimonia* and of the demands of the virtues or *aretai* – specifications which will *in practice* render happiness/eudaimonia the same as activity of the soul in accordance with virtue (*psuches energeia kat'areten*). Or such was Aristotle's doctrine.

9 Where Ross left a gap, something such as this from Aristotle will go into it. Equally, a less Aristotelian supplementation could be imagined, e.g. one based on the Kantian idea of the kingdom of ends. But the most important thing is that *something* reasonably detailed can be put there; that, at this point in his exposition, Ross is being not *evasive* but *allusive*, or so it may be hoped; and that those who accuse Ross of invoking intuition to solve the problems of moral epistemology are insisting on seeing him as offering a mysterious general answer to questions to which Ross in fact, both justifiably and explicitly, emphatically refuses a general answer. What Ross sees himself as offering piecemeal, or rather reminding us of piecemeal, are the commonplace answers (plural) of our ordinary moral cum practical knowledge, and the reasons this furnishes for the answers it provides. (Note that, contrary to what these accusers have been told about Ross, Ross scarcely mentions intuition.)

In Ross's picture, as I have filled it out, virtuous agents are seen as striving to determine which acts would discharge in the fullest possible measure various *prima facie* duties. Our *prima facie* duties represent the various claims that lie upon us. In the typical case, such claims arise from what we have done or received or contracted, or they arise from what we are (from our status, etc.). They are, moreover, real claims, not apparent claims. So now we come to the expression *prima facie*.

Ross was just as aware as all his critics have been of the disadvantages of the expression *prima facie*. In so far as he explains his reservations about the other term that he might have used, viz. 'claim' ('claim' is less misleading, surely, than Ross's terminology and its merits were urged upon him by Prichard), these reservations related *only* to *claim*'s not being quite general enough to cover all cases where Ross thought he saw a *prima facie* duty (e.g. the agent's duty of improving his own character). Why then does Ross persist with *prima facie*? (If we want to have Latin, then Susan Hurley's *pro tanto* would have been so much better.) And why does Ross use the equally (though differently) misleading noun-phrase 'conditional duties', if the claims made upon us of Rossian obligations are neither illusory nor hypothetical, but categorical [cp. RG 28] or categorically founded?

Well, perhaps the thought goes like this. Duties all *strive*, so to speak, to direct or appropriate the agent's choice of act. They all strive to get themselves adopted as what verdictively or all-in *ought* to be done. But unluckily (the thought goes) not all can be done. So not all will win the all-in verdict 'let this be done!' If this is a correct reconstruction, then Ross's unfortunate retention of *prima facie* and 'conditional' arises from his desire to suggest simultaneously all of the following: 'these are categorical claims', 'not all can be satisfied', and 'in deliberative mode we have to decide which duties, *verdictively*, ought to be performed'. Perhaps the saddest effect of the *prima facie* terminology is for it to have overlain Ross's expression of his key assertion that in many cases *prima facie* duty is rooted in the *sanctity* of a practice [RG 37] or in the inherent evil or wrongness of non-fidelity, of non-reciprocity, of unconcern for injuries done, or of unconcern for dependents, etc. But here let me direct you to Bernard Williams's old discussion of *prima facie* in his *Problems of the Self* (Cambridge, 1973) and direct you further to the admirable attempt of the logician E. J. Lemmon to persuade us, in Oxford's best linguistic mode, to distinguish more carefully than we usually do in philosophy (and Ross ever does) between duties, obligations and various other forms of commitment. See 'Moral Dilemmas', *Philosophical Review*, Vol. 71 (1962).

10 Back now to Ross's own defences against ideal or agathistic utilitarianism. Earlier, I committed myself to thinking it philosophically embarrassing to find Ross saying anything like this:

> Just as before we were led to recognise the *prima facie* rightness of the fulfilment of promises, we are now led to recognise the *prima facie* rightness of promoting the general welfare. In both cases we have to recognise the *intrinsic* [author's italics] rightness of a certain type of act, not depending on its consequences but on its own nature [RG 47].

And the thing I have complained I cannot believe is that there is any rightness at all – let alone intrinsic rightness – in acts ultimately promotive of the moral virtue of ethnic non-quarrelsomeness if the doing of these acts involves acts of ethnic cleansing, expropriation, murder and the rest. Ross cannot win even a Pyrrhic victory over consequentialism, I judge, if he commits himself to recognise any *prima facie* rightness at all (let alone intrinsic rightness) in promoting the general good simply *as such*, or if he relies on the existence of other *prima facie* duties to disable or render inert the *prima facie* duty to do acts of intrinsic good-promotion or virtue-promotion by doing acts that are themselves outrageous. Even as he criticised Moore, Ross surely needed to escape more cleanly and definitively from the charm of the idea, so relentlessly exploited by consequentialists of all colours,[14] that no act can be wrong the doing of which will increase the nett amount of intrinsic good in the world.

Let us begin on this matter by noticing two things: first that what Ross really needs when he formulates the duty of type [4] is to understand the content of the duty itself *as already qualified* by the other duties. It may seem to be a pedantry to insist that he cannot have what he needs to have here. But it is important. So long as Ross stays inside the framework that he has himself set up and so long as he recognises a *prima facie* duty to increase intrinsic good, he cannot qualify the *content* of the duty of beneficence in this way. For the *prima facie* duties in (1)–(6) are all co-ordinate. None can be formulated in a way that renders its content (contrast its final force) dependent on the content of the other *prima facie* duties. That the

---

[14] Cp. S. Scheffler: 'One thing they all share is a very simple and seductive idea: namely that ... what people ought to do is to minimise evil and maximise good, to try in other words to make the world as good a place as possible.' *Consequentialism and its Critics* (Oxford University Press, 1988), page 1.

duties will work in concert is owed to the balancing done by the agent who has the eye of experience, the *omma tes empeirias* (Aristotle NE 1147[b14]). Using that eye, he arbitrates the proper relative demandingness of the claims that he surveys. That eye cannot, however, change their given content.

The second thing to notice is that the directive 'Increase the nett amount of intrinsic good in the world' is not only completely mad. It is not only the recipe by which some of the most megalomanical crimes in the history of the world might have been justified. It is also different in content from the general directive 'Be beneficent'. If the injunctions of Ross's type (4) duty of beneficence corresponded to duties, the duties in question could not be the same as those to which one is directed by the imperative 'Be beneficent'. Listen to the words 'Be beneficent.' In English I take it that they mean more or less, 'Do the sort of thing a beneficent person would do.' The beneficent person is not simply one busy in producing good as such, still less one producing as much good as possible. The beneficent person is one who helps X, or rescues Y, or promotes this or that cause and does so *because* each of those things is in its own way an important and benevolent end. His acts are not directed at simply increasing the nett quantity of intrinsic good in the world.

The interesting thing about this divergence of view concerning beneficence is that it takes us all the way back to Ross's own original insight, 'The essential defect of the ideal utilitarian theory is that it ignores or at least does not do full justice to, the highly personal character of duty.' If we abandon some of Ross's subsequent formulations and insist on interpreting the type (4) obligation to beneficence as an obligation to act the part of the beneficent or benevolent kind of person, we can see the obligation in a new way. We can see it as a schema that generates countless more specific, as Ross would say *prima facie*, duties, duties most of which arise (often in a supererogatory or non-mandatory manner) from the agent's historic situation, arise from who he is, arise from who his putative beneficiary is, or arise from what goals he has already committed himself to promoting (say, education or music or whatever). In so far as there is a duty to beneficence, so construed, it is not derived from the supposed platitude of moral mathematics that a larger nett intrinsic good is better than a small one. That has nothing to do with it and Ross has no need to concede anything at all to this idea. It is derived from the kind of reflection that I have claimed Ross ought not to have taken so much for granted on the part of his reader and that I have already touched upon in further elucidation of the Aristotelian tag 'the judgement lies in perception'. This reflection could take the form of reflection on the ends of life for human beings who are seeking to live in eudaimonia with other human beings.[15] Or it could take the form of reflection about what conduct is to be expected of autonomous beings who live within a kingdom of ends, live that is within a systematic union under common objective laws of self-legislating beings that treat one another as befits self-legislating beings. Or it could have taken other forms. What is important is the size and shape of the space that Ross's theory can leave for such reflections.

11 This is not the moment to try to think all the way through the divers consequences of limiting and reformulating agathistic or type (4) *prima facie* duties of agents in the manner I have just advocated. I simply remark that I should not myself claim that it would have the effect of shifting Ross into the camp of those who seek to make the virtues somehow *foundational* of moral thought. For in matters of right and wrong Ross is best advised not to be a foundationalist at all.

12 Let me conclude by trying to carry one or two steps further the now revised Rossian disputation with consequentialism. Suppose someone said this: It is all very well limiting the type (4) obligation in this way. But the benevolent person as reconstituted is not *facing up* to the Balkan situation – just as he wouldn't, one fears, have faced up to the Nazi one. 'Even if he'd been in a position to shoot Hitler, he wouldn't have faced up to that either.'

My reply to this begins by pointing out that, in the Balkan case, the thing that one is being inveigled into is violence against the innocent. Resistance to Nazism need not have involved that. Second, the new dialectical situation, as I see it, is this.

1 The requirement of beneficence – the thing Ross calls the *prima facie* duty to beneficence (misleadingly so far as *prima facie* goes and somewhat indiscriminately, so far as the word 'duty' goes) – is not the same as the requirement to 'make the world a better place'. In its new form, it can generate some 'highly personal' concerns. (This is not to say it cannot inherit any of the charms so widely attributed to the would-be platitudinous injunction to 'make the world a better place'.)

2 Beneficence is *by its true nature* restricted, both in what it will attempt and in the means by which it will attempt that.

3 It seems unthinkable that a beneficent person could take seriously the consequentialistic representations that we considered in the Balkan example.

[15] Note however that the beneficent person is not as such readily identifiable with any Aristotelian stereotype.

All right. So much is obvious. But suppose it were still represented that the beneficent person *ought* to be taking the consequentialists' representations seriously, that the beneficent person as so far characterised, appears complacent, hide-bound, a veritable fainéant. Is there not any more to say here?

Well, I would say first that, if the consequentialist really wanted the beneficent person to take seriously the prospect of *doing that sort of thing*, then the consequentialist could no longer be in the friendly or advisory business of telling the beneficent person what it was right for him to do. He would have to be in the business of showing that there was *nothing else* for him to do, that there was nothing else that anyone could try out. He would have to be in the business of showing the beneficent person that that was what he *had* to do. This is a new discipline and a new dialectic. Surely though, if such a thing *were* shown – and the difficulty of showing it would be extreme, but if it were shown – then the questions of right and wrong, of obligation, of acts the doing of which would be morally praiseworthy because from a sense of duty, all these would long since have gone out of the window. Their place would have been taken by dire (alleged) necessity.

13 That is one answer to the charge. The second answer is partly inspired by Ross's very title *The Right and the Good*. The anti-consequentialist should remind the consequentialist of the state of the argument. The consequentialist has proposed an account of rightness. But on behalf of this account, the consequentialist offers (so far) no non-question-begging argument – either to the effect that we already believe his equivalence (we don't, and Ross has shown we don't) or to the effect that we are already committed to believe it. How *could* the second be shown? I am not certain. Until the consequentialists try to show it, I think it is a mistake to raise objections to their doctrine. It does not deserve objections. If one were to offer objections then people could object to the objections. But then we should lose track and forget that objections to objections do not give the consequentialists any argument *for* this equivalence. That would still be the thing we lacked. Pending the production of a non-question-begging argument *for* consequentialism, let me simply say that it may be best for the ordinary, passably beneficent, passably otherwise virtuous person's ideas of what is right to be permitted to stand. Contrary to consequentialist misrepresentations, this person is not concerned with his own virtue. He is concerned with what it would be right for him to do.

14 The consequentialist might say to Ross at this point (if Ross were to concur in this part of my defence of his position) that constantly agents rank the alternative courses of action that are open to them. If they rank alternatives, then they must do so in the light of something or other. Surely it would be irrational for them to prefer alternatives that secured worse outcomes, that is outcomes whose badness was already implicit in the rankings that the agents *already* make.

In practice, such arguments, when spelled out in particular cases, usually prove to *presuppose* consequentialism rather than to justify it. The chief point I want to make about them is this, however. In a context, we may well rank acts for their possibility in that context. That is agreed. But this ranking is one that we effect (or that is my suspicion) by applying all sorts of ideas that are not really valuational at all. We deploy here all sorts of ideas that fall under the *right* rather than the *good*, namely ideas of the sanctity of a practice, of the forbidden, of the taboo, of the *nefastum* or *atasthalon*. Such ideas are already involved by their whole nature with thoughts of the morally impossible. The capacity that we have to make context-specific rankings of alternative courses of action shows nothing then about the possibility of grounding the right in the good. It shows nothing at all about the analytical, conceptual or moral grounding of the consequentialists' foundational equivalence.

Consider. When someone draws back in horror from the suggestion that problems of race, hatred and prejudice can only be solved by acts of genocide, do we really need or want to describe things as follows?:

> the agent is devoted to a certain end E (racial harmony) valued at N and is considering an act (genocide) disvalued at M. But when the agent looks deeper into things, the difference between N and (N − M) shocks him, shocks him so much that he draws back in horror.

Horror at a mere difference! This is mad. The agent is not shocked by the difference between N and (N − M). That is just a number, very much like any other difference. Surely he is shocked at the nature of the act itself that is said to be disvalued at M. If 'disvalued' is the right word at all …. The ideas he is deploying are ideas of right and wrong, forbidden, *nefas* etc. The thought the agent is having is the thought of doing something like that! Once consquentialism had been argued for in a non-question-begging way, perhaps it could be argued such responses were to be discounted. But that is not the present situation.

15 These points ought to be all of a piece with Ross's point about the right and the good. But are they? The point we are looking for is not put explicitly into service, alas, in chapters 1 or 2 of *The Right and The Good*, where we most need it, or in the parallel passage in *The Foundations of Ethics*. In so far as we find it working explicitly in Ross, it occurs in chapter 4 of *The Right and The Good*, the chapter entitled 'The Nature of Goodness'. In that chapter it is lodged at an interstice in the highly wrought filigree of Ross's very Moorean discussion of the nature of the good and the toti-resultance of good from the other properties of things:

> In contrast with [certain other properties], value is a toti-resultant property based on the whole nature of its possessors. And this is true not only of 'good', the adjective which expresses intrinsic value, but also of 'right' and 'beautiful', which are often classed with it; though right does not stand for a form of value at all, and beautiful does not stand for an intrinsic form of value. [122]

'Right does not stand for a form of value at all. And wrong does not stand for a form of disvalue': this was really Ross's whole message, waiting there to be followed through. How one wishes he had said some more about it – and said it in chapters 1 or 2, in explicit opposition to Moore's agathistic consequentialism.

Is this the only place where Ross makes anything of the thought we attribute to him? Once we look, there are one or two similar remarks to be picked up. I conclude with one other:

> The rightness of an act, if the contention of our second chapter is correct, is intrinsic to the act, depending solely on its nature. But if we contemplate a right act alone, it is seen to have no intrinsic *value*. Suppose for instance that it is right for a man to pay a certain debt, and he pays it. This is in itself no addition to the sum of values in the universe. If he does it from a good motive, that *adds* to the sum of values in the universe. Whatever intrinsic value, positive or negative, the action may have, it owes to the nature of its motive and not to the act's being right or wrong; and whatever value it has independently of its motive is instrumental value, i.e. not goodness at all but the property of producing something that is good. [133]

To assess this, it is necessary, before one exercises the freedom to try to deploy Ross's finding in a less scholastic fashion, to remember that the intrinsic goods are for Ross knowledge, virtue and pleasure. It is true that, if the suggestion I have made to Ross be adopted and implemented, then Ross is no longer without defences against the suggestion that there is an unqualified *prima facie* duty to promote knowledge, virtue and pleasure. But there is so much more to say –

not least about the ideas that fall under the category of right, wrong, forbidden etc and about the point of the whole non-consequentalist scheme by which we still have to live. If only someone would *begin* there.[16]

16 Conclusion. Ross saw clearly that something was wrong with Moore's reductivism and his neutralism. He chased the weakness that he saw round and round the plate, but he never properly speared it. Maybe Ross thought his insight into the personal character of duty would fully suffice for him to secure one small and decisive victory over Moore – a victory on neutral ground that would lead into others over the whole field. But in order to win any decisive result at all, he needed a more accurate reconnaissance of the dispositions of the enemy to be defeated. And Ross needed to take more care to reckon or enumerate his own forces. Had he compared the forces available to him with all the forces that Aristotle or Kant were wont to deploy, he would have seen that by taking the enemy more seriously he had the power to win the whole campaign. For on the main point, he was right (I think). The mistake was for Ross to suppose there was a small victory he could win quickly on the enemy's own terms without radical reconstrual of the conception he had inherited from Moore of benevolence, without following through all the consequences of his own insights into the personal character of obligations not duties. Changing the metaphor yet again, I conclude by saying that Ross needed to take more care to get all his pieces on to the board, to take better stock of them and to use all of them. Nothing less would have sufficed. Moore was not to be defeated by anything so quick or humiliating as fool's mate.[17] Those like me who want to disbelieve consequentialism will have to purify Ross's critique before they resume it.

[16] The best remark I know about this comes (not at the beginning but towards the end, alas) in Philippa Foot's, 'Action, Outcome and Morality', in T. Honderich (ed.), *Morality and Objectivity: A Tribute to J. L. Mackie* (London: Routledge, Kegan Paul, 1985). My indebtedness to this article and its companion piece, 'Utilitarianism and the Virtues', *Mind* **94**, 1985 will be manifest.

[17] The text published here overlaps but does not coincide with the lecture given at the Royal Institute of Philosophy. In the text given here, I dwell mostly on an earlier phase of the debate about consequentialism than the Philippa Foot – Samuel Scheffler phase that consumed the major part of the lecture actually delivered. For criticisms and amplifications of some of the claims advanced here about Ross and Moore, see the comments that Jonathan Dancy and Stephen Darwall offered on the version of the present text that was published in *Utilitas,* 10(3) (November 1998).

Deontology and value

DAVID McNAUGHTON AND PIERS RAWLING

I

1 Morality and alienation

Integration and coherence are central values in human existence. It would be a serious objection to any proposed way of life that it led to us being alienated or cut off from others or from some important part of ourselves. Morality, with the strenuous demands it makes on us, is one area in which alienation is both particularly threatening and peculiarly undesirable. If morality cuts us off from some important part of ourselves then it appears unattractive, and if it cuts us off from others then it seems self-defeating. While there are few philosophers who take the radical view that morality is, by its very nature, an alienating force, a more common complaint has been that some particular moral theories should be rejected because the picture of moral thought which they offer inevitably leads to the alienation of moral agents. The main target of criticism has been consequentialism, but some deontological theories, especially Kantianism, have also come under attack.[1]

In this paper we revisit the problem. In part II we argue that act-consequentialism, because it has a limited conception of the form that moral reasons can take, offers a picture in which the agent is inevitably alienated from some of her reasons.[2] In part III we show not only how the kind of deontology we favour avoids this problem but also that it is immune to a different sort of worry about alienation often levelled against deontological systems.

---

[1] Three classic discussions are: M. Stocker, 'The Schizophrenia of Modern Ethical Theories', *Journal of Philosophy* **73** (1976), pp. 453–66; P. Railton, 'Alienation, Consequentialism, and the Demands of Morality', *Consequentialism and its Critics*, S. Scheffler (ed.) (Oxford University Press, 1988), pp. 93–133; B. Williams, 'Persons, Character and Morality', *Moral Luck* (Cambridge University Press, 1981), pp. 1–19.

[2] We argue here only against act-consequentialism, according to which, even in its indirect forms, the right act is the one which maximises (or at least sufficiently promotes) the good. Some of our objections apply to rule and motive consequentialism, but discussion of those will have to await another occasion.

David McNaughton and Piers Rawling

2 Two kinds of reasons

Reasons for acting can be divided into the agent-neutral and the agent-relative. An agent-relative reason is one in which reference to the agent is ineliminable if we are to understand the nature of the reason. My reason for insuring, say, one particular car is that it is *mine*, and any elaboration of my reason which omitted its relationship to me would fail fully to capture that reason. Many reasons take this form: that this is *my* child, *my* friend, *my* career, can all, in appropriate circumstances, figure ineliminably in my reasons for acting. Agent-neutral reasons, by contrast, contain no such ineliminable reference to the agent. My reason for giving money to Oxfam may be simply that it will help to relieve severe suffering.

Personal concerns loom large in our lives. Each of us is naturally especially concerned about his house, his career, his family, etc. Morality, however, seems to demand that we concern ourselves with the wider good. Morally speaking, no-one's welfare is any more important than any one else's. From here it is a short, and seductive, step to the thought that morality abstracts from the personal concerns that find expression in agent-relative reasons. What matters from the point of view of morality is the promotion of the good, irrespective of whose good it is. The aim of morality is the promotion of the good, impersonally conceived. Moral reasons will thus all be agent-neutral, since the fact that it is, say, my child rather than some other child who will be affected by my action cannot be morally relevant. Or, more accurately, ultimate or underivative moral reasons will be agent-neutral in form. There may indeed, from the moral point of view, be good reasons for me to devote more time to the welfare of my own children, but it will not be the fact that they are *mine* that is morally significant, but the fact that this is the most efficient way to promote some neutral good – the good, say, of each child enjoying a warm and partially exclusive relationship with one or more adults who occupy the role of parent. This line of thought thus leads to act-consequentialism, to the thought that the only consideration that bears on the rightness of an action is the difference that act will make to the amount of value in the world. Since the more value there is in the world the better, the natural conclusion of this line of thought is that the right act is the one which maximises value; the one that produces more good than any alternative open to the agent.

Nagel has pointed out that, contrary to the claims of consequentialism, there seem to be three areas of moral concern where agent-relative reasons play an ineliminable role: options, constraints, duties of special relationship.[3]

[3] T. Nagel, *The View from Nowhere* (Oxford University Press, 1986), p. 165.

Options A morally admirable agent may legitimately decline to help others if that would substantially damage her interests or disrupt her projects, even if the good to others is greater than the loss to her.

Constraints It can be wrong to perform certain kinds of action, such as lying or killing, even when, by so doing, we could make the world a better place. Crucially, it seems, it may be wrong for me to perform such an action *myself* even if I could thereby prevent someone else from performing more or worse actions of a similar nature.

Duties of special relationship I have an obligation to help *my* friend (child, spouse) – an obligation which does not extend (in the same manner or degree) to others. Crucially, it would in many cases be wrong for me to neglect, say, my children even if I could thereby bring about a net increase in the good by promoting good relationships between other parents and their children.

Deontologists characteristically maintain that in each of these areas we find moral reasons that are both agent-relative and underivative.[4] The act-consequentialist, by contrast, in so far as he admits such considerations as offering moral reasons at all, will regard them as derivative from the overarching duty of promoting the impersonal good. And if only derivatively morally relevant then only contingently so also. In circumstances where paying heed to some agent-relative consideration would not further the good then a virtuous agent would have no reason to pay heed to it. If there is moral reason to A, the consequentialist argues, it must be because there is some impersonal good that, as things actually are, A-ing furthers, directly or indirectly. But this line of reasoning, we now argue, threatens to alienate the conscientious consequentialist from those close to her. We shall consider the standard example of friendship.

3 Friendship

We suggest that the relationship of friendship is roughly characterised as involving at least the following three thoughts.

1 A true friend, when she helps her friend, does so for her friend's sake; she has no further end in view nor any ulterior motive.
2 Friendship is a moral relation. It involves a tie or bond on which both have the right to rely. Your friend has a right to expect more from you than from others just in virtue of being

---

[4] Strictly, on our view, only reasons to do with constraints and duties of special relationship are essential to deontology. Options are optional. Many deontologists include them, but some, like Ross, do not.

your friend and, if let down, will have been wronged. (In this respect, friendship is not like a personal project, where often the continuing interest of the agent is a central part of the reason for keeping up the project.)

3 Acts of friendship are not, in their purest form, done from a sense of duty. Ideally, the motivational resources of friendship should be found within the friendship itself.

So on what sorts of reason might a friend act? Suppose, to take a familiar scenario, your friend Sally is in hospital and feeling low. Why should you visit her? Your reason might be that she is your friend and you can cheer her up.[5] For the true friend such a reason, which includes the agent-relative thought 'she's *my* friend', is non-derivative and not instrumental to some further end. There need be no further reason why I should visit my friend than that she is my friend and needs cheering up, and my having the reason I do does not rest on any further consideration. (There can be cases where it would be a reason only in certain conditions. For example, if I am merely exploiting the friendship, then I have a reason to help her only when this furthers my ultimate goal. But then I am not a true friend.)

II

4 Alienation and consequentialism

Alienation can take different forms. Our complaint against act-consequentialism will be that it alienates the agent from her reasons. As a conscientious consequentialist she cannot fully acknowledge and act on all her reasons. We suggest that consequentialism faces her with a dilemma. Either she cannot acknowledge the reasons she needs to engage with if she is to experience the good of friendship, or she cannot always act on the fundamental reasons which drive her moral theory.

Direct act-consequentialism

Direct act-consequentialism says that, from the moral point of view, the only reason for doing anything is to promote the good. If there

---

[5] We take practical reasons to be facts, and often they are non-psychological, non-normative facts, such as 'she is my friend and is lonely'. The fact that you ought to help her is a normative fact, but is not itself the reason to help. (If someone asks, Why ought I to help her? the answer is not, Because you ought to.) Motivating states are psychological states of the agent: either belief–desire pairs, or perhaps just beliefs.

are other reasons around then we should only take them into account if acting on them promotes the good. 'It will cheer her up' is a reason which direct act-consequentialism can endorse, for this would be an instance of benefiting someone. And cheering her up will be the right thing to do if it will do most good, and thus be the act there is most reason to do. But what of the thought 'she's my friend'? Since this offers an agent-relative reason for acting, a theory that sees all reasons as reasons to promote agent-neutral value cannot include it. Reasons of friendship are invisible from this consequentialist viewpoint.

This remains true, even if the consequentialist concedes that friendship is an intrinsically valuable relationship. For then the consequentialist aim is to bring it about that, all else equal, as many people as possible are in rich meaningful friendships. So what can the direct act-consequentialist offer as a reason for visiting her sick friend? That she wishes to promote the good of friendship wherever it is to be found, and this is an instance of doing so. But then she wouldn't be a friend, because a friend is someone who does something *for the sake of her friend*. This brand of consequentialist seems alienated or distanced from her friend by her inability to act for the very kind of reason that constitutes the relationship of friendship. This makes direct act-consequentialism self-defeating: one of the very goods that it might hope to realise – the good of friendship – can only exist if agents do not act for the reasons which it, as a moral theory, can endorse. It fails to accommodate the first of our three thoughts about friendship.

Indirect act-consequentialism

Few defenders of consequentialism opt these days for the direct version. Almost all go indirect and suggest that the virtuous agent would do better not to employ consequentialist reasoning on each occasion of acting. Indirect act-consequentialism prescribes that the moral agent should develop dispositions to act from motives such as friendship. She may do better overall, in promoting the consequentialist goal, if she normally acts from such dispositions, even if they sometimes lead her to do a non-optimific act. Since, *ex hypothesi*, she acts from the right motives, she is no longer alienated from her friends.

If this answer seems convincing, it is only because the notion of having a 'disposition to act from the motive of friendship' is not adequately spelt out. Unless the agent is in the grip of some completely irrational compulsion, to be disposed to act from a motive is to see some considerations as reasons which favour that course of action. What is it to act from the motive of friendship? It seems that it must include seeing reasons such as 'She is my friend and I can cheer her up' as underivative reasons for acting. That I can cheer her up is indeed a reason for visiting someone who is sick, but that she is my friend is a part of the reason; a reason not only for visiting, but for visiting *her*, rather than some other sick person whom I might equally be able to cheer up.

Can the conscientious indirect act-consequentialist agent acknowledge the existence of such an underivative agent-relative reason? While all act-consequentialists agree that all underivative moral reasons are agent-neutral, they diverge on the question of whether there can be non-moral agent-relative reasons, such as a reason to care especially about my projects or my happiness. The line of reasoning that took us to consequentialism in section 2 can seem to rule out the possibility of such reasons. The fact that it is *my* happiness that is at stake may perhaps explain why I care about it so much, but how can it give me a *reason* for preferring my happiness to that of another, given that they are equally valuable? However, we do not have to decide which way the consequentialist should go on this issue, for either way he is in trouble.

If the only reasons for acting are agent-neutral ones then my reason for visiting my friend must be derivative: I only have reason to visit her because developing such a disposition is a means to developing a character that will lead me to do, in the long run, the most good of which I am capable. But I will only be capable of friendship if I believe that the reason for visiting her, that she's my friend, stands on its own independently of any extra support from the moral theory. If that's the case, then the successful moral agent must be deceived about the nature of her reasons for acting. She must falsely suppose that such agent-relative reasons stand on their own, independently of the support they get from their contribution to the theory-given aim. But a theory of reasons for action that works best only if agents have false beliefs about what their reasons might be imposes its own form of distance or estrangement. For the best kind of agent, on this theory, is one from whom the normative truth is hidden. Alienation from the truth is, in its own way, as unsettling as alienation from part of oneself or from others.

Better, perhaps, for the indirect act-consequentialist to accept that there are genuine non-derivative agent-relative reasons for acting, but that they are not moral reasons. Reasons of self-interest provide a model here. It seems plausible to suppose that I have a self-interested reason to eat when I am hungry, which is not a moral reason, and which is quite independent of any reflections about whether my eating would promote the general moral good. There might also be other, non-self-interested agent-relative reasons, expressive of our natural affections: reasons to care about those close to us that, while they have no moral force in themselves, might nevertheless be reasons an indirect strategy would encourage us to act on. If that were the case, I would not be mistaken in thinking that the fact that she is my friend is a reason for my caring especially about her. So the first of our three thoughts about friendship would be accommodated. Moreover, it seems that room could also be made for the third thought, that we should not help our friends out of a sense of duty. For while I would not be acting contrary to the dictates of morality in acting on this reason – that she is my friend – the reason itself is not an explicitly moral one and so, in doing it for my friend, I would not be acting from a sense of duty.

This gets us nearly all we need, but not quite all. For it fails to capture the second of our thoughts about friendship, that there is a moral tie between friends. If my friend lets me down, then my moral complaint is not, or not primarily, that she has acted wrongly in not expressing a disposition whose cultivation would maximise the good, but rather that she has wronged *me* in not treating me as a friend (morally) should. On the indirect act-consequentialist outlined above, the fact that she is my friend figures twice. First, it is a morally relevant but derivative reason for visiting. What is underivatively morally relevant is promoting the good; paying special attention to the needs of one's friends is an optimal strategy for achieving that goal. Second, it is a non-moral but underivative reason for visiting: that she is my friend figures underivatively among my reasons for acting, but it is not itself a moral reason. Whereas what we seem to need to capture the moral bond of friendship is rather the thought that the fact that she is my friend supplies a morally underivative reason to visit her. This thought is, of course, one that any consequentialist is committed to denying.

Whether or not indirect act-consequentialism can succeed in allowing room for friendship in the moral life, it buys what success it has in finding room for reasons of friendship at the cost of alienating the agent from his ultimate moral reasons – his guiding aim of maximising the good. Even if the agent is not in the habit of performing consequentialist calculations on each occasion of acting, he can still come to know that the disposition on which he is inclined to act will here lead him to do the wrong act. Take Railton's example of Juan and Linda who have a commuting marriage. Linda is a bit depressed and so Juan decides to visit her, even though he recognises that, taking everything into account, he could do more good by giving the cost of the air fare to Oxfam. It may still be that 'Juan should have (should develop, encourage, and so on) a character such that he sometimes knowingly and deliberately acts contrary to his objective consequentialist duty' (p. 121). For if he had developed some other character he would have made less overall contribution to the good. But this strategy saves the moral agent from being alienated from others only at the cost of alienating him from his ultimate reasons for acting, which he here recognises, yet must discount.

Indirect act-consequentialism might insist that Juan refrain from considering whether the act is right (i.e. whether it maximises value) to avoid this kind of conflict. Even if this were possible, it does not solve the problem of alienation, because this requires the agent steadfastly to refuse to contemplate those considerations which ultimately constitute his reasons for acting.

The only routes of escape open to the consequentialist are unattractive. He can claim that the theory is self-effacing, so that the best agent is one who believes the theory to be false, but we have already pointed out the alienating consequences of that move. Or he might deny that the fact that an action would produce the most value in itself gives an agent most reason to do it. He has more reason, perhaps, to act in accordance with those rules or dispositions which will, in the long run, better promote the good than any other set of rules or dispositions he might have adopted.[6] But in that case it is hard to see that he is any longer an *act-*, rather than a motive- or rule-consequentialist. There must be some content to the distinctive act-consequentialist claim that the act that produces the most value is the *right* one; but denying that this is the act that one has most reason to perform apparently evacuates the claim of any content.

Our conclusion is that consequentialism faces a dilemma. Direct act-consequentialism alienates us from our friends. Indirect act-consequentialism alienates us from our ultimate reasons for acting.[7]

III

5 How (our version of) deontology enables agents to avoid alienation

A deontologist has no problem with the second thought concerning friendship. Because deontology avers that one has duties of special

---

[6] The act-consequentialist might argue that giving the money to Oxfam would not be right if it would *change* Juan's character in such a way that the long term consequences of giving to Oxfam rather than visiting Linda were not optimific. But Railton explicitly rules out that suggestion (Railton, 'Alienation', p. 121).

[7] For a different but equally telling critique of Railton's paper, see D. Cocking and J. Oakley, 'Indirect Consequentialism, Friendship, and the Problem of Alienation', *Ethics* **106** (1995), pp. 86–111.

relationship, it can allow that the fact that I stand in a particular relationship to another person can be an underivative moral reason to help them. Deontology need not deny that the fact that an act will make things go better is also an underivative morally relevant fact. What it denies is that it is the only underivative morally relevant fact. In the case of duties of special relationship, the other has a claim on me in virtue of the relationship in which we already stand.

> [Others] stand to me in the relation of promisee to promiser, of creditor to debtor, of wife to husband, of child to parent, of friend to friend, of fellow countryman to fellow countryman and the like; and each of these relations is the foundation of a *prima facie* duty.[8]

The thought is, to take a simple example, that if I have promised someone that I will A then that gives me a reason (though not necessarily an overriding reason) to A, independently of considerations of the amount of good I might do by A-ing or refraining from A-ing. So deontology has no difficulty accommodating our first two thoughts about friendship.

The very success of deontology in capturing the second thought about friendship may seem to render it unable to accommodate the third. Is the deontologist not also in danger of alienating himself from his friends, by thinking of helping his friends as a duty which morality imposes upon him? (This is not the same kind of alienation as we were discussing in the case of consequentialism. The problem here is the inappropriate intrusion of moral thoughts into the motivational structure of one's deliberation. It is thus not a problem peculiar to deontology.) To talk of duty here makes it sound as if you visit your friend in hospital from a sense of duty; but this is characteristically unpleasant for both parties. You should surely be visiting your friend out of friendship. If it is the thought that you have *moral* reason to visit your friend in hospital that motivates the visit, then the act of visiting is not the best expression of friendship. In a perfect act of friendship, it seems, thoughts of duty, or of what morality gives one reason to do, should be absent. You visit Sally solely because she is your friend and she would welcome a visit.

What is it to act purely out of friendship, and can a deontologist allow that the morally good agent acts out of pure friendship, rather than from a sense of duty? The first thought about friendship was that my reason for visiting my friend will be simply and solely: she is my friend and she would welcome a visit. But what the deontolo-

---

[8] W. D. Ross, *The Right and the Good* (Oxford: Clarendon Press, 1930), p. 29.

gist holds need not conflict with this. For deontology also holds that the reason you should visit this person is that she is your friend and would welcome a visit. It may seem that, in talking of duties of friendship, the deontologist must be claiming that your reason for visiting must be that you ought to visit sick friends – that you have a duty to do so. But this is a mistake. That something is my duty, or that I ought to do it, is not the reason why I should do the action. The reason is always some other relevant or salient fact or facts. That you ought to do it cannot be the reason why you ought to do it. So if the complaint is that the deontologist cannot offer as a reason for visiting the reason that the true friend offers, then the complaint is unfounded.[9]

Someone may object as follows. The deontologist holds that I have a *moral* reason to visit my friend in hospital, whereas in true friendship one does not think of this as a moral reason at all. So they cannot be the *same* reason. Thus, on the deontologist's picture, the morally good person cannot be a true friend. This criticism rests on the assumption that reasons come, as it were, pre-labelled. They present themselves as moral, or prudential, or of some other variety. A reason of one kind cannot be identical with a reason of a different kind. But on our view there are just reasons for acting; that my friend is in hospital and needs cheering up is a reason for me to visit her. The morally good person can, and should, act for this reason.

What then distinguishes moral from prudential reasons? There are various points of view from which we can assess situations: the moral point of view, the prudential point of view, the point of view of the interests of my department, or my faculty, or my university etc. From each point of view, some reasons will be endorsed and others discounted. Thus, from the self-interested point of view, the fact that you will benefit from my sacrifice is discounted or, if admitted, only admitted as an instrumental reason: I have a reason to benefit you only because it will benefit me. Reasons may, of course, be salient from several points of view. From the point of view of friendship and from that of morality, that a friend is in hospital and needs cheering up is a reason to act.

If the virtuous agent visits her friend just because she is her friend and needs cheering up, then in what sense is her action governed by moral considerations? In adopting the moral perspective, the agent is alert to reasons that are visible from that perspective. We have been supposing that the agent is acting rightly in visiting her friend. But there could be cases where there were moral consid-

[9] We owe this claim to Philip Stratton-Lake who argues for it in 'Why Externalism is not a Problem for Ethical Intuitionists', *Proceedings of the Aristotelian Society*, 99 (1999), pp. 82–3

erations on the other side that made it wrong to visit. If there were, then the moral agent would, assuming they are not hidden from her, be aware of them. So the following counterfactual is true of her: she would not visit if there were morally good reason not to. The virtuous agent is guided by morality in that these kinds of counterfactual are true of her, but that does not mean that thoughts about duty enter into her thinking where it is right for her to visit her friend. She just sees the reason to visit and 'straightway she acts'. There is nothing in her pattern of motivation that suggests alienation.[10]

Suppose, however, that she explicitly wondered whether there might be a competing moral consideration and so asked herself whether it was morally permissible to visit her friend. Does that degree of reflection induce alienation, rendering her incapable of acting on the original reason? We think not. Suppose that reflection reveals that there is no competing reason, or none sufficient to cast doubt on the rightness of her visiting, then she will still be acting on the original reason: this is my friend who needs help.

The case that does seem to involve alienation is the one where I do not want to visit – perhaps I have other things I want to do more, or I know that my friend is crotchety when ill – but then I decide that I should visit, because this is what duty requires. This pattern of motivation seems, from the point of view of friendship, distinctly second best. What one wants in a friend is someone who does not have to call on the sense of duty to make them do things that friends do willingly. It is not, however, the specific appeal to the motive of *duty* here that is alienating; rather, the alienation results from my need to appeal to a consideration beyond the reason that my friend needs help, to bolster my flagging motivation. It would be just as alienating to appeal to the motive of friendship to get myself to go. There is something equally distancing about being visited by someone who is motivated only by thoughts about what friendship requires.

A willingness to take moral considerations seriously is only alienating where thoughts about duty are needed to motivate one to do what is right, when thoughts about the reasons that make the act right are insufficient on their own. But thoughts about considerations of friendship are equally alienating when they are needed to motivate one to do what is friendly, when thoughts about the reasons which make the act friendly are insufficient on their own. True friends need no such additional motivation, but then neither do ideal moral agents.

[10] This is not a specifically deontological solution, any more than the problem is specifically one for deontology. We find it, for example, in Railton, 'Alienation', pp. 111–12 and S. Scheffler, *Human Morality* (Oxford University Press, 1992), p. 32.

David McNaughton and Piers Rawling

Deontology endorses personal relationships in a way that consequentialism cannot. Ross sounds preachy with his talk of duties of special obligation, as if Rossian agents only engage with friends out of a sense of obligation. But this need not be. Since duties are not themselves reasons, obligation only obtrudes when friendship flags. However, friendship is not vitiated should the Rossian agent contemplate reasons of friendship from within the moral perspective – the special moral ties between friends will show up there, but the reason for helping a friend remains simply that she is a friend in need.

Consequentialism is a theory with a different structure. Its sole moral aim is to maximise (or at least promote) the good. The problem is to get agents to do this. In order to achieve the good of friendship, agents are precluded from viewing the relationship solely in terms of its agent-neutral value. Indirect act-consequentialism acknowledges this, and suggests that we eschew thoughts of value when being friendly. However, this poses a problem for the indirect act-consequentialist in cases of conflict, when friendliness runs counter to maximising the good. Here the agent can neither acknowledge nor act on her deepest moral reasons, from which she is alienated.[11]

[11] We are grateful to Roger Crisp and Brad Hooker for comments on an earlier version of this paper.

Beauty and testimony

ROBERT HOPKINS

1 Kant claims that the judgement of taste, the judgement that some particular is beautiful, exhibits two 'peculiarities'. First:

> [t]he judgement of taste determines its object in respect of delight (as a thing of beauty) with a claim to the agreement of *every one*, just as if it were objective.[1]

Is the judgement in fact objective? Since Kant thinks that the judgement of taste not only demands the agreement of all, but is *justified* in doing so, his answer seems to be yes. This impression is borne out by his account of our engagement with beauty, which makes central the necessity, under the right conditions, of shared responses to beautiful things. Since it does all this while maintaining that beauty is just a capacity to elicit a certain affective response, Kant's view is reasonably seen as offering a modest form of objectivism about beauty. And this construal of his position is complicated, rather than thwarted, by his use of the term translated here as 'objective'. For, although Kant means something distinctive by that term, and indeed claims that the judgement of taste is *not*, in that sense, objective, these views dovetail with the broader position just described (see below, section 2).

The second peculiarity is this:

> Proofs are of no avail whatever for determining the judgement of taste, and in this connection matters stand just as they would were that judgement simply *subjective*.[2]

Judgements of beauty cannot be proven, and as one example Kant cites the 'proof' given by the testimony of others. Anyone who finds that others admire what he finds not to be beautiful, will stand his ground. He:

> clearly perceives that the approval of others affords no valid proof, available for the estimate of beauty. He recognises that others, perchance, may see and observe for him, and that, what many have seen in one and the same way may, for the purpose of a theoretical ... judgement, serve as an adequate ground of proof for him, albeit he believes he saw otherwise, but that what has

[1] Kant, *Critique of Judgement*, trans J. C. Meredith (hereafter CJ) section 32.
[2] CJ, section 33.

209

pleased others can never serve him as the ground of an aesthetic judgement.[3]

Although Kant here discusses the complex case where the opinions of others conflict with the subject's own, nothing in the rest of the passage suggests that this complexity matters to him. So he thinks that the testimony of others does not provide me with 'proof' for thinking something beautiful, even if I have not yet had the chance to form my own opinion. Further, as his comments about the 'theoretical' case makes clear, Kant does not mean anything particularly stringent by 'proof'. He means no more than *decent grounds for* the proposition in hand. Finally, he seems to have in mind the force for me of others' judgements alone, and not as reinforced by any reasons their makers might have for them. At least in this part of his discussion of 'proofs', his claim concerns, not aesthetic *argument*, but the giving of aesthetic opinions. In short, Kant is saying that concerning beauty, unlike many other observable matters, the considered opinions of others do not provide decent grounds for my own judgement. As we might say, questions of beauty do not admit of testimony.

Is Kant right? I will argue that to a large extent he is, but that this creates difficulties for his account. In particular, this aspect of his second 'peculiarity' is in tension with his first, the acknowledgement that aesthetic judgements have some measure of objectivity. For, to put the issue too crudely, if there is something to know about a thing's beauty, why can't I learn it from someone else? Now, as is suggested by the way Kant presents his two peculiarities, he himself recognises certain tensions between them. However, the rest of the *Critique* only tackles the tension between the objectivity of aesthetics and the absence of proofs of *other* kinds. The issue of testimony is forgotten. Dealing with it raises matters Kant left untouched. But the point of considering this issue extends beyond the rational reconstruction of Kant's own view. I suggest that accommodating the truth about testimony concerning beauty sets a serious task for any aesthetic theory (see section 10).

2 It will help to begin with a little more exposition. Let us start with the unsettled business of Kant's use of 'objective' and 'subjective' (or their German equivalents). The judgement of taste is *not* objective in Kant's sense, in that it is not made on the right sort of ground. For its ground is the subject's *pleasure* in the object, and pleasure is, for Kant, the only 'subjective' sensation. That is, pleasure is the only sensation which cannot be combined with a concept

[3] Ibid.

so as to yield a representation, be it of states of the external world, or states of the subject himself.[4] But if my judgement that something is beautiful is based simply on my pleasure in that thing, a pleasure which in itself does not represent that thing as being any particular way, how then can I justifiably demand that others respond to the object in the same way? This question lies at the heart of Kant's thinking about beauty.

To gain some sense of the question's urgency for Kant, contrast what he takes to be the situation for ordinary empirical judgements. Normal cognition involves the combination of sensations with concepts. The sensations are 'objective' in his sense, in that when so combined with concepts they constitute representations of how the world is – that the thing before me is a certain shape or colour, or that I myself am hungry. Concepts are in effect rules, ways of ordering the sensory input. When I judge that the world is thus and so, my claim on this agreement of others stems from the fact that I have ordered my sensory manifold under a certain rule. If they possess the concept, i.e. if they know the rule, and if their sensory manifold parallels my own, they must accept that the object in question falls under the concept.[5] But in the case of beauty matters are quite otherwise. There, my judgement is made solely on the basis of my pleasure in the object, the 'subjective' nature of which precisely excludes the sort of consideration just deployed. Whence, then, my legitimate demand on the agreement of all?

Kant's answer begins from the thought that the pleasure which grounds the judgement of taste has a distinctive source. It is produced when the imagination and the understanding stand in a special relation, a relation Kant describes as their being in 'harmony'. The nature of the faculties so related, and that of the relation itself, is obscure, but Kant's basic idea is that beautiful objects engage the very same capacities deployed in normal cognition, but without those capacities producing their usual outcome. In the appreciation of beauty, although no concept is applied, no rule found under which to subsume the thing, the object strikes the cognising subject as being suitable for being so processed. This allows Kant to answer his central question. For the judging subject's pleasure stems from the way the object affects his cognitive system and, Kant thinks, there are good reasons *a priori* for thinking that it must affect every other cogniser's system in just the same way, producing pleasure. Thus it is that the judgement of taste can legitimately lay claim to

[4] CJ, sections 1 and 3. For careful discussion of these complex issues, see Eva Schaper, *Studies in Kant's Aesthetics*, (Edinburgh University Press, 1979), chapter 2.

[5] Kant, *Critique of Pure Reason*, e.g., A105–6.

the agreement of all, which is to say, to their likewise responding to the object with pleasure, should they encounter it. And this even though pleasure, the 'subjective' sensation, is our only guide to beauty.[6]

These claims raise many questions, but not ones we need answer. It is enough to note some connections between Kant's view and the theme of objectivity. Even here, our discussion will not be exhaustive, in part because it is a complex question quite what objectivity amounts to, and very plausible that traditional debates over it concern several distinct notions, which interrelate in far from obvious ways.[7] Further, it is clear that Kant's view contains more than one strand relevant to such questions. Given these complications, space allows for just two observations.

First, consider the demand Kant is centrally concerned to vindicate, for the agreement of all in the judgement of taste. Objectivity requires at least a subject matter the nature of which is not determined by *particular* judgements made about it.[8] Any such subject matter which my judgement concerns should be accessible to your judgement too (you may not be able to *know* about the issue, but you can at least judge concerning it). And if I have rightly judged how things are, your judgement should conform to mine (and *vice versa*). Thus that my judgement should demand your agreement, and that that demand be legitimate, seem minimal conditions on the objectivity of our discourse. Second, consider Kant's explanation of how that demand can be legitimate. Its legitimacy rests on the source of aesthetic pleasure, in our nature as cognisers. Given this source, we are, under ideal circumstances, guaranteed to respond to an object in the same way, with pleasure or otherwise. Of course, Kant acknowledges that other factors may intrude so as to prevent our responses being alike.[9] But, provided they do not do so, we shall find the same things beautiful. Thus our taking things to be beautiful exhibits a discipline grounded not in accidents of our nature but in our mere capacity to cognise. It is surely plausible that, where claims to objectivity centre on conformity in response, the more deeply rooted the conformity, the stronger the claim.

This is enough to make at least initially plausible my claim that

[6] CJ, sections 21, 35–8; Introduction, section VII.

[7] This is convincingly argued in C. Wright, *Truth and Objectivity* (Harvard University Press, 1994).

[8] It does not, of course, require a subject matter independent of our *collective* responses, including judgements. Or rather, not every form of objectivity requires this.

[9] See the discussions below of 'interest' (section 3) and dependent beauty (section 7).

Kant's view offers a modest objectivism about beauty. More detailed questions concerning objectivity can be considered if our main topic, testimony about beauty, requires it (see section 10). Before turning to that topic, note that Kant's account allows him to explain why judgements of taste do not admit of 'proof' of at least one kind. Kant denies that there are principles of taste, general claims citing some property definitive of, or conducive to, beauty from which, coupled to the premise that a given object has that property, we could deduce that it is beautiful.[10] Were the judgement of taste grounded in normal concept application, there would have to be such principles. For if finding something beautiful involved applying a rule, there would have to be features, common to all beautiful things, the possession of which is what constituted their fitting the rule. Since judgements of taste are not grounded in this way, it is at least left open that there is no feature common to all things which affect our cognitive capacities in the way described above.

However, showing there to be no proof by principle is quite different from showing there to be none by testimony. For testimony centrally concerns the force for others of my judgement alone, not its force when supported by arguments. Even if there are no principles of taste, the question remains whether a judgement of taste can provide others with reason to adopt it. After all, in many matters, my judgement alone gives you reason to accept what I say, as when I tell you that my new house has three bedrooms. Is this so for beauty, and if not, why?

3 I begin by considering some explanations, before examining what there is to explain. This may seem premature. However, it is not always easy to separate one's views of explananda from possible explanations. This temptation is especially strong for one impressed by Kant's account of beauty. For *prima facie* that promises to explain, in any of several ways, a particular construal of the facts. This is that testimony over beauty is not possible at all. Below (sections 4–6) I reject this. But the apparent ease with which Kant's view explains why matters should be so exerts a powerful pull towards taking them to be. So let me dispel the impression that any explanation is on offer here. The easiest way to do this is to assume for argument's sake that testimony over beauty is not possible, and to ask why, in Kant's terms, this should be.

A first attempt at explanation makes the most direct use of the materials above. One of Kant's main claims is that the ground of

[10] CJ, section 34. See also Mary Mothersill, *Beauty Restored* (Oxford University Press, 1984).

the judgement of taste is the judging subject's pleasure. This claim by itself renders impossible testimony over beauty. For your telling me that some object is beautiful brings me no opportunity to take pleasure in that thing, and so offers me no ground, of the kind Kant considers necessary, for judging its beauty. Hence the failure of testimony.

The difficulty with this suggestion emerges most clearly if we consider an analogy. Beauty is not the only property we judge on the basis of a response on our part. Judgements of colour, to take one example, are likewise grounded in a response, here a perceptual response, to the object. The judgement that something is, for instance, red, is grounded in its looking a certain way. Now, if someone tells me that some item is red, his testimony offers me no opportunity to respond to the coloured object in the appropriate way – I can hear his claim without anything looking red to me. Does it follow that testimony over colour is impossible? It does not – if we can accept anything on testimony, it is simple observation claims, such as that some particular item is a certain colour. What, then, is the source of this difference between colour and beauty?

In a way, this question is easy for the explanation to answer. In the case of colour, the subject's judgement must be grounded in *someone's* response to the object, but not necessarily his own. This is shown precisely by the possibility of testimony about colour. In the case of beauty, in contrast, the judgement of taste can only be made on the ground of the *judging subject's* pleasure. But are we here offered an explanation of testimony's failure, or a redescription of it? The possibility of relying on testimony over colour just is the possibility of using another's response to the object as ground for one's own judgement. We have no understanding of what is distinctive about beauty until we know *why* judgements of it must be made on the basis of the judger's own responses.

Someone might dispute the analogy with colour in either of two ways, each generating a new explanation for the failure of testimony concerning beauty. The first notes that judging colour is straightforwardly a case of applying a concept and that, as we saw above, Kant is eager to distinguish appreciating beauty from concept application. As a result, 'aesthetic judgement affords ... no knowledge of the Object'.[11] And, where there is no knowledge, there is nothing to learn from testimony.

As it stands, this explanation moves too quickly. Whatever exactly Kant means by denying the presence of knowledge in the aesthetic realm, he certainly thinks that one can have warrant for a judgement of taste. For that is what he means by his most basic

[11] CJ, section 15.

claim, that pleasure is the 'determining ground' of the judgement that something is beautiful. But if one person can be warranted in judging something beautiful, why can't a second person acquire warrant for that belief on the basis of the first's say-so? Testimony's failure for beauty just is the failure of such acquisition to occur. Kant, it seems, is committed to terms rich enough to generate our problem, whatever he says about knowledge.

There is undoubtedly more to this first contrast between beauty and colour. Kant's claims about their differing relations to 'knowledge' are really ways of summarising the fundamental differences discussed above (section 2). Appreciating something's beauty is not a matter of finding out about it via some modification of my state which serves to represent that thing. I discover its beauty through my pleasure, and that feeling is, in Kant's phrase, 'referred to the subject'.[12] My pleasure is not brute, it reflects the fact that my faculties are in harmony; but that fact too fundamentally concerns my state, not the nature of the object (save in so far as it puts me in that state). In the colour case, in contrast, although I find out about colour via a response on my part, that response is 'referred to the Object', that is, it combines with a concept to represent some property of the item.

However, are these further differences relevant? They concern the differing sources, in the case of colour and of beauty, of a normative demand made in each – the demand for the agreement of all.[13] But, whatever its source, the mere presence of that demand in the aesthetic case is sufficient to generate our problem. If the maker of a judgement of taste is, on the basis of his pleasure in an object, justified in demanding from everyone agreement as to its beauty, why isn't anyone of whom agreement is justifiably demanded equally justified, *on the basis of the original judger's pleasure*, in giving that agreement? This is the fundamental formulation, within Kant's framework, of the problem of accounting for the failure of testimony over beauty. Our discussion this far has served simply to bring us to the point at which we have focused this problem clearly. Note that the problem is generated precisely by the demand for agreement, enshrined in Kant's first 'peculiarity', which is the central strand in his attempt to develop an account of beauty as objective. Nothing in the first proposal for demarcating beauty from colour has shown how to solve that problem.

This stress on the normative demand raises one last hope for that first proposal. For what exactly is it that the maker of a judgement of taste demands from every other person? Is it (a) pleasure in O, on

[12] CJ, section 1.
[13] CJ, section 18.

encountering it; (b) a judgement that O is beautiful, on encountering it; or (c) a judgement that O is beautiful, *prior to* any such encounter? Kant swings between (a) and (b), but surely it is (c) that would be required for testimony concerning beauty. If Kant does not think that the maker of a judgement of taste is justified in demanding (c), that is why, he should say, testimony fails for beauty.

There is no escape here. Compare colour. There, the testifier demands, on the basis of his experience, that everyone (α) on encountering O, respond perceptually to it as he does; and (β) agree, on encountering O, that it is (say) red. But he also demands (γ) that everyone accept that O is red *prior* to experiencing it. How can he do this, if they lack any grounds for judging O's colour? By *telling them* its colour, and letting his word serve as their ground. Why, then, can he not do the same when beauty is the topic? That is precisely our question. It is no answer simply to stipulate that the judgement of taste lays claim, from all, to (a) or (b), but not (c). The last two differ solely in whether contact with O is necessary for the other to give his 'agreement', and our question all along was why, in the case of beauty, such contact should be needed.

What of the second disanalogy between beauty and colour? This is that there are complications unique to the case of beauty. Here, according to Kant, the key response is pleasure, but it must be pleasure stemming from the right source – the distinctive state of our cognitive system described above. In particular, the subject's pleasure in the object must not stem from its satisfying his 'interest', as Kant puts it.[14] It must not, for example, spring from his self-congratulation in liking such arcane and difficult items; or from his pride in his country, for having produced the thing in question. Now, it is hard enough in one's own case to be sure that no such factors sully one's pleasure in the object. How much harder, then, to know this of someone else's reaction. And perhaps Kant can explain the failure of testimony in these terms. For beauty, but not colour, the response of another cannot ground my judgement, since only with colour can I be sufficiently confident that the other's response was of the right sort.

This, then, is the third explanation. One difficulty is that it takes as central phenomena which are peripheral to testimony. It focuses on my difficulty in knowing the source of my informant's judgement. But in its purest form testimony involves my forming a belief about some issue simply on another's say-so, without concerning myself about his grounds for that judgement. Even setting that anxiety aside, the proposal fails. It is simply unclear that, when the issue is the source of pleasure in something's beauty, my access to

[14] CJ, section 2.

the facts in another's case is much worse than in my own. Certainly Kant says very little of a positive nature about how I might ascertain the source of my own pleasure. He seems to reject the idea that, when my pleasure does have the appropriate, purely cognitive, source, I can directly experience that fact. Rather, the only manifestation in consciousness of that cognitive state is the pleasure itself.[15] If so, it is hard to see how there is a difference in kind between the first- and third-person case. More importantly, it is implausible that I could never know enough in the case of another. For one thing, this itself I could learn by testimony. If you simply *tell* me that your pleasure stems from no interest of yours, and if you have been sufficiently rigorous in your inquiry to know that, why should I not acquire that knowledge, simply by believing you? Of course, when you tell me that something is beautiful, you are making a rather different claim. But if the latter implies, or perhaps implicates, the former, my epistemic position will be the same.

A fourth proposal picks up on this idea about what is implicated about the judger's state. Perhaps the speech act of claiming that something is beautiful 'implicates an avowal'. That is, perhaps it gives rise to a conversational implicature, in Grice's sense, that the judger takes, or has taken, pleasure in the object in question. If so, no other person can earn the right to offer that judgement simply in virtue of what is said to him. For, as noted before, it is obvious that hearing testimony about an object's beauty does not allow one to take pleasure in it. Thus if I have not experienced the thing, but attempt to claim that it is beautiful on your say-so, I have not taken the pleasure in it which my claim implicates. My claim is not one to which I am entitled, and any who hear it, once they discover the facts, are likely to 'feel not just annoyed, but as if [they]'d been lied to'.[16]

This proposal has clear affinities with the first. Unlike the first, it promises to explain *why* my right to a judgement of taste requires my pleasure in the object judged. My judgement conversationally implies my pleasure in the object, and that is why I need to have taken such pleasure. Indeed, I suspect that much of what the proposal asserts is true. However, it gives a hostage to fortune. Implicature only occurs in the context of *claims* about beauty, speech acts of asserting that some thing or other is beautiful. Of course, if there is to be testimony at all, there must be at least one

---

[15] This reading is defended in P. Guyer, *Kant and the Claims of Taste,* 2nd edition, (Cambridge University Press, 1997), pp. 88–97.

[16] Mothersill, *Beauty Restored*, p. 160. Mothersill's book is the source of the phrase 'implicate an avowal', and of the proposal offered in this paragraph. See esp. pp. 85, 159–60.

such speech act, but there need not be two. The epistemic interest of testimony centrally concerns the right to form the *belief* that p on the basis of what others tell me, not the right to go on to pronounce on the topic in question. Appeal to implicature may explain the oddness of claims about beauty based on the testimony of others, but it cannot explain that of beliefs so based. So, if the failure of testimony in this area extends to belief, the implicature account is defective. It can at most cover some of the phenomena, and is not likely to be the deepest explanation of those. For if we had an independent explanation of why testimony cannot ground beliefs about beauty, facts about implicature might very well emerge as consequences of this.

Of course, all this counts for nothing unless testimony's failure in the aesthetic realm does indeed extend to belief. It is time to ask whether this is so, and more generally quite what we need to explain. Before doing that, let us quickly reject a final proposal.

We can avoid the pitfalls of last explanation by making a claim about the *content* of the judgement of taste. For this, unlike implicature, is common to the spoken judgement and the belief it expresses. We should claim that the content of a judgement that O is beautiful is in part that O evokes a pleasure response. So far, this is not implausible, and Kant, at least, would accept as much.[17] Now we want this claim about content to explain something about the judgement's grounds, i.e. why they must include the *judging subject's* pleasure in O. So we must further claim that the content is that the judger takes, or has taken, such pleasure. However, this move, although it seems the only one left to us at this stage, is fruitless. It accommodates the absence of testimony for beauty only by surrendering any pretensions to objectivity. To note just one consequence of the proposal: if it is part of the content of someone's belief that some object O is beautiful that he takes pleasure in it, he is no longer in a position genuinely to *disagree* with someone who denies O's beauty.

4 In considering whether beauty admits of testimony, there are various situations we might discuss. We have already noted (section 1) the contrast between cases in which the hearer (H) does not already have an opinion on the matter on which his informant (T) testifies, and those in which he does. In the former, T's testimony that p, if

[17] Kant certainly thinks the judgement of taste has content, since otherwise he can hardly consider it to be warranted. For a plausible reconstruction of his view on what that content is, see A. Savile, *Aesthetic Reconstructions: The Seminal Writings of Lessing, Kant and Schiller* (Oxford: Blackwell, 1987), chapter 5.

it gives H any reason to believe p, gives him the only reason he has; in the latter H has other reasons, for or against. We will concentrate on the former, since it focuses our problem in its purest form. A second distinction is between cases in which H and T are equally well qualified to judge on matters of the kind in question, and those in which T is more expert than H. The latter situation is especially interesting for aesthetics, since it offers one model of the relation between the critic-connoisseur, be it of nature or art, and those who hope to learn from him. None the less, in what follows I concentrate on cases in which H and T are equally qualified to judge the beauty of whatever sort of thing is in question. Again, this case is, I think, basic. In passing, I will attempt to indicate how my claims might extend to the question of expertise.

Preliminaries aside, is it ever legitimate for the testimony of another, my equal in expertise, to carry weight in my thinking about whether a given thing is beautiful? In particular, how sharp is the contrast in this respect between beauty and other observable matters? (We will continue to take colour as our example.) I think that there is an important contrast to draw. However, to get to it, we need to steer a course through conflicting intuitions.

On the one hand, it seems H can acquire some grounds for belief that some object O is beautiful on the basis of T's testimony. Suppose I have never seen, or looked at pictures of, the Picos De Europa, but that you tell me they are beautiful. Doesn't this give me some warrant for believing that they are beautiful? Perhaps we have walked many mountain ranges together, and I have always found your taste in such matters to be rather refined. Suppose I then plan a holiday in the Picos, perhaps sacrificing some other project I had been contemplating. In doing this surely I need not be acting irrationally, not even if I cite as my main reason for going the beauty of those mountains. And doesn't this suggest that my plan is based on a belief, in the beauty of the Picos, that is not entirely groundless?

On the other hand, there is a powerful pull towards the idea that all I can really be doing is *going to see whether* your claim is true. Perhaps your testimony gives me *some* reason to think the mountains lovely, but does it give me sufficient to justify my forming the belief that they are? (No doubt how much warrant is sufficient varies with context, but it is hard to think of a situation, where the putative belief concerns beauty, in which testimony ever meets this context-determined limit.) Odder still is the idea that I can thereby come to *know* that the mountains are beautiful.[18] And in these

---

[18] Let us set aside Kant's idea (above, section 3) that quite generally aesthetic matters are not capable of being 'known'. My claims are plausible independently of Kant's rather theory-laden views on the topic.

respects, testimony concerning beauty contrasts with testimony on other matters. Suppose you have visited the Asturias and tell me that their regional flag is a distinctive shade of purple. Provided I have no reason to mistrust you, this gives me sufficient grounds for the belief. And, provided you established your belief in an appropriate way, perhaps by observation, the belief I form constitutes *knowledge* of the flag's colour.

There is another aspect to the contrast here. As Kant himself notes in the passage on testimony with which we began, in non-aesthetic matters the opinions of others can combine, so that the warrant provided by their testimonies taken together outstrips that provided by any one of them taken alone. Kant notes that this can provide sufficient warrant to overturn the hearer's own, contradictory observations; and that this is not so when it is beauty in dispute. We might add that combined testimony on a non-aesthetic matter can also provide sufficient warrant to leave the hearer, when he has not observed the matter in hand, in a better position than any of his informants.[19] Several witnesses to a crime might think that the perpetrator wore a red top, but, given the speed and upsetting nature of the events, not be at all sure. The inspector in charge of the case, having interviewed each, might be justified in believing the assailant's top to be red, and more so than any of his informants. It is very hard to construct an analogous case in the aesthetic sphere. Suppose that a painting combines a heady Romanticism with a luscious look. Many viewers, although inclined on balance to find it very beautiful indeed, might be left with some doubt as to whether it is in fact beautiful at all, so large loom those features which, in the end, might be taken as faults. In such a case, can the testimony of several such viewers leave someone who has not seen the picture in a better position than each of his informants? I think not. At best, he is left no worse off, in his warrant for believing the painting beautiful, than each of them.

There are many factors we might vary, in these examples, in the hope of closing the gap between aesthetic and other matters. We might in particular consider the various ways in which, on matters of beauty, T may be a more or less suitable informant for H.[20] But even if such manoeuvres achieve something, they hardly bridge the divide completely. For in non-aesthetic matters no such rigorous selection of informants is needed. Complete strangers, of whom I know almost nothing and in whom I have no reason to place any

[19] This point, and a similar example, can be found in C. A. J. Coady, *Testimony* (Oxford: Clarendon Press, 1992).

[20] This need not be to reintroduce the issue of expertise. We might merely consider cases in which T and H are in various ways alike.

particular trust, can pass on to me their knowledge of, say, the direction of my hotel, or the result of today's big match. Their testimony
gives me ample warrant for the belief I form, despite my ignorance
of their character or intent. So even if another's testimony can
sometimes do more, by way of justifying my belief in something's
beauty, than I have allowed, the contrasts with other matters stand.
At the least, then, enough has been established about testimony
concerning beauty to vindicate the criticisms levelled at the proposals
of section 3. For the contrasts here are with other, response-involv-
ing, observable properties, such as colour; and they concern the
warrant testimony provides for *belief* about a thing's beauty. We
must find another explanation for testimony's failure.

First, however, we need a tighter grip on the phenomenon. We
have as yet done nothing to reconcile the conflicting intuitions
described above, and nothing to give the phenomenon a formulation
sufficiently precise to allow explanation to begin. In the next two
sections, I offer a more theoretical description of the facts.

5 To make progress, we need to consider in a little more detail the
nature of testimony. There are two main accounts of how testimony
operates.[21]

One account, which I will call the *evidential model*, finds its
crispest expression in Hume.[22] On this view, H, the hearer's, warrant
for believing what his informant T testifies to is given by an inference. The inference has three premises. The first is that T says that
p. The second appeals to the correlation, as established by H's past
experience, between (i) utterances by informants of some kind to
which T belongs, on the topic of the kind to which the claim that *p*
belongs and (ii) the truth of those utterances. The third concerns
the prior probability that *p*. Provided appropriate versions of these
premises are available, H can make an inductive inference to the
conclusion that *p*. Of course, the view need not claim that anyone
learning from testimony in fact makes such an inference. Here, as in
other cases in which reasoning provides one's justification for belief,
it suffices that H *could* so infer, were he to put his mind to it. And
the degree to which he is justified in his belief that *p* is the degree
to which some such inference, available to him, would support that
conclusion.

The rival account is harder to focus. The best formulation of it

---

[21] The accounts which follow are not the only ones available. But they
exemplify the two poles between which any account must position itself.
Since they are also the most plausible accounts I know, I will not compli-
cate matters by discussing alternatives.

[22] Hume, *Inquiry Concerning Human Understanding*, chapter IX.

known to me is given by Tyler Burge.[23] He distinguishes between justifications and entitlements. Both are sources of warrant for one's beliefs. Entitlements are warrants lying in grounds which one need not, in order to be warranted, be able to articulate. Justifications, in contrast, 'involve reasons that people have and have access to' (Burge p. 459). Sources of entitlement, for Burge, include perception, memory and testimony. Thus we already see one difference between the account emerging here and the evidential model. For by insisting that the warrant testimony provides is just the warrant delivered by the inductive argument outlined above, the evidentialist makes testimony a matter, in Burge's terms, of justification, not entitlement.

There is more to Burge's view. When T tells H that p, the default is that H is entitled to believe him. Unless there are special grounds for suspicion, H is under no epistemic obligation to assess T's credibility, his past performance in giving witness on the issue in hand, or anything of the sort. So it is not just that, for Burge, H need not formulate the second premise above; unless the question arises, he need not incur any commitments on this or related matters. Finally, if H does form the belief that p on T's say-so, and if T was himself entitled to, or justified in, that belief (by perception, memory, argument, or whatever), then H inherits T's warrant for believing that p. And this, even though H perhaps lacks any knowledge of T's grounds for that belief. Of course, the evidential model too allows for this last, as any plausible account of testimony must. But on that model, H overcomes his ignorance of T's grounds for believing that p by making use of grounds of his own own – his knowledge that T has proved a reliable enough informant on such matters in the past. On Burge's model, H inherits warrant without having grounds of his own to cite – as the idea that testimony is an entitlement precisely allows. So Burge sees testimony as a way for T's warrant to be passed on to H, via the *a priori* epistemic right H has to believe T unless there are reasons for not doing so. I will call this view the *transmission model*.

There is an asymmetry between the ambitions these two positions can reasonably entertain. Advocates of the evidential model have thought that this is the only way in which testimony could conceivably operate. Advocates of the transmission view need not, and should not, be so uncompromising. We clearly *could* reason as the evidentialist suggests, since the inference he describes is merely one instance of a more general pattern of reasoning we sometimes use, i.e. standard induction. The only question is whether testimony

[23] Tyler Burge, 'Content Preservation', *Philosophical Review*, 1993, pp. 457–88.

between us does in fact operate in this way, and in particular whether the evidential account can cover both the particular things we do know by testimony, and the sheer scale of our dependence on the word of others. (Of course, someone holding the transmission view might argue that reasoning along evidential lines, for all that it could, and perhaps does occur, does not merit the name of learning by 'testimony'. But, for our purposes, this would be merely a matter of terminology.)

If the transmission model must accept that the evidentialist might be right about at least some of our thinking, this opens up an interesting possibility. Perhaps, although the transmission acount fits most of the testimony we rely on, in some areas matters operate as the evidentialist suggests. I suggest that beliefs about beauty constitute just such an area. If we make use of both models of testimony we can sharpen the contrast, with respect to testimony, between beauty and other matters, and reconcile our conflicting intuitions about whether testimony over beauty is possible at all.

6 In what follows, I will simply assume that the transmission model is coherent, and that it provides the right account of by far the greater part of our dealings with testimony.[24] Since this includes testimony about colour and other observable properties, one part of the contrast I want to draw is in place, albeit without argument. I want to concentrate on beauty, and suggest that here the transmission model does not apply. Instead, to the extent that beauty admits of testimony at all, it does so on evidential lines. This will enable us to see how – at least in a central class of cases – another's testimony can give me *some* ground for a belief that something is beautiful, without that ground being at all powerful.

From the conflicting intuitions marshalled in section 4, we can at least extract this. It is hard to believe that T's testimony that O is beautiful offers H *no* support for that proposition; but, equally, it is hard to believe, at least in standard cases, that it offers him *much*. Indeed, the stronger the epistemic notion we apply here (Does H gain sufficient ground to form the belief? Could he be better warranted in that belief than several uncertain informants? Could it overturn the warrant provided by his own experience? Does he gain knowledge?), the harder it is to think that it applies to H's state. A consequence of this is that H's warrant will, in standard cases, be far weaker than T's. Of course, T's warrant might itself be weak or

[24] For defence of this assumption, see Burge, 'Content Preservation', Coady, *Testimony*, F. Schmitt, 'Justification, Sociality and Autonomy', *Synthese*, **73** (1) (1987), 43–85 and D. Owens, *Reason Without Freedom*, draft 1998.

strong. But, in at least many of the cases which concern us, it will be perfectly healthy. If T has judged O beautiful on the basis of experience of O, T is in an excellent position to hold that belief. Even so, our intuitions suggest, H will still acquire no more than very weak support for the proposition that p.

This disparity, between T's warrant and H's, is something only the evidential model can accommodate. For it takes H's and T's warrants to derive from quite different sources. The latter depends on whatever grounds T has for his belief, the former on the strength of the best inductive inference, of the form described above, available to H. It is clear that there is no reason for the strength of these two warrants to be linked. T's warrant will depend on his current situation, H's on reasoning available to him largely concerning T's past record, or that of informants relevantly like him, in communicating truths. It is also clear that H's warrant might, across different situations, vary to any degree. For the support the inference yields for its target conclusion is in part determined by at least one matter which itself admits of continuous variation. This is the strength of the past correlation, as experienced by H, between claims, on the part of the relevant body of witnesses, on the given topic, and their truth. So it is at least consistent with the evidential model that the warrant provided by testimony about beauty be as weak as it is, and that it often be far weaker than the informant's warrant.

The transmission account, in contrast, cannot accommodate these observations. Since on that account H inherits T's warrant for the testified belief, H must be justified in holding that belief to the same degree that T is. But in the standard cases of testimony about beauty, T's warrant will be strong, and H's weak. And that is our reason for thinking that testimony about beauty, whatever else it involves, does not operate on transmission lines.

One might wonder if things are so cut and dried. Couldn't the transmission model claim that H inherits a *portion* of T's warrant for believing that p, a portion so small that usually H cannot know that p, or even perhaps have sufficient warrant to form the belief? I don't think so, since these modifications are entirely *ad hoc*. These claims can't be made for testimony on just any subject matter, since on many topics testimony does indeed provide us with knowledge, or fully warranted belief, and thus with warrant of at least roughly the same strength as that of our informants. So the proposal must be that we alter the account to allow for such partial transmission of warrant, even though for topics other than beauty it applies unchanged. This amendment is not needed to save the account altogether, since we are simply assuming that it holds for testimony on most topics. It is motivated by nothing more than the desire to stretch the account to cover our conclusions concerning beauty. The evidential model, in contrast, can accommodate the weakness of testimonial support on questions of beauty without revision, let alone revisions of an *ad hoc* kind. We should conclude that the transmission model does not apply to beauty.

However, this argument requires one point of elucidation and one qualification. The point of elucidation is in response to a worry. The proposal is that we reject transmission testimony over beauty on the grounds that, standardly, when beauty is the subject matter, H's warrant is considerably weaker than T's. The worry is that the same grounds serve to cast doubt on my assumption that transmitting testimony does occur, indeed is the norm, for other subject matters. True, if I take your word on the colour of something, or a stranger's word on the direction of my hotel, my warrant is perhaps not considerably weaker than my informant's. Certainly, in such situations I will often have sufficient warrant to *know* what I am told. But is my warrant *as* strong as my informant's, supposing his belief to be formed in first hand experience of the matter? This is not obviously the case, and if not, it seems that the form of argument above, if legitimate at all, threatens to prove that transmitting testimony fails for every topic, not just for beauty.

This is a general objection to the transmission model. I will suggest the main lines of the response I favour, although developing it fully would take us too far afield. What makes it plausible that, in the sort of case just described, H and T are not equally well off epistemically? It is thoughts such as this. If the stakes are high, T is in a better position than H. If, for instance, each is persuaded to wager large sums on whether p (the proposition to which T testifies), T will reasonably bet rather more than H. But does this show that, prior to that gaming situation, H had less warrant than T for the belief that p? Or is it rather that the gamble with high stakes alters which aspects of each's condition are epistemically relevant?

I suggest the latter. Raising the stakes makes it very important to be right about whether p. This leaves H and T wanting not merely to be entitled to the belief that p, but to *know* that they are entitled to it. Now, on Burge's view, entitlements, whether provided by perception or by testimony, are defeasible. That is, there are conditions the holding of which would undermine that entitlement. For perception, such conditions include the malfunctioning of T's perceptual apparatus; for testimony, they include hearing that p from someone who is deceitful, or is himself deceived, about whether p. To be entitled, it is not necessary to know that these defeating conditions do not obtain.[25] But to *know* that one is entitled may indeed

[25] Burge, 'Content Preservation', p. 468.

require just this. Since the two sets of defeating conditions differ, we can see that it may well be harder for H to establish that he is entitled than for T to do so. Hence our sense that the epistemic positions of the two differ. However, this difference is merely potential, except when it is important to be right about whether p (and perhaps in other special circumstances). It in no way suggests that in normal conditions there is any (further, actual) difference between T and H's epistemic positions, and in particular that the latter is less warranted in the belief he acquires from the former.

The qualification the argument requires is as follows. I have spoken here as if the support testimony offers for beliefs about beauty must always be weak. But what of the cases, the possibility of which we considered earlier (section 4), where H's informant is in some way specially suited to him? If it is indeed possible for such an informant to provide H with strong justification for beliefs about beauty, we need to say a little more.

Conceding this possibility leaves the argument just given intact, but restricted in its scope. It applies only to those cases, by far the more common, in which no such special 'suitability' of T to H obtains. For those cases the conclusion stands that testimony works on evidential lines, if it works at all. But what of the other, exceptional, cases? Here, we are supposing, the warrant for H's belief is strong. Since there is here no obvious disparity between the strength of T's warrant for the relevant belief, and the strength of H's, it is possible that on these occasions transmission testimony is the source of H's warrant. However, the evidentialist can also hope to account for these cases. For perhaps T's 'suitability' to H just amounts to T's having in the past judged beauty just as H himself does, when he finally experiences the object in question. If so, there is a strong past correlation, from H's perspective, between T's claims about beauty and their truth; and that strength would be inherited by the support for T's current claim which an evidential inference offers.

I will not attempt to settle which account best fits these putative exceptions. I am only convinced of their possibility by the thought that, if evidential testimony over beauty is possible at all, as it seems it must be, then in principle it could in special circumstances offer the strong support here contemplated.[26] So it is hard for me to reject the evidential account of these cases, in favour of the transmission view. In what follows I will speak as if transmitting testimony never occurs for beauty. But, since I have offered no argument for this last

---

[26] David Owens drew my attention to this.

element in my description of the phenomena, I will attempt not to rely on it in what follows.[27]

7 I have argued that beauty does not admit of testimony in the form standard for other matters, i.e. testimony as transmission. At most, it admits of testimony as evidence, as input to a Humean inference. Even then, the support provided for the testified proposition is usually weak. Earlier I rejected the most obvious explanations, from within Kant's scheme, for the purported failure, *tout court*, of testimony for beauty. Now the facts have been focused more sharply, it is time to attempt a better explanation.

There are several explanatory strategies we might adopt, but there is space to consider only one. I concentrate on this because it is, I think, both the most natural and, in the end, the most promising. Although there are different versions of this strategy, they all begin from the fact of disagreement over beauty. It is very tempting to try to explain the contrast between aesthetic and other matters thus: beliefs about, say, colour can be acquired by transmission testimony, as beliefs about beauty cannot, because people disagree over the beauty of things, as they do not over their colour.

One attraction of appealing to disagreement is that we may anyway need to use it to explain the phenomena above. Why does evidential testimony about beauty in general provide only weak support for the testified belief? If disagreement is common, the explanation is straightforward. The prevalence of dispute means that H will be hard-pressed to identify T as belonging to a type the members of which he has always experienced as in agreement. But since, when two subjects disagree, both cannot be right, this undermines the correlation, as experienced by H, between the claims about beauty made by subjects of that type and the truth of those claims.[28] Hence, except in special circumstances, the support an evidential inference would offer to any claim now before H will be relatively weak.

[27] We might construe expertise in aesthetic matters along the lines here proposed. On this view, the expert is one whose aesthetic credentials are sufficiently well established for his testimony to provide strong evidence for a Humean inference to the truth of his claims. If there are 'experts' in beauty, whose testimony has special force, the proposal offers a plausible way to accommodate that.

[28] Can the modest objectivist framework we are working within here allow for the notion of *truth*? I see no reason why not, for at least some such notion is not of much metaphysical import (see Wright, *Truth and Objectivity*). Even if that claim is wrong, other notions could readily be substituted here – at the limit, just that of succeeding (or failing) in *legitamately* making a demand of all.

Now, it is quite another question whether disagreement can explain why transmitting testimony about beauty is not possible. Perhaps the strategy's success with evidential testimony will encourage optimism on this score. However, before we can explore the prospects for this approach, we need to settle an important preliminary. We are interested in explanations consistent with Kant's modest objectivism about beauty. So we must first ask how far his scheme can accommodate disagreement.

Kant can certainly allow that certain kinds of disagreement occur. If I consider O beautiful, but you do not, this might be because my judgement or yours (or both) is prompted by pleasure in O which is based on some interest, some desire or other idiosyncratic feature of that person (section 3 above). Alternatively, it may be that we are in fact making judgements of different kinds, without realising it. For Kant allows that what is apparently talk of beauty *simpliciter* is sometimes really talk of the object's suitability to some end. This is the source of his famous distinction between free and dependent beauty.[29] An end can be grasped only by applying a concept, and it is central to the account of beauty explored above (section 2) that the pleasure grounding the judgement of taste is not dependent on the application of concepts. So the two judgements must be of different kinds. Thus we find Kant readily acknowledging that, if one person judges O independently of thoughts about an end it might serve, while another judges it in terms of such thoughts, their disagreement, even if each talks of beauty, is only apparent.[30]

Beyond these sources of conflict, Kant cannot allow for disagreement. If neither of us is pleased by O because of some interest, and if neither is tacitly judging O's suitability to some end, then Kant cannot see how we can disagree over O's beauty. For the pleasure each of us feels should then have its source in the object's effects on our cognitive system – its putting the faculties 'in harmony' – and Kant's central thought about how agreement is justifiably demanded from every one is that, what has the effect on one, must have it on all. Since the interestedness of a pleasure removes the warrant it provides for a judgement of taste, and since judgements of dependent and of free beauty cannot really conflict, Kant thus has to deny that *there can be genuine disagreements over free beauty in which both parties are warranted in their judgements.*

8 The preliminary over, we can ask how exactly the fact of disagreement might explain the failure of transmitting testimony concerning beauty. There are several possibilities. We start with two

[29] CJ, section 16.
[30] Ibid.

which rely on the relative *prevalence* of disagreement to distinguish the aesthetic from the non-aesthetic, transmission-involving, case.

First, one might think that the relative prevalence of disagreement over matters of beauty raises issues which must be left to lie, if there is to be testimony along Burgean lines. Burge devotes 'Content Preservation' to explaining how there can be an *a priori* entitlement to believe the claims of others. That entitlement is not only defeasible, in that conditions may hold which undermine it (section 6 above). It is also vulnerable in its status as *a priori*. If the testimonial situation raises questions about T's right to his belief, or the sincerity of his claims, then clearly H cannot be entitled *a priori* to believe him. He must consider these questions, and their answers can at best be known *a posteriori*. The relative prevalence of disagreement in aesthetic matters, as opposed to ordinary empirical ones, seems to force H into precisely such *a posteriori* investigations. For, if disagreement is common when beauty is the topic, how can H simply take for granted that T is a reliable guide to the beautiful? He must examine T's credentials, and that alone prevents him being entitled *a priori* to the testified belief, in the way Burge describes.

Although this explanation applies readily enough to Burge's official view, it bypasses the real issue. For I think that Burge's claims for the *a priori* status of testimonial entitlement should be seen as distinct from the rest of his account. Thus far I have concentrated on Burge's idea that testimony works through an entitlement to believe what one is told, an entitlement by which the testifier's warrant for his belief is passed on. Whether or not this entitlement is *a priori* seems a separate matter. Why should that entitlement not hold even if H has to earn the right to it by settling certain issues *a posteriori*? Our being entitled to believe what others say if the question of their competence or trustworthiness does not arise is quite consistent with our being entitled to even if it has arisen, provided those questions receive a satisfactory answer. Answering such questions may require H to formulate claims, for instance concerning T's general truthfulness or reliability, of the sort which could form the basis for a Humean inference as to whether to believe his claim that *p*. But H can consider these matters without thereby undertaking any such inference, and without his warrant to believe that *p* stemming from the fact, if fact it be, that some such inference is available to him.[31] My suggestion is not that all transmission testi-

---

[31] What then is the role of those *a posteriori* beliefs? H's answering the questions about T satisfactorily is a necessary condition, once they have arisen, for his reasonably letting his belief conform to T's. Provided that condition is met, his warrant lies, as on the unmodified Burge model, in whatever T's warrant consists in. Compare: in special circumstances, I may

mony involves an entitlement *a posteriori*. That proposal might not be coherent, and certainly would not allow transmission to do some of the work Burge wanted, e.g. allowing for the scale of our dependence on what others say. My thought is only that some testimony involves such an *a posteriori* entitlement. I see no reason for Burge to deny that.[32] If not, while the prevalence of disagreement over beauty may force certain questions on H, its doing so does not explain why T's testimony to him cannot involve the transmission of warrant between the two.

There is a second way to use the prevalence of disagreement to explain transmission's failure for beauty. If disagreements over beauty are common how can H be entitled to take T's word on whether O is beautiful? For there could easily be a second informant offering a contradictory view. If H is entitled to believe both, then he is entitled to believe both that the thing is beautiful and that it is not. This is unacceptable. Since H is related to each of his possible informants in just the same way, it seems he must either be entitled to believe both, or entitled to believe neither. The former possibility we have ruled out, and so it is the latter which obtains. But this is just the possibility that, for beauty, transmitting testimony does not occur. No such obstacle holds in the case of such 'theoretical' matters as the colour of things. Disagreement is possible there, but rare. Thus the possibility of contradicting informants is not live, as it is in the aesthetic case; and hence no parallel problem for transmission holds.

This explanation has an appealing simplicity. However, it is insufficiently directed at the explanandum, the impossibility of transmission. We can approach this issue by asking exactly what is supposed to be 'unacceptable' about H's situation, were transmission to hold. It seems it can only be that H might end up *taking himself* to be entitled both to believe that O is beautiful and to believe that it is not. In particular, transmission would not have the more serious consequence, that H would really be entitled to contradictory

[32] One reason why Burge does not consider this possibility is that he is in part exploring whether one can learn matters *a priori* from testimony. In 'Content Preservation' the matter in question is that testified to (see esp. note 4; cf. 'Interlocution, Perception and Memory' *Philosophical Studies*, **86**, 1997, 21–47). Elsewhere it is the existence of other minds – see 'Reason and the First Person', in C. Wright, B. Smith and C. Macdonald (eds), *Knowing Our Own Minds* (Oxford: Clarendon Press, 1998), pp. 243–70, esp. 262ff.

have to decide whether to trust my memory; but, if I do reasonably decide to do so, my warrant for the remembered belief stems from the entitlement memory brings, not from any justification my deliberations might offer.

beliefs. For transmission simply hands on to the hearer any warrant the informant had. The Kantian framework within which we are working dictates that only one of H's two conflicting informants could in fact be making a warranted judgement of free beauty (section 7). So there is at most one warrant, for a belief genuinely about (free) beauty, for H to inherit. Even given transmission, then, the *appearance* of conflicting entitlements is the most that can be involved.

If this is the unacceptable possibility, declaring transmission to be impossible doesn't help. What would help would be if no one ever adopted any belief about beauty on the basis of another's testimony. But universal agnosticism is not the same as the absence of transmission. Hearers need to form beliefs if testimony is to work by *either* transmission or evidential means. And provided they do form such beliefs, when beauty is in question, it makes matters no worse whether they do so by transmission or by inference. Transmission could not generate any conflict worse than that between warrants apparently available to the subject, for the reason just given. And evidential testimony can equally generate conflicts of apparent warrants, as when H's contesting informants both have an equal claim, given their past performance, on his credence. So the explanation is not of why transmission, in particular, fails to obtain.

There are certainly responses available to the explanation at this point. For one thing, it made play with the notion of the prevalence of disagreement. That was what was to differentiate beauty from other matters. Perhaps it will also help differentiate transmission from evidential testimony, in the aesthetic case. Perhaps, that is, evidential testimony threatens to generate a conflict in apparent warrants, but in far fewer cases than transmission would. This would be so if few informants in fact make equal claims, given their past performance, on our credence. Another reply would be that transmission threatens to generate a conflict between apparent warrants of greater strength than that promised by evidential testimony. For we saw above (section 7) how disagreement weakens the support evidential testimony offers to beliefs about beauty, but transmission promises the hearer the same warrant which the informant enjoys.

However, these responses raise more questions than they answer. The first simply draws attention to the problematic role played by prevalence in the original argument. How exactly does the threat of more of a given unacceptable consequence act to frustrate the mechanisms which would generate it? The second leaves us wondering why the *strength* of apparent warrants for conflicting views should matter. And this in turn raises the more serious question why a merely *apparent* conflict of warrants is problematic at all. That my entitlements seem to conflict simply tells me that I should try to find out how matters really stand. I should undertake the sort of investigation discussed earlier in this section, into the general reliability of my informant, or the disinterestedness of his judgement of taste. I argued above that the need to do this does not prevent that informant from passing on to me his warrant for his belief, provided my investigations find in his favour. Such investigations do not render transmission impossible, so how does the need to undertake them do so? Moreover, it is not clear that this need is even actual. The explanation does not claim that every informant is actually contradicted by another, just that he might be. Even if the likelihood of this occurring is higher than in non-aesthetic matters, it is not obvious that this possibility compels those who hear testimony over beauty to investigate their informants.

9 Where does this leave us? Our two explanations for the failure of transmission testimony for beauty have come to nought. They join our earlier Kantian (section 3) attempts, which were directed at a cruder explanandum. Other, quite different, approaches to the problem are available to Kant. I doubt, however, that they promise much. Should we then be pessimistic about the prospects for explaining the phenomena in any way? Or does all this serve to show that we need to reject Kant's basic framework before progress can be made? Neither response is appropriate. I will end by saying something about why it would not help to adopt a fundamentally different approach to beauty (section 10). First let me lift the gloom a little by offering, very tentatively, some suggestion as to how, in roughly Kantian terms, we might proceed.

What is it about transmission testimony that prevents its holding in the aesthetic realm? In essence, transmission allows the thoughts of one subject to fall under the rational control of the deliberation, or other epistemic operations, of another. For just that is effected when H adopts T's belief, and inherits whatever warrant he has for it. Transmission thus breaks down the barriers which separate rational subjects. Of course, there are still distinct *loci* of belief; but warrant spans these *loci*, so that what is accessible only to one, such as his perceptual experience, can rationally underpin the beliefs of another. Perhaps this partial dissoloution of separateness is the source of transmission's untenability in aesthetic matters.

We can pursue this thought by returning to the last explanation. The moral of its failure is this. If the prospect of merely apparent conflict is insufficient to explain why transmission should be impossible, we should appeal instead to the more serious threat, that of genuine conflict between H's entitlements. It is this which transmission testimony over beauty would render possible, and the need to avoid this consequence which prevents such testimony obtaining. Obviously, since transmission does occur elsewhere, the threat of genuine conflict must be specific to the aesthetic case. If we can show this to be so, we need no longer appeal to the prevalence of disagreement to distinguish the ordinary from the aesthetic case – the difference will be one of kind, not degree. But to make room for this possibility, we need to surrender a key part of Kant's framework. Transmission merely passes on warrant. If H is to be in possession of conflicting warrants, it must be possible for the warrants of separate subjects to conflict, so that transmission can then pass both on to H. So we must abandon Kantian orthodoxy and allow that two subjects can be warranted in holding different, but genuinely conflicting, beliefs about something's beauty. The central idea of the explanation is that this is made tolerable by the separateness of the rational subjects in question; whereas, were transmission to obtain, the conflict of warrant could occur within a single thinker, and that is what cannot be sustained. The central difficulty in building an explanation on these lines is to reconstruct Kant's framework so as to allow for genuine, warranted disagreement, without abandoning altogether the spirit of his view.

How, in outline, might we try to do this? The crucial notion, I suggest, will be that of a *sensibility*, a set of dispositions determining one's response, pleasure or otherwise, to the aesthetic object. Different subjects may be equally warranted in their conflicting judgements of a thing's beauty because the pleasure of each is in part determined by her sensibility, and sensibilities differ. How, then, can each also justifiably demand from the other agreement, in both pleasure response and judgement? This is the hardest question of all for the proposal (as it was for Kant's original account). I speculate that, if anything can provide the answer, it is the thought that sensibilities are not simply different, but ordered. Some are more refined than others. The demand each subject makes of the other is not simply to feel about O as she does, but to develop the sensibility to be able so to feel. (Obviously, the notion of a hierarchy of sensibility will need explicating without reference to an independently established order of beauty, on pain of abandoning the most alluring feature of Kant's view, what I have called its modesty.) How can both be warranted in that demand, if the sensibility of one is more refined than that of the other? I have no properly developed answer. Perhaps the question can serve simply to underscore the difficulties the proposal faces. I acknowledge that those difficulties are considerable. My thought is only that there is enough promise in this line of thinking for complete pessimism about explaining transmission's failure to be unreasonable.

10 How general is the problem of accounting for testimony concerning beauty? Is it dependent on particular aspects of Kant's view? Many of his ideas promise to bear on this theme, as we saw in section 3. Examples include his stress on pleasure as our guide to beauty, on experience of the object as the necessary context for that pleasure, and the need for the pleasure to be 'disinterested'. These ideas may not, in the end, suffice to explain testimony's failure; but they hardly hinder that explanation. If any feature of Kant's position is to blame, it is surely, as I began by suggesting, his modest objectivism. It is scarcely plausible that a less modest, more metaphysically committed objectivism would fare better. Thus the direction in which to look for alternative solutions to our difficulty is towards positions rejecting the objectivity of beauty. Perhaps these views offer simpler and more obviously successful explanations than that sketched in section 9.

I am sceptical. Now that we have refined the explanandum, there are no plausible anti-objectivist moves that would help.

Initially, we so characterised the problem as to encourage optimism about a subjectivist solution. We took it (section 3) that beauty did not allow for any form of testimony. Kant's difficulty in explaining this sprang from his insistence on the judgement of taste legitimately demanding agreement from all. For it was this which sustained the problematic analogy with colour, and which fuelled my 'fundamental formulation' of the problem. If we reject the idea that judgements of taste do legitimately make that demand, we may hope thereby to render the explanatory problem more tractable. And, as noted (section 2) such a rejection might well amount to denying any objectivity for beauty.

Now, however, the situation is quite different. Our task is not to explain why there is no testimony for beauty, but why there is only testimony of the evidential form. It is at least *prima facie* plausible that testimony's two forms require the same basic resources. Either form involves the acquisition of warrant for a belief from someone else's asserting that belief. So if there is to be testimony at all, statements in the relevant discourse must be assertions, and must admit of warrant. We could readily explain testimony's failure if judgements of taste are not genuine assertions, or if, though they are, they can never be warranted. And of course, there are forms of subjectivism which, applied to beauty, would make precisely these claims – respectively, expressivism and some form of error theory.[33] However, adopting any such view will be pointless, given the task

[33] For the former, see A. J. Ayer, *Language, Truth and Logic*; for at least an analogue, in ethics, of the latter, see J. L. Mackie, *Ethics, Inventing Right & Wrong*.

now before us. For unless judgements of taste have the disputed features, there can be no evidential testimony concerning them; and, if they have them, it is as problematic as before why they don't allow for testimony by transmission.[34]

This argument may seem to sever altogether the link between the problem of testimony about beauty and the question of objectivity. It does not do so. For one thing, I have not argued that the presence of testimony requires only that of assertoric content and warrant, or that, whatever else may be needed, the missing ingredients are the same for both testimony's two forms. This is enough to leave open the possibility that more subtle moves in the objectivity debate might indeed help explain the facts about beauty and testimony. For another, the suspicion that the two themes remain linked can be reinforced by returning briefly to the 'solution' sketched in section 9.

That solution attempts to retain one of Kant's objectivity-bolstering claims, that the judgement of taste legitimately demands the agreement of all. But it abandons Kant's insistence that there can be no warranted genuine disagreements about (free) beauty. In doing this, it may indeed surrender an objectivist component of his position. For that insistence of Kant's is closely related to the claim that beauty meets what Crispin Wright has called the 'cognitive command constraint'.[35] The basic idea behind this is that, in objective discourse, it is *a priori* that disagreement stems from a cognitive failing on the one part of one side or the other. In the case of beauty, if no disagreement can be warranted, then, when it occurs, at least one view must be (in part) determined by factors which undermine warrant. And what is a cognitive failing, if not a warrant-undermining determinant of belief? Since Kant also thought that it is *a priori* that his ban on warranted disagreement holds, talk about beauty precisely meets Wright's constraint. If banning warranted disagreement is the only way to meet this constraint, and if meeting that constraint is central to vindicating beauty's claims to objectivity, then the solution of section 9, which rejects the ban, undermines those claims.

It is a delicate question whether this threat will be realised. Whether the ban is the only way to meet Wright's constraint is not

---

[34] Sophisticated variants of these subjectivist views will attempt to account for a good deal of the appearance of assertion and warrant in our talk of beauty, (see S. Blackburn *Spreading the Word* (Oxford: Clarendon Press, 1984), chapter 6 and *Essays in Quasi-Realism* (Oxford University Press, 1993). These variants will face a version of the problem above. They need to explain how it can be that evidential testimony about beauty seems to be possible, when transmission testimony does not.

[35] Wright, *Truth and Objectivity*, pp. 92–3. Cf. chapter 4.

clear. It turns on whether sensibilities, as the driving sources of dis-agreement, can be so only by being, in effect, cognitive failings, at least on the part of one party to the dispute. Whether meeting Wright's constraint is necessary for objectivity is also uncertain. Wright suggests so,[36] but he does not argue for that view, and I suspect that the case in point will precisely make the question look more difficult. We need not settle these hard questions. It is at least clear that the proposal of section 9 entangles us afresh in issues of objectivity.

I have tried to argue that there is a problem in explaining beauty's susceptibility, or otherwise, to testimony. Kant touched on the difficulty, but did not solve it. His view made the problem prominent, by its admirable attempt to acknowledge the objectivist tendencies in our thinking about beauty. But the problem faces other positions too, and in particular cannot be solved by leaping headlong into subjectivism. For the truth about testimony over beauty is more subtle than Kant allowed, and that subtlety frustrates simple sub-jectivist explanations. None the less, my suspicion is that questions about testimony over beauty and objectivity remain linked. If that suspicion is misplaced, no matter. My main hope is that others will take seriously the task of explaining why testimony over beauty, while not entirely impossible, is so only in a limited form.[37]

---

[36] Ibid., pp. 148, 175.

[37] Thanks are due to members of the Birmingham Philosophy graduate seminar, to Anthony O'Hear, David Owens, Tom Pink, and Anthony Savile. My greatest debt is to Barrie Falk, who brought the third critique alive for me. This paper is dedicated to his memory.

The Sirens' serenade

ANTHONY SAVILE

How are the beautiful and the good related? A popular answer to this ancient question takes it that to call something beautiful is just to bring it under the most general term of favourable aesthetic assessment and that since the good is in general what we reflectively want then, crudely put, the beautiful is the good's aesthetic dimension. Following this train of thought, we avoid the suggestion that there is any intimate connection between the beautiful and some more narrowly conceived moral or ethical good, since that is, again crudely put, restricted to the good's practical dimension, a dimension supposedly alien to aesthetic concerns.

For us today the *locus classicus* of this relaxed way of thinking is to be found in some lines Frege wrote just over a hundred years ago: 'We want to have in sight a goal to strive towards: we want some point to aim at that will guide our steps in the right direction. The word "true" can be used to indicate such a goal for logic, just as can "good" for ethics and "beautiful" for aesthetics'[1]. So for Frege it seems, while the beautiful and the ethically good and the true can all be seen as species of what we strive for, the goals of three of life's most wide-ranging activities, there may be no internal relations between them, no reason to think that they are otherwise closely linked.

Undoubtedly there is something in Frege's suggestion that matches a common way of expressing ourselves in the face of almost anything that brings us aesthetic delight. We have had a beautiful holiday in beautiful surroundings in beautiful company, indicating, I suppose, that each of the said items was to us a source of undisputed pleasure for its own sake. In such reports the word 'beautiful' is used in an entirely anodyne way as the most general term of aesthetic praise, and that will explain very nicely the almost boundless extension of the term. It says so very little and so can be applied easily without the risk of dissent in almost any situation given only that the object in view elicits a favourable response. The suggestion also fits long-established elucidations of beauty reasonably well. Early scholastic thinkers, notably of the Franciscan order, took it to be what pleases and cannot fail to please; much later Kant held it to be a source of universal and necessary disinterested

[1] In Frege, 'Logic' (1897) in *Posthumous Writings* (Chicago, 1979), 128.

delight. Frege may well have seen his predecessors as struggling towards his own broader characterisation

Nevertheless, it may seem as if the anodyne way of talking is a corruption of something far more demanding. The beauty of Couperin's *Leçons de Ténèbres* or the Star of Bethlehem (*ornithogallum pittospermum*) in flower seems to be of a different order than the beauty of a well-turned Question in the House or of a slick advertisement for your friendly local bank, not just different in degree, but different in kind. If we want to mark a special place for such paradigms as my two it will be as well not to reserve the term 'beauty' for the broad generic idea. We have an expression for that already one might say, to wit, 'aesthetic success', and we hardly need to abstract one from elsewhere where it may already be comfortably in place.

A different reason for resisting Frege's thought is provided by the commonplace observation about so much of the art of our own time in which beauty as traditionally understood has been firmly marginalised. Aesthetic success by contrast has surely been achieved, in the eyes of many at least, in ways that earlier thinkers (Frege included I dare say) could scarcely imagine. To preserve something of the traditional usage of the term is a precondition of our being able to say what it is that we moderns have turned our backs on. It is also a precondition for asking whether our backs have been advisedly so turned. Here we should not say on Frege's behalf that what we have turned our backs on has been a particular conception of the beautiful, on the sweetly cloying and sentimental images of the late nineteenth century, say, and to insist that our contemporaries have never abandoned pursuit of beauty conceived of in Fregean terms as aesthetic success. That would be to under-estimate the revolution that has taken place. Something far more general than a recent nineteenth-century inheritance has been jettisoned, without abandoning concern for the aesthetic itself.

We may perhaps detect some hint of this narrower and now rather neglected notion in the scholastic characterisation of the beautiful as what pleases and *cannot fail to please*, as they put it: *id quod natum est placere*; *id quod ex essentia placet*. We may also sense it in Kant's qualification of our delight in the beautiful as a *necessary* delight. Admittedly, it is just possible to see such phrases as these as simply marking the requisite public and shared nature of our favourable responses to what we hold beautiful, but for which publicity the proposed elucidations might miss even the anodynely conceived mark. However, in the case of Kant at least, even if the necessity to which he adverts does serve that important function, taken as what he calls 'exemplary necessity' it also serves to pick out what he called 'a kind of duty' to take delight in what is truly beautiful. The scholastics' phrases also seem to be more exigent than is required simply to rule out mere fortuitous accord in our responses to beautiful things (as if that were even the sort of thing that might have occurred to the thirteenth century mind anyway).

An idea closely related to Kant's, maybe even to that of the mediaeval scholars too, has become something of a commonplace today in the form of the normative claim that beauty is essentially what *merits* the response of pleasure or whatever attitude of favour one's tongue lights on, and while there is room enough to attach this qualification to Frege's own suggestion his own words do not indicate that he himself had thought of doing so. His own suggestion appears less normative than the one we have retrieved from Kant.

The fundamental difference between the normative commitment of Kant and the descriptive one of Frege can be nicely illustrated by reflecting on the story of Odysseus' passage with the Sirens. Their clear and mellifluous song entranced all who heard it. So, as far as being such as to please universally and infallibly no song from ancient times had as good a claim to supreme beauty. Yet, Homer tells us that Circe was well enough disposed towards Odysseus to warn him of the danger he ran in harking to their chant and to convey to him how little the pleasure to which he looked forward was merited. On that score the sisters' production was certainly *not* beautiful and indeed it may have been utterly loathsome, no matter what it sounded like in men's ears. Such adverse judgement is, I fancy, intimated by the description Circe offered of the nymphs' chosen abode (*Ody.* xii. 44–6). In Chapman's somewhat expansive version it runs:[2]

And then observe: They sit amidst a mead;
And round it runnes a hedge or wall
Of dead men's bones: their withered skins and all,
Hung all along about it; and these men
Were such as they had fawned into their Fen,
And then their skins hung on their hedge of bones.

The adverse judgement is intimated by Homer, I say. However, I am aware that the thought that the girls' mephitic environment

---

[2] What Chapman takes six lines to do Homer manages in (less than) three:

ἀλλά τε Σειρῆνες λιγυρῇ θέλγουσιν ἀοιδῇ
ἥμεναι ἐν λειμῶνι, πολὺς δ' ἀμφ' ὀστεόφιν θὶς
ἀνδρῶν πυθομένων, περὶ δὲ ῥινοὶ μινύθουσι.

bears on the aesthetic quality of their song is an obscure one, and I shall not be able to dispel it until I reach the very end of my talk.

What then should we to say of Odysseus' own judgement? Pursuing the normative conception, the right thing must be that the song appeared to him (and to others who heard it) to be supremely beautiful, although in fact it was not so. We need the distinction between *true* beauty, as attested by the senses, and a *mere appearance* of beauty, which Odysseus enjoyed, likewise attested by the senses. To make the distinction between the two we have to be able to give substance to the idea of the response of delight as merited or unmerited as the case may be. Circe's charitable warning illustrates this. It does not suggest how it should be done.

Taking the distinction between genuine and merely apparent beauty on trust for the moment we may use the thought that Homer's story provokes to contest one form of aestheticism that exerts constant appeal – often under the title of 'formalism' – namely, that a mere specification of how something sounds, or looks, or strikes the spectator from a narrowly sensuous (*scilicet* 'formal') point of view must ultimately be what the defining response of our aesthetic pleasure is directed at. If that really were the truth of the matter it would be difficult, impossible even, to understand how we could say that the earlier sailors' judgement of the song was mistaken. For as far as sensory input goes there is surely too little available to give purchase to the thought that the approbation or disapprobation that it calls forth is either merited or not. As long as we find ourselves generally taking delight in some appearance or other we are bound to suppose it earns the accolade. Whether the Sirens' song is produced in the best of intentions or the worst, whether by evil figures or benign water sprites can make no difference to its aesthetic quality. That idea, I believe, is one that we must resist. To do this we do not need to deny that in certain far remote circumstances a song having the same 'appearance' or sensory input as did the Sirens' song could indeed be genuinely beautiful. That admission does not stop us saying that as far as mastbound Odysseus and his earplugged men go, they would still not have been missing a true beauty even if the girls had been amorously taken with Odysseus and had sung their song simply to encourage him and his men on their homeward way.

This reflection may seem so counter-intuitive that its effect may rather be to threaten the idea that the beautiful is what merits our favour than to exemplify it. That is, while that doctrine does indeed serve up a way of thinking about the Sirens as we might wish, it does so in a way that seems to beggar belief. Surely, people are wont to say, there can be no significant aesthetic difference between objects that present the subject with the same sensory input, be that visual input or auditory, or whatever. Since we can imagine the Sirens singing the very the same song either malevolently or benevolently, its beauty, which is after all a feature of its appearance to the senses can hardly be altered by the moral disposition with which they sing it. There is confusion in this way of thinking.[3]

First, under the influence of the idea that the aesthetic is closely allied to the sensory, it identifies what we perceive and judge from the aesthetic point of view with something that is shorn of anything that cannot be captured in terms of sensory input. Making that assumption a name is found for that input. We are inclined to call it 'the appearance' or 'the image' of the object that is experienced, and then the object is said to be beautiful in the light of its presenting the spectator or the audience with a felicitous appearance or image – one, say, which we find ourselves unable to take in without favour. Thus generations of luckless mariners experienced the Sirens' song, and, unable to resist the charm of its appearance as it fell upon their ears, they sailed to their deaths. Its beauty was quite lethal.

It is notable in this way of thinking that what is thought of as the proper object of our aesthetic judgement is not so much the song as the appearance that the song presents. Better put, perhaps, the beauty of the song is entirely dependent on our response to something else, namely an appearance which has been identified with unadorned sensory input. Yet one ought to say appearances conceived of like this are not objects of perception at all, and it can not be they that are beautiful or not, but the song itself that the sailors heard. This point acquires focus as soon as one sees it mirroring a fateful false step in philosophy's reflections about our perception of the world around us.

Heroes such as Descartes, Locke, Berkeley, Hume, Leibniz and the author of the first edition of the *Critique of Pure Reason*, have thought of the proper objects of perception as impressions or sensations or representations, objects distinct from whatever it was that gave rise to these appearances. In their wake successive cohorts of undergraduates have sweated to explain how starting from that obvious-seeming and often uncontested truth we could possibly acquire perceptual knowledge of the world around us. Release from the trap only came as we learnt to say with Thomas Reid that while

---

[3] The confusion may lie in the thought about what we can imagine. After all, if it was the appearance of the song that had that effect on the sailors, it might be supposed to have the same effect if sung by the good hearted as by the bad. Only the good hearted may be expected to know that and to remain resolutely and virtuously silent. A change of heart would require that they change their tune.

we have the sensory experiences and sensory input that we do, they are not what we perceive but are merely the stimuli whose occurrence is the perception of their distal causes. Now just as it is a mistake to say that the true character of what we perceive depends on the nature of the representations with which we are immediately presented, so too it is mistaken to suppose that the aesthetic character of what the sailors heard must lie in the sensory input with which they were presented. It isn't, for what they were immediately presented with was the song, and its aesthetic character depends on much more than the nature of the auditory stimuli whose occurrence enabled them to hear it.

The mistake is a pervasive one, not the sorry possession of philosophers alone. Most of the major museums today do a thriving trade in retailing faithful replicas of some of their choice possessions. At least they are sold as faithful and indiscernible replicas, and that selling point is often supported by information about recent strides forward taken by the technology of laser scanning and so forth which at last has enabled us to produce resin-based objects with exactly the same appearance as this or that masterpiece in their collections. The sensory input of the original and of the replica is the same, so the appearance is the same, so the aesthetic quality can scarcely be different. At £34.99 that little Egyptian figurine must be a bargain. When it is unpacked at home however it looks quite wrong, even though the sensory input is unchanged.

Am I then saying that our aesthetic appreciation of things has nothing to do with appearance? Certainly not, only the appearance that matters must not be identified with sensory input. Rather, we are concerned with things from the aesthetic point of view when we focus on the way in which they present themselves to us in experience. The sailors of the Odyssey judged the Sirens' song to be beautiful on the basis of what it sounded like to them, the way in which they experienced it and the way in which they felt themselves drawn to that terrible fen. As soon as we put it like that we can see that there is ample scope for us to say that the appearance that something has, the way it presents itself to our eyes or ears, will depend in large part on the beliefs we have about it. I see something, or hear something not as a bare representation but as having a history and a character, and the way in which I think about its history and its character impinges on the experience that I have of it, and on my assessment of it as beautiful or not. My knowledge that the figurine is a mass produced replica enters into my experience of it and accounts for my judgement of it as somehow tawdry.

A vivid example of this important truth is provided in an autobiographical sketch of Thomas De Quincey's called 'The

Affliction of Childhood'. When he had just turned six his slightly elder sister and loved playmate Jane died. He records that:

> with her death there was connected an incident which made a most fearful impression on myself, deepening my tendencies to thoughtfulness and abstraction beyond what would seem credible for my years. If there was one thing in this world from which, more than from any other, nature had forced me to revolt, it was brutality and violence. Now, a whisper arose in my family that a female servant, who by accident was drawn off from her proper duties to attend my sister Jane for a day or two, had on one occasion treated her harshly, if not brutally; and as this ill-tempered treatment happened within three or four days of her death, so that the occasion of it must have been some fretfulness in the poor child caused by her sufferings, naturally there was a sense of awe and indignation diffused through the family. I believe the story never reached my mother, and possibly it was exaggerated; but upon me the effect was terrific. I did not often see the person charged with this cruelty; but when I did, my eyes sought the ground; nor could I have borne to look her in the face; not, however in any spirit that could be called anger. The feeling which fell upon me was a shuddering horror, as upon a first glimpse of the truth that I was in a world of evil and strife.

Let us suppose that the story never did reach his mother's ears, or that if it did she did not believe it. Mother and son would have received nearly enough the same sensory stimuli in encountering the serving woman, but given the difference in their beliefs about her the experience they had of her was markedly different. Her appearance to Thomas was unbearably horrible, unpleasant in the extreme; to his mother she appeared quite neat and unalarming. For the two of them the aesthetic character of their experience was radically different, but what they perceived, the serving woman going about her business was the same, and the input to their perceptual systems likewise.

As I express myself in these terms you may suspect that I am preparing myself to recommend some version of aesthetic relativism. The aesthetic character that things have depends on how they appear to us in our experience, and our experience of them depends on our beliefs and expectations and so forth about them. So won't it be the case that the aesthetic character of the things we experience is different according to the differences there are between the beliefs and expectations that perceiving subjects have about them? Hence the Sirens' song was beautiful to the sailors who succumbed to its enchantment, but to someone predisposed against them by their ghastly taste in garden design – remember the bony hedges draped with rotting human skins? – it would not have been beautiful, but loathesome. If that were where my thought was tending then I should hardly be able to retain the idea that the beautiful must merit favour. For however the song fell upon sailors' ears, however beautiful it struck them in the light of their beliefs as they sailed closer and closer, on that score it fell short. Yet saying what I have just said, how can I resist the thought that given their beliefs the Sirens' singing was indeed truly beautiful?

Obviously enough we would say that De Quincey's experience of the family servant took the form that it did because he believed it to be true that she had maltreated his sister. His mother's experience depended on her assumption that nothing was amiss being true. Consequently, the correctness of any aesthetic judgement they may have found themselves making that went beyond how the woman struck them personally can hardly be understood except by reference to the facts of the case. A mistaken belief about the object of my attention will not prevent the object appearing to me in the light of that belief, but it may mean that I am in thrall to an apparent rather than a genuine beauty. So I suggest that it does make good sense to say of the deluded sailors as they approached the fatal fen that the song they heard appeared beautiful to them but was not really so. It was not really beautiful because in some way that we have still to explore, their response to it was less than fully informed. Among other things perhaps they believed that harking to it carried no risk and that their experience of the song was deformed by that falsehood. The threat of relativism can be staved off, that is, if one deploys the idea of a fully informed and knowledgeable response to the objects of one's attention and insists that it is that which determines whether they genuinely possess the aesthetic properties one wants to ascribe to them or whether they merely appear to have those properties.

You might think that Homer's own tale counts against me here. For surely Odysseus *was* fully informed about the Sirens, informed by Circe, that is. She told him what would happen if he didn't stop up the ears of his comrades and if he didn't prevent himself from seizing the tiller by having them tie him securely to the mast. The knowledge that he had apparently made no impact on the way he experienced the song, or so the tale goes. Odysseus found the song just as enchanting as his ignorant predecessors had done; still he found it beautiful. So again it seems that the fully informed experience of the song was one that no man could resist, and its appearance to *informed* Odysseus could be nothing other than the appearance of a song that was truly beautiful. Even so, we still shan't say that it merited that devoted response.

I am inclined to think that all Circe told Odysseus was that it was dangerous to listen to the Sirens, and, notoriously, the thought that some activity is a risky one adds spice to the way a certain sort of man regards it. Certainly the truth that it is risky or dangerous to undertake a particular activity need not detract from its worth. It would be wrong to deny on that score that mountaineering is a manly sport or that someone who had traversed a particularly hazardous route up some peak had made a beautiful ascent. No, what Circe had failed to draw to Odysseus' attention was that the Sirens' serenade was calculated to lure him and his men to their deaths, where the expression 'was calculated to' does not so much express an assessment of risk as imply a moral assessment of the nymphs and their design. They were through and through wicked and the aesthetic character of their song was imbued with their wickedness so that anyone who perceived that and experienced the Sirens' singing in the light of that perception must have found it loathesome.

Still, you might think, Odysseus wasn't stupid. And Circe knew he wasn't stupid. He must have been able to work out for himself from her warning that those girls were naughty girls, yet even possessed of that presumptive knowledge he still needed to be fastened to the mast, and still found the singing to be alluring. So it seems that moralising the situation does not serve. The trouble here lies not in the moralisation of the situation but in the inadequacy of the moralisation that I have lent it with my rather flippant attribution to Odysseus of the thought that the girls were naughty. For that suggests that they were up to no more than a bit of lighthearted mischief which one might easily enough condone as long as one doesn't get caught up in it. But of course that is not how we should think of them at all.

One might also reflect here that the more fully thought through assessment of those monsters, in the absence of which Odysseus would not have been in my way of talking fully informed, could not come about all at once. It would have needed closer acquaintance with them and the suffering they had inflicted on their earlier victims for it to be firmly anchored in his breast. In just the same way we might say our own historical distance from the Claudian Emperors makes it hard for us to make their awfulness vivid to ourselves without study and the exercise of imagination. Merely being told by Suetonius that they were a bad lot will not quite do the trick. However, I suggest that had Odysseus had that closer experience, or else exercised his imagination with effect – perhaps he should have read his Homer – then the information Circe provided would have allowed him to reorganise the way he thought about the bewitching Sirens. Not only would he then have regarded it as frivolous to speak of them as I just did as naughty, but his horror of them, akin to De Quincy's horror at the serving woman, would not have made it possible for him to hear their song as beautiful. Since we know this moral assessment of the Sirens to be correct, neither Odysseus nor anyone else in that well-anchored informed state could have listened to their song with delight. Hence it was anything but beautiful. We may even think it right to suppose that in that well-anchored and informed condition Odysseus could have afforded to steer his vessel himself and dispense with his hempen bonds while sailing by.

I introduced the Sirens to illustrate the difference between the descriptive and normative view of beauty and to point up another view of it than the one Frege offered us. But it is not at all certain that I have succeeded on the latter point. After all I have already more or less admitted that the advocate of the Fregean view can say that I have pointed accurately enough to a general constraint on aesthetic success but not to a preferential focus within the broader spectrum. Going normative you might say is something that the Fregean can perfectly well envisage even if Frege himself did not. This observation is accurate enough and, since my earlier reservations about the generic concept of beauty still stand, it shows that work of further specification still remains to be done. Nevertheless the labour we have put in already may not be entirely wasted since it does allow me to point to one illusion that underlies one way in which practising artists of our own times have sometimes sought to revolutionise their art.

A thought that many have found appealing – as a programme I would tentatively attribute it to Marinetti, though I am happy to accept correction on that score – is that a purely aesthetic interest in the material of the world is blocked by the practical context in which it impinges on us. A viable project for the artist is to allow the beholder to view it out of context and for itself, so to speak. Decontextualising the processes of decay, say, the wounds of war, the wreckage of traffic accidents, discovers in these things an aesthetic purity that the artist can reveal. Keeping the practical implications of the subject matter at bay by his distancing manoeuvres the artist allows true beauty to shine through. But this is nonsense. For there is, I repeat, no pure appearance that the beauty is the beauty of; what has the aesthetic quality that is on display must be the process of decay itself, the wounds of war and the wreckage of the crash. But then decontextualising is merely a name for ignoring the true nature of what we are shown, sensitivity to which alone allows us to form a sound aesthetic judgement of what we see. The decontextualising programme is mirrored well enough in an image of the wised-up, fully informed Odysseus musing to himself that the true beauty of the Sirens' song was really only appreciated by those lucky fellows who ended up as bones and rotting skin hung on the nymphs' garden hedge. That, I have argued, is entirely false.

What then should the step forward be? The weakness of the present position is that my speaking of beauty as what merits our favour has been given no content apart from the negative one that it must sustain delight in the full knowledge of what it is. Seeing the Sirens' song as a manifestation of their corrupt nature and grasping the idea of corruption as we do, delight at their singing is unsustainable. But we must say more than that since otherwise it might be that anything may be beautiful that we find pleasure in and which isn't badly flawed in one way or another. Yet that is hardly distinguishable from the anodyne notion that I started with and desired to replace. It is less the idea of beauty as what merits our favour than of what does not repel it, and that is quite a different matter.

One source of the difficulty philosophy has encountered at this point must be located in the very undemanding nature of the response in terms of which it has been customary to discuss the subject. From antiquity to our own day favour, pleasure and delight have been the recurrent favourites, and perhaps it takes too little to merit them. I am not quite sure why it has seemed so natural to talk in such terms, but I surmise that it may have something to do with a kind of professional distaste philosophy has for passion. It is as if to talk about passion dispassionately we have to talk in dispassionate terms. The trouble is that once we do that the subject matter tends to leach away. Someone who was not a philosopher and who understood this well was Cyril Connolly, and I find some remarks he made at the start of an essay of his entitled 'In Quest of Rococo' highly suggestive. He wrote:

> One can describe a passion only in terms of passion. Many years ago I noticed that certain works of art brought tears to my eyes. Lines of Horace, Dryden, Rochester, Pope, the last paintings of Watteau, Mozart's *Voi che sapete*, while in the summer of 1938 two small buildings – Palladio's Roman theatre at Vicenza and the Amalienberg pavilion outside Munich – were added to my list ...What had they in common? Perfection or the ideal of perfection – a lyrical conception of humanity, a response to all that is transitory and fugaceous, a calligraphy of farewell.[4]

[4] In Cyril Connolly, *Previous Convictions* (Hamish Hamilton, 1963), pp. 48–60.

Anthony Savile

Connolly's tears were scarcely tears of pleasure or of delight, I think; more plausibly they were tears occasioned by the felt recognition that something he longed for and perhaps even feared impossible was realised. Tears of joy, one could perhaps say with some understanding of their appropriateness. What makes them appropriate is what they are recognition of, to wit, the perfection experienced in the poetry or in the building or, looking back to my own two paradigms, perfection in the Star of Bethlehem or in Couperin's *Ténèbres*. In all such cases I surmise we respond with joy to something like the experience of an ideal as realised in the object we call beautiful, and that is clearly something far more specific than is needed to accommodate the generic and Fregean notion even when that is adjusted to make room for the normativity I have insisted on in ruling out the Sirens' chant as a worthy paradigm. But is this revised characterisation of the beautiful plausible? Is it even coherent?

As for its plausibility, that you must test against your own experience, your own and that of others who have tried to capture in words what has most deeply moved them in their aesthetic moments. This is not a matter of rigorous proof; only of acceptable description. Perhaps some confirmation of its correctness though can be had from a figure very different in temperament from Connolly. I have in mind Simone Weil, who spoke of her own paradigms, the finest English and Provençal poetry, as eliciting what she called 'a joy which by reason of its unmixed purity hurts, a pain which by reason of its unmixed purity brings peace'. Although she doesn't explicitly speak of the sense of perfection that brings pain and peace, I find it hard to understand her readiness to talk of the unmixed purity of her joy except as a response to something like perception of unalloyed perfection in the poetry that so moved her, painful like the unshaded brilliance of the sun, yet joyous because so ardently desired.

Let me suppose that you will not reject my tentative description out of hand as untrue to our lives as lived. You may think that the real test it has to sustain is of coherence. Not that it is inherently self-contradictory, for if it were that it would not even get past the first stage of scrutiny, but that it just does not cohere well enough with other things that we think and say about the beautiful. A first thing one may say is that my suggestion fits in too badly with the history of our reflection about the subject. To this my response must be that it does no more than redress the balance of a tradition that for a long time has supposed that once it is allowed that the beautiful is not in the seventeenth and eighteenth century way of speaking a 'real' property of objects, once it is admitted that to call something beautiful is not to bring it under a concept, that it is not to make a 'logical' judgement about it, as Kant put it, then we can do nothing more than elucidate the concept from the side of subjective response. However, it is easy to forget that there is a long tradition too that finds enlightenment in asking what the subjective response of joy or delight is response to without supposing that that can only be a fully objective, 'real' property of objects. William of Auvergne for one, a significant figure in thirteenth century aesthetics, had it that the beautiful is that goodness or decor that pleases our sight and inward vision and that we call bad things ugly which our minds abominate and spit out.[5] For him the pleasure of our inward vision is provoked not by a 'real' quality of the object but by its goodness or decor; what our minds spit out is not 'real' (to wit, primary) quality but the ugly object's badness.

A far greater figure than the Bishop of Paris was Kant, and we should not forget that one of his principal struggles in the *Critique of Judgement* was to find a suitable internal object of our aesthetic delight that makes the rose or the statue a truly beautiful one, one that demands and requires our loving approbation. The form of finality that such things were said by Kant to enjoy, their purposiveness without a purpose, is certainly obscure in its detail, but it is analogous enough in structure both with William's goodness and decor and with my own suggestion about perfection to allow me to deny that all connection with history has been lost. Indeed, in one way the suggestion I am offering you is very close indeed to another famous claim of Kant's in this same area which has puzzled and intrigued his readers. I have in mind his assertion in the penultimate section of the *Critique* that beauty is the symbol of morality and that that is what ultimately underpins beauty's place in our spiritual economy. What has puzzled and intrigued has often been how Kant could say such a thing since to us it seems so obvious that beautiful things are not symbols, let alone symbols of morality. That retort assumes too quickly that we understand him.

As Kant means it, a symbol is nothing other than an individual thing that can be presented to experience and which has a structure analogous to that of some Idea that experience cannot grasp. We might say that as a symbol a thing of beauty condenses a way of thinking, and gives us some assurance that that way of thinking is adapted to the world. My speaking of our joy in the beautiful as prompted by the recognition of an ideal as realised in the particular

[5] 'Hanc bonitatem vocamus pulchritudinem seu decorem quam approbat et in qua complacet sibi visus noster seu aspectus noster interior. Malum autem turpe dicamus de turpidine quam per se respuit et abominatur mens nostra.' *De Bono et Malo*, 206 (ms. Balliol).

object is plainly continuous with that. If we baulk at Kant's suggestion that what beauty symbolises is what he sees as the necessity and universality of the moral law, we would not be moving so very far from him in spirit to say that the beautiful is a symbol of the good, where that notion is not restrictively a moral one but designates whatever it is that we most care about and which can be presented to experience in perfect and condensed form. Were I to vie with Kant for a snappy slogan, instead of saying that the beautiful is the symbol of morality I should suggest it is the perfect appearance of the good. Right or wrong, there is no break with history here[6].

A more direct dissatisfaction finds matter to quarrel with in my suggestion that the response of joy or awe is a response to experienced perfection.[7] That, it is felt, makes no sense, or if it does make sense it is suggestive of a falsehood, not a truth. We cannot surely divorce the idea of perfection from the thought of what it is that is perfect, yet those things we find beautiful are very rarely perceived as perfect of their kind. Just think how silly it would be to suppose that Kant's ideal of beauty, a beautiful man or woman (Cf. *Critique of Judgement* §17), is one whose perfection one judges in their appearance. Interestingly, it is again Kant who has the right thing to say here. Effectively we find our awareness of the person, the way they present themselves to our experience, a condensing of an ideal we cherish, a condensation we experience without hesitation or resistance. The perceived perfection is not *of* the man or woman, it is perceived *in* them. The perfection we judge ourselves to confront is not straightforwardly the perfection of the flower, of the man or woman or of the natural scenery, rather it is of some good that these things are experienced as embodying and which can only be articulated in the particular case. To quote Simone Weil again: 'Beauty is a carnal attraction that seizes the flesh demanding passage to the soul'.[8]

Speaking in this rather opaque way I might be thought to have abandoned an assumption that I have been making implicitly all along. This is the assumption that our judgements of beauty are properly evaluable as true or false. For on my account of the matter there seems to be nothing in the objects we call beautiful that answers to the perfection I say we are sensitive to, nothing that is

---

[6] To dispel anxiety that comes with the term 'symbol' we do well to remember its etymology which suggests no more than that the beautiful 'runs along with' the good, or *latine* that it 'concurs' with it.

[7] Cf. Simone Weil again: 'distance is the soul of the beautiful'; 'all other objects of desire we want to devour, it we want to be'.

[8] Quotations from S. Weil are all from *Gravity and Grace*, (Routledge, Kegan and Paul, 1952), pp. 136–137.

beyond our readiness to make the judgement that we are confronted with true beauty. Criteria are unavailable. Now I do not suppose that this is the place to argue this well-trodden issue. But it is in place for me to say that I do not accept this. There is no inconsistency between acknowledging that there is nothing to guide us at the end of the day in thinking that something is beautiful or not except reflective judgement and supposing that our judgement may be right or wrong and the assertions it encourages us to make true or false. So here I merely state my position and leave it at that. However, given what I have said already there is good reason to use the eruption of this topic as a point of leverage for a last visit to the Sirens.

Suppose it be allowed that there is something right in the idea that those things we find supremely beautiful condense perfectly in their appearance a certain ideal. Notoriously the ideals we commit ourselves to, often in the name of love of the good, differ from time to time and differ from society to society. Is it so certain that as the Sirens were found by Odysseus's precursors to condense to perfection an ideal dear to them their song was not a beautiful song after all? A carnal attraction that passes directly to the soul seems to describe exactly how the song was experienced by those men, and perhaps by Odysseus too.

Rather than reiterate what I have already said I shall respond to this thought by adverting to a film that has attracted philosophical attention, to Leni Riefenstahl's *Triumph des Willens*, the striking documentary she made of the 1934 Nuremberg rally. Of it Mary Devereaux has recently written: 'At once masterful and morally repugnant, this deeply troubling film epitomises a general problem that arises with art. It is both beautiful and evil. ... It is this conjunction of beauty and evil that explains why the film is so disturbing'.[9] Now certainly the film was an instant artistic success. As Devereaux reminds us, it won the 1935 German National Film Prize and the Gold Medal at Venice. It also won the Grand Prix at the 1937 Paris Film Festival. It is also plain what it is about it that encourages her to call it beautiful. She observes that Riefenstahl displays great skill in gripping the spectator's attention and in 'generating some of the enthusiasm and excitement felt by rally participants' and that she used the devices of theme and characterisation, symbolism and point of view to tell a story – the story of the New Germany – that created a powerful vision of Hitler and National Socialism.

[9] Mary Devereaux, 'Beauty and Evil; the case of Leni Riefenstahl's *Triumph of the Will*', in Jerrold Levinson (ed.), *Aesthetics and Ethics, Essays at the Intersection* (Cambridge, 1998), pp. 227–256.

That vision, Devereaux goes on, is one in which the military values of loyalty and courage, unity, discipline and obedience are wedded to a heroic conception of life and elements of German *völkisch* mythology. In Riefenstahl's hands, an annual political rally is transformed into a larger historical and symbolic event. *Triumph of the Will* presents the Nazi world as a kind of Valhalla, 'a place apart, surrounded by clouds and mist, peopled by heroes and ruled from above by the gods'. Seen from the perspective of the film, Hitler is the hero of a grand narrative. He is both leader and saviour, a new Siegfried come to restore a defeated Germany to its ancient splendour.

This description conveys very well how the film manages to condense or embody an ideal in a cinematic experience of great power. In particular it must have made that ideal seem real (or realisable), indeed it may well have seemed to Riefenstahl herself an ideal which right-minded patriots of the day would gladly embrace, and which her film would encourage them to adopt. But is it really beautiful? Does it merit our unresisting admiration. Not surely once we view it from the point of view of the fully informed judge. As Devereaux herself observes it is a morally repugnant film, the song I would say of a latterday Siren, and one which cannot entrance us (however much we may admire the artistry with which it was made) once we have seized what it is that is so repulsive about the ideal that it embodies. It is that informed moral perception that absolutely inhibits the passage of what captivates the flesh on its way into the soul.[10] Whatever it may be that is so troubling about this film it can-

[10] We do well to remember Hume here who declares that his good judges, who are above all men of sound understanding (apart from being practised, discriminating and unprejudiced) are thought of as possessing a developed moral sense that gives them the edge over classic tragedians and enables them to attain an aesthetic estimation of those authors that is superior to that of the best contemporary critics. The view I have been proposing is entirely in line with Hume's thought. 'The poet's *monument more durable than brass*, must fall to the ground like common brick or clay, were men to make no allowance for the continual revolutions of manners and customs, and would admit of nothing but what was suitable to the prevailing fashion. Must we throw aside the pictures of our ancestors because of their ruffs and farthingales? But where the ideas of morality and decency alter from one age to another, and where vicious manners are described, without being marked with the proper characters of blame and disapprobation, this must be allowed to disfigure the poem, and to be a real deformity. I cannot, nor is it proper I should, enter into such sentiments. ... And where a man is confident of the rectitude of that moral standard by which he judges, he is justly jealous of it, and will not pervert the sentiments of his heart for a moment, in complaisance to any writer whatsoever' ('Of the Standard of Taste', para. 31).

not be its extraordinary conjunction of beauty and evil. Those who recognise its evil must deny its beauty; and those who miss its evil will merely take for beauty a false semblance of it.

There may appear to be a difference here between Homer's originals and the latterday version. I took it that the marine creatures' song was loathsome because once fully informed we could not avoid hearing their singing either as an expression of their nature, like the ghastly hedge that they had constructed around their meadow or as the intentionally chosen instrument of their wicked designs on Odysseus and his men. The latterday Siren sought to enchant the masses with a message that was corrupt in itself. But does this difference make a difference?

Earlier on I observed somewhat obscurely that the environment the Sirens had made for themselves intimated an adverse judgement of their song and I also said that that song was imbued with their evil character. One way of understanding this idea that I might have encouraged would be to think that informed as we are of the sisters' moral character we cannot but see what they have made as awful. Their garden and their song express their awfulness just as they are experienced in the light of this knowledge. Their song is imbued with their wickedness just because correct judgement of it depends on its being heard in the light of the knowledge we have of its origin. That was not what I meant though and if that were all there were to it I could not say, as I have done, that their song would still not be beautiful even if it had been sung from the purest of motives. And as far as the garden went the girls presumably constructed that for their own delight and our revulsion at their construction depends as much on the nature of its materials as on their way of gathering them.

A more satisfactory approach opened up by the last part of my talk is to say that garden and song both express an ideal which is through and through rotten, yet which is just the sort of thing that would delight their authors' perverted minds.[11] The ideal that spoke to them will have been one of their own domination over the world of men and of humankind. Putting it like that the song already has a character of its own that lends itself to their wretched design and

[11] Perhaps we should not forget that the Sirens were not human and that they were only doing what came naturally to them. So maybe the judgement of perversion should be revised for that is arguably a judgement that is implicitly relativised to the kind of thing under consideration. However, that will not affect the ugliness of their song, since the ideal that their singing expresses is one that cannot but repel us, and the terms 'ugly' and 'beautiful' are terms that relate to specifically human values and valuations.

does not acquire its character from the design with which it is sung. The ideal that it embodies is one that we cannot reflectively endorse, though as the Riefenstahl example shows, it is one that is liable to exert power over the unwary. We can see why the unalerted mariners should have sailed to their deaths. If the sailors were moths to that flame the flame was no purer as it burned at sea than it was on celluloid. The difference there is between the old Sirens and the new makes no difference to that.

At the start I asked what was the connection between the beautiful and the good and rejected the idea that beauty simply is the aesthetically good, the good in the supposedly sealed-off domain of sensory appearance. In its place I have proposed that once we do justice to the beautiful by allowing it a specificity that marks it out from other qualities of things we find aesthetically engaging, the only way we can account for the way it merits or demands our devotion must lie in the way we find it giving body in perception to a reflectively sustainable ideal or good to which we are already at least dimly sensitive. At the same time I have tried to make it plausible that our sensitivity to the good in question can be taken in a way that is central to our understanding of beauty while leaving little room for any unwelcome relativism and doing nothing to impugn the thought that our best, fully informed, judgements that this thing or that is beautiful can lay claim to truth.

Misplacing freedom, displacing the imagination: Cavell and Murdoch on the fact/value distinction

STEPHEN MULHALL

The view that matters of fact and matters of value are categorically distinct, and that any credible account of ethics must begin from an acknowledgement of that distinction, has been a constant topic of debate in analytical moral philosophy throughout the twentieth century. It is not, however, as simple as it may at first appear to establish an uncontroversial articulation of the view under discussion, because in the course of the debate's evolution that view has been defined in a number of very different and not obviously equivalent ways.

Moore gave new life to this venerable Humean theme when he accused Mill and Spenser of committing the naturalistic fallacy – of defining the meaning of 'goodness' (a word he took to denote a non-natural property) in terms of words denoting natural properties, such as pleasure or happiness. For Moore, however, the fallacy in the naturalistic fallacy did not essentially turn on its proponents' reliance upon references to the natural realm; for the same basic error would have been committed by anyone who proposed to identify the property of goodness with another non-natural property. Fundamentally, the problem was one of attempting to define the undefinable: goodness could not be equated with any natural or non-natural property because Moore believed that goodness was a simple and hence essentially undefinable property – one whose essence could therefore only be intuited. Since this line of reasoning was based on a startlingly implausible vision of definition as exclusively a matter of breaking a given *definiendum* into component parts, and since it resulted in a global interdict which made no essential reference to any alleged criterial difference between the natural and the non-natural realms, it is multiply ironic that Moore's intuitionistic identification of a naturalistic fallacy should so often have been the immediate source of contemporary moral philosophy's fervent belief in a distinction between fact and value.

Even as that belief re-rooted itself, however, it was redefined; for after the impact of logical positivism and the more general linguistic turn in analytical philosophy, the belief in a distinction between fact and value came to be expressed as the belief in a distinction between descriptive and evaluative propositions – or, as this thesis was more pithily put, in a gap between 'is' and 'ought'. Stevenson's work, for example, makes a sharp separation between the factual and the emotive elements of moral disagreements, so that on his view complete agreement on the facts of the given matter could co-exist with complete disagreement on the evaluative attitudes they elicit in individual observers. Hare's adaptation of this emotivist vision identified key logical constraints upon those who committed themselves to a specific evaluation of any particular state of affairs, but explicitly argued that no such specific evaluative judgement could be derived from a set of factual premises without the addition of an evaluative premise – and his perennial problem with the fanatic (e.g. the sincere Nazi who is prepared to acknowledge that he should have been subject to extermination had he been a Jew) makes it clear that imperatival logic together with a clear view of the facts offers no significant constraint on an individual's initial choice of evaluative premises.

However, it is not at all obvious that the fact/value thesis and the is/ought thesis should be treated as equivalent. To do so would amount to assuming that every evaluative judgement is a judgement of obligation or duty, and that every descriptive judgement is essentially non-evaluative. The former assumption presupposes what is at the very least a highly controversial view of morality; the latter faces problems with McDowell's and Williams' thick moral concepts (judgements about, for example, courage or prudence at once describe and appraise the situations to which they apply, and the two functions are not even analytically separable). As for the is/ought distinction taken on its own terms, Hare quickly found himself faced with counter-examples such as Searle's promise-maker, certain facts about whose utterances (i.e. her uttering certain English words in certain circumstances) appear to entail conclusions about how she ought to behave. Do we really want to say, as Hare suggests in response, that learning how to employ the concept of promising involves acceding to a logically separable moral principle? We shall return to this question below.

The discontinuous recent history of the thesis about fact and value, taken together with the accumulation of lines of criticism directed at each of its very different articulations, suggests that it will be exceedingly difficult to find a formulation of it that is at once clear and plausible; and this has no doubt contributed to the decline in its popularity amongst contemporary moral philosophers. But this exercise in genealogical criticism leaves unaddressed the root cause of its past popularity, and of its continuing intuitive appeal both to philosophers and to morally reflective individuals; for it still seems to be the case that many of those who engage with the thesis find it difficult to shake off a sense that it must be getting at something undeniably true, even if that something turns out to be trivial rather than fundamental, a matter of common sense rather than metaphysics. In this essay, I will argue that we can make some progress in addressing this diagnostic question by examining the work of two of the earliest and most penetrating critics of this thesis – Iris Murdoch and Stanley Cavell. For their writings aim not only to turn us away from adherence to the thesis, but also to help us understand who we are to have been seduced by it in the first place.

1 Fact and value: the ubiquity of morals

Iris Murdoch was making clear her objections to the fact/value thesis from the outset of her career as a philosopher, most significantly in a series of papers in the 1950s.[1] But the theme continues to dominate in her most recent, and most substantial, philosophical text, *Metaphysics as a Guide to Morals*;[2] and in that book, it becomes clearer than ever before just why she takes the thesis so seriously. For in her view it runs counter to the following fundamental idea:

> The moral life is not intermittent or specialised, it is not a peculiar or separate area of our existence ... [W]e are all always deploying and directing our energy, refining or blunting it, purifying or corrupting it ... 'Sensibility' is a word which may be in place here ... Happenings in consciousness so vague as to be almost non-existent can have 'moral colour' ... ('But are you saying that every single second has a moral tag?' Yes, roughly.) (MGM, p. 495)

Those who believe in the fact/value distinction are committed to thinking of our states of consciousness as only intermittently or partially engaged with moral value, since in their view values generally and moral values specifically form an essentially distinct region of our experience (or at least an analytically distinct aspect or dimension of it). Certainly, in so far as our experience is directed at the factual, its focus and orientation must be capable of being understood in terms that are entirely value-free. For Murdoch, however, this fails to acknowledge that all our states of consciousness and action presuppose discrimination, and any such discrimination is subject to moral evaluation:

[1] Now collected in Conradi (ed.), *Existentialisists and Mystics* (London: Chatto and Windus, 1997).
[2] Iris Murdoch, *Metaphysics as a Guide to Morals* (London: Chatto and Windus, 1992) – hereafter MGM.

Stephen Mulhall

> The moral point is that 'facts' are set up as such by human (that is moral) agents. Much of our life is taken up by truth-seeking, imagining, questioning. We relate to facts through truth and truthfulness, and come to recognise and discover that there are different modes and levels of insight and understanding. In many familiar ways *various* values pervade and *colour* what we take to be the reality of our world; wherein we constantly evaluate our own values and those of others, and judge and determine forms of consciousness and modes of being. (MGM, p. 26)

The element of this claim that challenges the fact/value thesis most intimately is Murdoch' correlation of truth and truthfulness; for this reflects her Simone Weil-inspired conviction that human fact-seeking activities are imbued with evaluative structure and significance – that the concept of truth is internally related not only to reality but also to beauty and goodness.

The most obvious of these links is activated when the object of one's truth-seeking consciousness is another person. In this case, perceiving truthfully, perceiving the reality before one, means coming to see that person as one's other (possessed of consciousness, moral judgement and value, functioning as a unique kind of limit on one's actions) and coming to see her as she truly is (with a particular nature or character, with a particular array of needs and wants, with a particular claim upon us). Both aspects of this task require the overcoming of one's own limitations or distortions, the eradication or transcendence of whatever egoistic fantasies might be blocking one's capacity to perceive the reality or truth of the other person; both, in effect, require that one transform the texture of one's consciousness, making it more responsive to reality and less permeated by illusion. In short, accurate perception here entails acknowledging the moral claims the other makes upon us, and accurate perception is itself a moral requirement.

Murdoch sees a parallel set of connections embodied in the process of coming to appreciate beauty in art and in nature. The idea here is that learning to appreciate beauty is a matter of learning to attend properly to beautiful things, which means learning to contemplate both their integrity or unity, their independent reality, and often learning to contemplate the aspects of reality to which they direct us by their truthful representation of the world:

> Art is informative and entertaining, it condenses and clarifies the world, directing attention upon particular things ... Art illuminates accident and contingency and the general muddle of life, the limitations of time and the discursive intellect, so as to enable us to survey complex or horrible things which would otherwise

258

> appal us … It calms and invigorates, it gives us energy by unify-
> ing, possibly by purifying, our feelings. In enjoying great art we
> experience a clarification and concentration and perfection of our
> own consciousness … Great art inspires because it is separate, it
> is for nothing, it is for itself. (MGM, p. 8)

The thought of Simone Weil behind this paean of praise is that to
recognise an object as beautiful is to refrain from consuming it, to
want it not to change; the experience of the beautiful thus places a
check on the ego's desire to ingest reality, to project its own fantasies
and desires upon the world in which it finds itself. It works to disrupt the self's addiction to illusion and its refusal to accept reality
as it truly is, and thereby purifies our consciousness.

Murdoch goes on to make parallel claims about those of our
activities which bring us closer to the facts, to the way things really
are. Academic scholarship, the labours of historians and scientists,
craftsmanship or technical skill of any kind, even the simple capacity to attend without distraction to what is presently within our field
of perception – all these activities are imbued with value not only in
the sense that they presuppose a particular articulation of the relevant field of attention (a conceptualisation which gives expression
to a particular set of interests, concerns and values), but also in that
they all depend upon recognising the constraints of the real and of
truth. Their proper exercise therefore amounts to a disciplining of
the self, a refusal to cover over reality by fantasy or self-deception.
In this sense, a devotion to truth is necessarily a devotion to truthfulness, and that means to a transcendence of egotism – a deepening capacity to place the self properly in the world, which can only
be done by recognising the reality and value of that which is not the
self.

The vision of morality that emerges from these kinds of consideration is one which suggests that 'spiritual pilgrimage (transforma-
tion-renewal-salvation) is at the centre and essence of morality,
upon whose success and well-being the health of other kinds of
moral reaction and thinking is likely to depend' (MGM, p. 367).
The essentially egoistic energies that permeate and generate the texture of the self's everyday inner life (energies explored in Freudian
psychoanalysis) can be transformed only by transforming their orientation; they must be re-directed, away from the ego and its interests and towards that which is not the ego. The broadest characterisation of the various techniques by which this transformation can
be effected is that of attending to particulars: we must either attune
our consciousness to its objects, or (if we fail) those objects will be
attuned to one's consciousness, to its fantasies and distortions – for

on Murdoch's account, the reality of our world is determined, the facts are set up as such, by the morally inflected discriminations of our consciousness. In this sense, every subject has the objects she deserves.

Since such discriminations can be thought of as generating pictures or images of the world, and since Murdoch holds that imagery is fundamental to human understanding, she often puts the point in terms of the imagination. She talks of 'a continuous breeding of imagery in the consciousness which is, for better or worse, a function of moral change' (MGM, p. 329); she also suggests that the creative imagination is the best available model for thinking or conceptualising as such (MGM, p. 306), and then distinguishes between two different aspects or modes of its activity.

> [There are] two active faculties, one somewhat mechanically generating narrowly banal false pictures (the ego as all-powerful), and the other freely and creatively exploring the world, moving towards the expression and elucidation (and in art celebration) of what is true and deep ... [I]n ordinary situations imagination appears as a restoration of freedom, cognition, the effortful ability to see what lies before one more clearly, more justly, to consider new possibilities, and to respond to good attachments and desires which have been in eclipse. (MGM, p. 322)

Hence the progress of our spiritual pilgrimage is a matter of discarding false or less-adequate images of the moral life in favour of more truthful ones – a process which often feels like deprivation, since it demands that we deprive ourselves of consoling pictures of reality in favour of ones less gratifying to our egos. In general, however, these images of the moral life imply a certain kind of transcendence and unity. '[T]he idea of perfection haunts all our activities' (MGM, p. 428): every time we cleave to a new picture of reality, we become at once certain that it cannot be of the ultimate reality, and so cannot be our stopping place. As finite creatures, we can never lose the sense that our moral perception is capable of further refinement, so the purification of our consciousness can never attain perfection; but neither can it shrug off its demands, and the progress we make is towards a deepening sense of the interrelatedness of the demands put upon us by moral values and dispositions – a sense of life and reality as hanging together, as making sense of a kind we have not yet begun to fathom except through a glass darkly, but to which we can always come closer than we presently are.

Of course, those wedded to the fact/vale thesis will be happy to admit that this perfectionist picture of human moral existence provides one possible perspective from which human beings might evaluate the situations and states of affairs they encounter; but it is no more dictated by the content and structure of the common, factual world we all occupy than by any other internally consistent evaluative perspective. They would, for example, dismiss Murdoch's accounts of what it is to perceive persons and artworks as confusing a description of what such entities actually are with one possible evaluative attitude that might be taken towards them. From this perspective, Murdoch's articulation of her perfectionist vision fails to create any difficulties for the fact/value thesis that are not created by any other moral vision; it simply provides us with one more example of the sheer variety of moral frameworks that we can impose on reality – one more token of the logically distinct(ive) type 'evaluative judgement'.

Before accepting this conclusion, however – before bracketing off the precise content of Murdoch's account – we should look a little closer at her 'moral interpretation' of human fact-seeking activities. Can we effect a separation within that account of her moral interpretation of such activities from an evaluatively neutral description of them, in the way her opponents proposed to treat her account of persons and artworks? Just how easy is it to construct an account of truth-seeking that divorces it from truthfulness, or one which divorces the idea of truthfulness from that of overcoming the self's misrepresentations of reality, or which divorces the idea of the self's mistaking what is real from that of the self's remaking of reality in the image of its own desires? But even if it were possible to argue plausibly that, for example, scholarship's demands on the scholar are not inherently ethical ones, the critical point for Murdoch is that this would be only one position in a debate over how properly to characterise the business of truth-seeking, over what it is to seek, find and have respect for the facts, and so over what the realm of the factual essentially is. And this in turn implies that our very characterisation of the realm of the factual is itself open to evaluative contestation – that how we think of the factual in relation to the evaluative is not itself value-neutral, and so that supposedly non-committal talk of a 'common factual world' upon which we project our differing evaluative attitudes is in reality the expression of a specific evaluative perspective.

We can begin to see more clearly of which perspective it is the expression if we ask ourselves what would be lost from Murdoch's moral vision if it were to be reformulated in the terms proposed by those wedded to the fact/value thesis – if we were to conceptualise her account of persons, artworks and truth-seeking as the expression of one possible attitude that we might adopt towards phenomena whose essential nature can be specified in evaluatively neutral terms. For, if there is a common thread to Murdoch's account of these matters, it is her stress on the disciplining or withdrawal or abnegation of the self, upon its overcoming of its inherent tendency to impose its will on reality; she aims to articulate a vision of the self as denying itself in order to let that which is not the self find its proper place. If, however, we attempt to express that vision in the terms of the fact/vale thesis, if we characterise it as one or more or less popular projection of an evaluative attitude upon our common, factual world, then it appears as one amongst a number of possible ways in which the human will imposes itself on reality. This characterisation of her vision creates such an extreme contradiction between its content and its new form that it is bound to be entirely unacceptable to its proponents. For in effect, we represent a vision of the need to overcome human wilfulness as merely one more efflorescence of the human will; and even if one were inclined to argue that this might in the end be the truth of the matter, in so doing one would hardly be offering a value-neutral characterisation of that moral perspective.

As Cora Diamond has pointed out in a penetrating and perceptive recent essay,[3] this is why Murdoch objected from the outset to the form of representation of any and every moral view that was imposed by proponents of the fact/value thesis in the name of scientific neutrality in ethical theory. The very terms in which those theorists gave expression to other moral views distorted a significant range of them, because the form of representation they proposed itself embodied the specific moral vision of the theorists – one that Murdoch identified as Protestant and Liberal because of the centrality it afforded to the idea of human freedom. Any and every human moral perspective was characterised by them as one possible way of evaluating a common factual world because that characterisation secured the fundamentality of the human capacity to choose one's own moral values; it built into their very conceptualisation of morality the idea that reality did not and could not force a specific moral value or vision upon us, whilst preserving the idea that our exercise of this freedom took place in an arena constituted by a shared, commonly perceptible and describable world. As a consequence, any moral visions which centred upon the idea that moral values might be the result of a kind of perception of reality, or that moral concepts are prior to the exercise of our capacity to choose and so provide the terms in which we can think about any such exercises of the will (Murdoch offers as examples certain forms of

[3] '"We are Perpetually Moralists": Iris Murdoch, Fact and Value', in Antonaccio and Schweiker (eds), *Iris Murdoch and the Search for Human Goodness* (University of Chicago Press, 1996) – hereafter WPM.

Christianity and Marxism, but we might add forms of perfectionism such as her own to the list) – such moral visions would appear as a kind of caricature or parody of themselves, with their most significant convictions variously mangled or watered down.

For Murdoch, then, the fact/value thesis is a meta-ethical expression of a liberal and protestant ethical vision of the centrality to human flourishing of the free exercise of the will. Her objections to it are thus not so much to the importance it assigns to human freedom (although she would certainly contest the absolute priority the thesis appears to confer upon it) as to the assumption that this priority merely reflects the value-neutral facts of the matter – whether with respect to the logic of moral discourse of the ontology of value in relation to the factual realm. Indeed, she is even happy to acknowledge that reminders about the difference between factual and evaluative claims can form a critical part of our repertoire as reflective moral agents. When, for example, someone argues that a particular action must be morally permissible since statistics show that people are constantly doing it, we can and should point out to her that she is using a concealed premise – that what is customary is right. This, we might say, is one grain of truth in the fact/value thesis; but on Murdoch's account we are then criticising our interlocutor not because she has failed to appreciate a logical gap between factual premises and evaluative conclusions, but because she has failed to appreciate the full range of possibilities open to her. We are reminding her that the facts do not dictate that she must perform the customary action that she is contemplating, that she can legitimately refrain from performing that action and so that she must take responsibility for performing it if she decides to do so. As Diamond puts it,[4] the implication is that she may be attempting to evade responsibility for her actions, and we are attempting to prevent her from doing so; but to confront her in those terms is to criticise her morally, not to accuse her of a logical or ontological error.

We might, however, argue further that on Murdoch's account there is a deeper truth of which the familiar philosophical idea of a distinction between fact and value is a distorted expression. As we have seen, proponents of the fact/value thesis commit themselves to the view that ethical discourse is a specific domain or subset of human discourse more generally, a particular branch or department of human thought and speech with its own distinctive structure and relationship to other such departments. And it is part of Murdoch's moral vision that human experience and thought is inherently or ubiquitously moral – that values can and do pervade and colour every aspect of our consciousness of the world. But this conflict

[4] WPM, pp. 80–2.

should not be viewed as a dispute over whether or not there is a distinction between fact and value, with Murdoch denying its reality; it is rather a dispute over how best to characterise or locate that distinction. For, as Diamond has stressed, if moral thought and values are ubiquitously present to consciousness, then they are by that very token distinct from factual matters, which are precisely not ubiquitous in that sense. Factual judgement-making might be said to be a family of cognitive practices. Historians, biologists, physicists and others each apply distinctive practices of justifying and criticising assertions, compiling and assessing evidence, establishing facts and understanding; each thereby distinguish themselves from one another, and establish a distinct subject-matter or disciplinary field. In effect, then, for a particular subject-matter to be a particular subject-matter, and thus a recognisable part of the ramified business of human cognitive activity, is for it not to be ubiquitous to consciousness and practice; so if morality is ubiquitous it must be distinguished from any such cognitive activity. Moral value is not the object of cognitive activity in the way biological or historical facts are the object of cognitive activity; it is not one subject-matter amongst others.

Diamond attempts to give a more positive account of this difference in the following passage:

> If value is said to be ubiquitous, this is in fact tied to the way in which our experience of the world can bear morally on any situation, can shape our vision of what the situation is. There is no limit to how objects of our attention *can* cast light on a situation (no limit that could be set in advance); a fundamental form of moral rationality is the *interpretation of something or other into practical life* – the interpretation into practical life of some fact or person or story or proverb or principle. (WPM, pp. 108–9)

These words encapsulate a radically different conception of the forms of human moral understanding and moral reasoning; for Diamond's Murdoch-inspired vision does not differentiate factual from evaluative reasoning in terms of a specific kind of premise or a particular pattern of inference. Interpreting things into practical life has no distinctive structure or principles because it is fundamentally not based on the following of some pre-given set of rules; it depends upon imagination, the ability to see connections, the creative shaping of one's sense of how aspects of human experience hang together or fail to do so.

Recognising that such interpretation is at least one fundamental form of moral reasoning has a double implication. It casts doubt on any attempt to distinguish moral thought and discourse as a branch or department of human thought and discourse; and it thereby casts doubt on the idea that moral philosophy is a branch or department of philosophy more generally. Once again, Diamond's Murdochian point is not that all philosophy is moral philosophy; it is rather that moral philosophy is not identifiable as one philosophical sub-discipline amongst others, one to be distinguished from those others in terms of (the distinctive properties and structure of) its subject-matter. If we cannot *a priori* exclude the possibility of interpreting any given phenomenon into practical reasoning, then we cannot prohibit moral philosophers from exploring the relevance for practical reasoning of any apparently non-ethical subject-matter or discipline with which philosophers concern themselves; and if we cannot assume in advance that any given branch or mode of philosophising has no ethical significance, then neither can we assume that it cannot itself be subject to ethical assessment. As Murdoch might have put it, if metaphysics can be a guide to morals, morals can be no less a guide to metaphysics.

In effect, then, just as the supposedly value-neutral meta-ethical fact/value thesis turns out to embody a distinctive ethical vision of the primacy of human freedom, so the supposedly value-neutral methodological conception of moral philosophy as one branch of philosophy itself works to exclude from the attention of those working in that field any moral views which contest that same distinctive ethical vision. This should not be surprising; for, if moral value is ubiquitous, it can hardly fail to shape and be shaped by the way in which human beings characterise the moral dimension of their lives and by the ways in which they characterise its systematic study. In short; if we are perpetually moralists, then there can be no such thing as meta-ethics in the standard value-neutral sense of that term; and moral philosophers cannot be thought of as having removed themselves from the ethical fray even at the most abstract level of their self-understanding.

2 Is and ought: claims, commitments and modes of self-presentation

Soon after Murdoch's first systematic published critique of the fact/value thesis, Stanley Cavell took issue with those who defended the linguistic variant of that thesis – the belief that there exists a logical gap between factual and evaluative statements, or that no ethical or imperatival conclusion can be derived from exclusively factual premises.[5] For Cavell, this thesis depends upon its being obvious

[5] Cavell's criticisms were first published as chapter XII of *The Claim of Reason* (Oxford University Press, 1979) – hereafter CR; but that chapter, essentially as it stands in CR, formed part of Cavell's Ph.D dissertation, submitted in 1961.

that we cannot infer 'We ought to do X' [O] from 'We promised to do X' [R2] unless we also grant the ethical proposition 'We ought to keep promises' [R1]. It is true that O cannot be derived from R2 alone; and let us assume that it can only be derived from R2 with the addition of R1. This will only establish the thesis if the step from R2 to O is *inferential* and Cavell denies that it is.

He utilises a non-ethical example to make his point. Suppose that, whilst I am playing chess, a friend advises me that I ought to castle now [O], and, when I ask why, replies that castling will neutralise my opponent's bishop and develop my rook [R2]. Does O follow from R2? It is surely absurd to say that it would follow if we added the premise that: Whenever castling will neutralise a bishop and develop a rook, then you ought to castle. My friend is not saying anything like that; she's just saying that castling is the best move *here*. And she can display why she thinks that in the form of further premises: With my rook in play I can trap my opponent's queen in two moves [R3]; with the queen gone I can win in four moves [R4]. From R2, together with R3 and R4, it follows (in terms of ordinary logic and a knowledge of chess) that: castling now will win [R5]. Does O follow from R5? Or is my friend making the further assumption that I want to win? Does O not follow from R5 without accepting the major premise: If you want to win, then you ought to castle? But again, my friend didn't mean anything so absurd: her advice is that castling will win *here*, not just any time. Does logical rigour then require the premise that: If you want to win, you should do whatever will win? But is that intelligible? Is it chess?

Cavell concludes that there is no major premise that could bind R5 to O: but that is not because a special sort of logic or psychology is needed to bridge the gap between them; it is rather because there is no gap to be filled – the step is not the conclusion of an inference.

> The gap which looks open on paper is closed in the *act of confronting* the player. To get a hint of what function 'ought' has, it should be noticed that any of R2–R5 could directly have been used to advise the player to castle: which of them you say depends upon what you think the person doesn't see, and how many steps you take in your proof will depend on how much it will take for him to see what you see ... If he cannot counter these 'factual premisses', whose *point*, in that context, is to advise him (and it wouldn't (grammatically) *be* advice unless you thought they would further his position), then unless he actually makes the move, or gives a good reason why he does not, then he either has not understood you, or has not mastered the game. (CR, p. 317)

Misplacing freedom, displacing the imagination

Cavell's claim is that the content of the original claim 'You ought to castle now' is completely specified by the reasons you are prepared to give in its support; any proof available for any of the reasons R2–R5 is simultaneously a proof of O. Choosing O, choosing to say 'You ought to ...', adds nothing whatever to the content those reasons specify, but rather determines the mode of that content's presentation. The mode of presentation of the content is not, in these kinds of case, itself the subject of inference – any more than it is when we present a conclusion by saying 'I most emphatically aver that ...' or 'let there no longer be any doubt that ...' or 'You will be awed to learn that ...'; and we would not expect to find within the speaker's proof of conclusions presented in such ways a premise presented in a parallel way – we would not, for example, wish to maintain that an awe-statement cannot be deduced from premises none of which contain the word 'awe'.

What, then, is the significance of choosing O rather than any of R2–R5 in our chess example? According to Cavell, whether you say R5 or O depends upon how you conceive the position of the player, and upon what position you take towards him. Saying 'ought' in such a context implies that there is an alternative, more or less definite, that the person you are advising might take, and against which you are taking a stand. Here, Cavell's specific criticisms of the is/ought thesis make contact with the more general conception of moral discourse and moral rationality that he develops in part III of *The Claim of Reason*.

In his view, what makes science rational is not the fact of agreement about particular propositions, or about the acknowledged modes of arriving at it, but the fact of a commitment to certain modes of argument whose very nature is to lead to such agreement; and morality is rational on exactly the same ground, namely that we commit ourselves to certain modes of argument – but in this case ones which do not lead in the same ways (and sometimes do not lead at all) to agreement about a conclusion. We can, in other words, agree to disagree about a particular conclusion whilst continuing to share our commitment to certain modes of argument – modes which, unlike those of science, permit reasonable disagreement as well as reasoned agreement. To talk of shared modes of argument in morality is, however, to imply that there are constraints on what are deemed pertinent considerations in a moral debate; individuals may be free to determine the significance they attach to any such consideration, but its relevance is out of their hands. It is in attempting to sketch out the structure of these shared modes of moral argument, these canons of relevance, that Cavell introduces the idea of a moral agent's cares and commitments.

Stephen Mulhall

For Cavell, a person's commitments are implications of what she says and does. If, for example, someone makes a promise then she is committed to performing a course of action; if she does not, she must explain why the circumstances in which she found herself justified her failure to honour that commitment, why she could not have given advance warning to those relying on her, and so on. Promising is not peculiar in this respect: expressing an intention, giving an impression, not correcting someone's misapprehension – all are ways of committing oneself to an action; and on Cavell's Austinian view of speech, any utterance whatever carries similar implications. Each such case will provide non-arbitrary and impersonal constraints upon the agent concerned; and, by the same token, unless my attempts to challenge someone about her behaviour take her budget of commitments as its reference point, then my challenge is morally incompetent.

Similarly, what human beings care about is not entirely arbitrary or unstable. One might object to the weight Antigone placed upon her relationship with her brother, but it would be incompetent to deny the relevance of care for one's close relatives; and it would be similarly incompetent to convince someone to break her promise on the grounds that it would be very time-consuming to keep it. Cavell's idea here is not that care-related reasons must relate to a moral agent's *existing* cares; after all, a crucial part of moral disagreement involves convincing one's interlocutor that there are things (values, people, responsibilities) that she should care about, even though her present intentions and behaviour show that she does not. There are, however, grammatical limits to the reasons that can then be cited, constraints upon what it makes sense to exhort someone to care about and upon how they might intelligibly justify a decision to reject or downplay them – constraints that vary according to the nature of the proposed object of care, of the interlocutor's other declared concerns and values, and so on. These constraints may be multiple and circumstance-relative, but they are neither vague nor arbitrary.

For our purposes, however, the key point to note is that the need to speak to someone's cares and commitments when confronting them morally controls not only the substance of one's reasons for so doing, but also their form or mode of presentation; and, here, the specific force of 'You ought to do X' comes into view. According to Cavell, it would be odd to say to a chess-player 'You ought to move the queen in straight lines' but correct to say 'You must move the queen in straight lines', and unexceptionable to say 'You ought to castle here'; this is because 'ought' implies that there is an alternative which the player would be justified in taking but which you are advising her (for specific reasons) to forego. What this pattern implies for moral debate is that, if I say 'You ought to do X', I imply that there is an alternative, morally justifiable action that my interlocutor might take but which I am advising against; whereas if I say 'You must do X', I imply that my interlocutor has no choice in the matter.

If, however, my reason for advising that X be done is that it is something to which my interlocutor is *committed* by virtue of other things she has said or done, then it would make no sense to present X as something she ought to do. That would imply that not doing X would be justified except in these specific circumstances, when in the case of the necessary implications of action precisely the reverse is true. Honouring the implications of a previous action is not something which needs to be supported by specific reasons from case to case; such implications rather form the given background of commitment, determining the course of action which the agent *must* follow, except when specific reasons support the claim that in this particular situation she ought not to do what she has committed herself to doing (presumably because there is something she should care about more). In short, when X is an implication of an agent's previous actions, it would make sense to advise her that she ought not to do X, but not to advise her that she ought to do it. Conversely, it would make sense to say that she must do X (when reasons exist which support the idea that the commitment should be overridden, but the speaker wishes to assert that they are not sufficient for so doing, i.e. that there really isn't an alternative); but it would not make sense to say that she must not do X (because when doing X is an implication of a previous action, it always exists as a legitimate alternative to not doing X).

These grammatical points lead to the following conclusions. First, when one's reason for advising that a certain action be done depends upon its being something to which the person addressed is committed, then 'must' rather than 'ought' is the appropriate mode of presentation of that reason; and, second, when one advises a person that she 'ought' to perform a certain action, the reason upon which that advice is based must relate to that person's cares rather than to her commitments. As Cavell summarises the matter:

> In both games and morality, there are two main sorts of reasons with which we may be confronted: the one I might call a 'basis of care' – it provides whatever sense there will be in your confronting someone with what he 'ought' to do; the second I call a 'ground of commitment' – it grounds what you say 'must' be done in that person's commitments, both his explicit undertak-

ings and the implications of what he does and where he is, for which he is responsible. (CR, p. 325)

And, of course, these canons of relevance will also shape the response of the person thus confronted. The terms in which any competently entered moral query about a given action must be articulated must also be the terms of any competently entered moral defence of that action; and the mode of presenting that defence (e.g. describing one's actions as something one must do rather than something one ought to do) will carry analogous implications about the speaker's conception of the position being defended.

We can see these constraints at work in the exchange over the chess-board from which Cavell started his critique of the is/ought distinction. The proponent of the distinction attempted to re-establish the gap between the advice to castle now and its supporting reasons by arguing that the force of those reasons depended upon the assumption that the player being advised wanted to win – that that is what the player cares about. This objection implicitly acknowledges the need for a link between ought-claims and a basis of care, but it assumes that whether or not a player of chess cares about winning is an entirely open question – an utterly arbitrary or contingent matter. In reality, however, if the player responded to this advice by saying 'I'm not trying to win', she could only mean that she was not fully playing (but rather testing a new gambit, teaching someone, throwing the game). In other words, caring to win is part of what is implied by describing what is done as playing chess; if that description is rejected, only certain kinds of alternative description can intelligibly be applied to what is being done; and each such description implies an alternative basis of care (e.g. for the pupil's confidence, or for a bribe).

A critical difference between games and morality begins to emerge here. A chess-player can competently reject advice competently grounded in what she must care for as a chess-player only by rejecting the assumption that she is (genuinely, fully) playing a game of chess; within the arena of play, what counts as her responsibilities and concerns are marked off by the rules and principles of the game, by those specific institutional inflections of the grammar of human cares and commitments. In morality, one's position is not determined by any such rules and principles; which values we are to honour or create, and which responsibilities we must accept or accept that we have incurred, is precisely a problem for us – a matter which it is ultimately up to us to determine. This personal responsibility does, of course, have its limits; its focus remains that of the nature and range of one's cares and commitments, and its exercise must therefore answer to the grammar of those concepts. This is why Cavell emphasises that the logic of moral debate (unlike that of debates about games) distinguishes between the relevance of a basis of care or ground of commitment and the weight to be attached to it. The former is not open to personal assessment, but the latter is; so a moral agent is obliged to respond to a competently entered objection to her action, but she is not obliged to accept the significance that her interlocutor gives it. Accordingly, the response she does make – accepting it, contesting it, denying it – reveals not what the logic of moral debate determines as an adequate basis for her claim or action, but what she personally regards as adequate.

It follows that any disagreements over modes of presentation in such a context give expression to a disagreement over what position the agent concerned is (is really, or should be) taking responsibility for; and the mode of presentation in terms of which the agent eventually accepts responsibility for what she does importantly determines what it is that she is accepting responsibility for.

> What you say you *must* (have to, are compelled to ...) do, another will feel you ought to do, generally speaking, other things equal, etc., but that *here* you ought (would do better) *not* to. (That is a much more usual conflict that the academic case of 'You ought to do X', 'You ought not to do X'.) What you say you *must* do is not 'defined by the practice', for there is no such practice until you make it one, make it *yours*. We might say, such a declaration defines *you*, establishes your position. One problem of the freedom of the will lies in what you *regard* as a choice, what you see as alternatives you can take, and become responsible for, make a part of your position. This is a deeply practical problem, and it has an inexorable logic: whether what you say that you 'cannot' do you in fact will not do because of fear, or whether out of a consistent conviction that it is not for you, in either case that is then *your* will. If the alternative is blocked through fear, then your will is fearful; if from single-mindedness, then it is whole. It is about such choices that existentialists say, You choose your life. This is the way an action Categorically Imperative feels. (CR, p. 309)

A position you must take is one to which there is no alternative; one that you ought to take is one amongst others, each with something to be said for them. To present your position in such ways is to define it by defining your sense of its relation to other positions, to place yourself in a particular space of moral options, and so to place yourself in relation to those who would plot that space differently or would have you place yourself differently in it. But this placing is yours alone to do; the logic of moral argument offers no impersonal background on to which one's responsibility not only for the choices one makes but for the range of choices one regards as available can be sloughed off. What it does provide, however, is the possibility of accounting for one's choices, by engaging in modes of explanation and defence which not only make reasoned agreement on that choice a real possibility, but also ensure that a sense of mutual respect, of mutual moral intelligibility, might survive eventual disagreement over the rectitude of a given choice.

> Morality provides *one* possibility of settling conflict, a way of encompassing conflict which allows the continuance of personal relationships against the hard and apparently inevitable fact of misunderstanding, mutually incompatible wishes, commitments, loyalties, interests and needs, a way of mending relationships and maintaining the self in opposition to itself or others. Other ways of settling or encompassing conflict are provided by politics, religion, love and forgiveness, rebellion and withdrawal. Morality is a valuable way because the others are often inaccessible or brutal; but it is not everything; it provides a door through which someone, alienated or in danger of alienation from another through his action, can return by the offering and the acceptance of explanations, excuses and justifications, or by the respect one human being will show another who sees and can accept responsibility for a position which he himself would not adopt. We do not have to agree with one another in order to live in the same moral world, but we do have to know and respect one another's differences. (CR, p. 269)

On Cavell's account, therefore, the difference or distinction which truly matters in this area is not the wholly illusory one between 'is' and 'ought', but that between 'ought' and 'must' (and between 'ought' and 'desirable', and so on through the range of available such modes of presenting the position one is taking on a moral question). Offering one's reasons for advising someone that she ought to do something does not amount to justifying one's view that she *ought* to do it, but rather one's view that *that* is what she ought to do. The advice will be competent in so far as those reasons have a basis in something the agent does or should care about; and the form of their presentation will be competent in so far as they acknowledge that the action is one to which there are morally viable alternatives. The mode of presentation of the advice serves to define the position of the advisor with respect to the choice the agent faces, and so with respect to the agent; and the form and content of the agent's response to that advice will help to determine whether and how their relationship is to continue.

Misplacing freedom, displacing the imagination

Despite first appearances, Cavell's objection to the is/ought theorist is very different in nature from those (briefly mentioned above) developed by such philosophers as Searle. Principally in opposition to claims made by Hare, Searle argued that it was possible to derive an 'ought' from an 'is' whenever one could draw upon what he termed 'institutional facts' about language. His favoured example was that of making a promise: and his argument was that, from a premise describing a person's utterance of certain English words, together with a number of other premises which consisted either of tautologies or statements of fact relating to the use of the English language, one could draw the conclusion that the person was committed to doing what he promised to do. Searle treated the case as an example of performing a speech-act in the Austinian sense of that term – of doing something by saying something: in this case, making a commitment.

Is not Cavell's reliance upon the logic of moral discourse merely another instance of such a general 'ordinary language' strategy? Two critical points speak against this suggestion. First, Searle happily accepts the is/ought theorist's claim that an inference is required to link descriptive premise with evaluative conclusions: he merely denies their claim that no such inference is possible. He thus accepts the fundamental background assumption of the is/ought controversy that Cavell rejects. Second, Searle's construction of the relevant inference depends upon his assumption that making promises is a linguistic practice or institution; it is the facts which follow from the existence of the relevant institution that give him the premises he needs to reach his conclusion – and it is this idea of institutional facts that Hare fastens upon in his reply to Searle, arguing that the notion begs the question against him by conflating two phenomena (meaning-rules and moral principles) that he argues are logically distinct. Cavell's position bypasses this controversy by rejecting from the outset the idea that promise-making is a linguistic practice or institution.

He is happy to describe it as a social action occurring against a definite social ground; and his account relies upon the fact that promising has a grammar – that not just anything one does will amount to making a promise. But he denies that promise-making is conventional or social in the way that institutions characteristic of particular societies are conventional; in particular, he denies that promising is a form of activity specified by a system of rules which defines offices, roles, moves, penalties, defenses and so on. Being a promisor is not an office – there is no special procedure for entering it (no oaths!), no established routes for being selected or training yourself for it, and so on; on the contrary, any competent adult can take on this 'office', and can do so merely by putting himself in it with respect to anyone equally competent. Similarly, in learning what a promise is, we learn what defences it is appropriate to enter, and when, should we not keep it. But these do not form part of a specific set of rules that distinguishes promising from other social and linguistic institutions; they are just the defences we learn in learning to defend any of our conduct which comes to grief – the excuses, justification and explanations (Cavell calls them elaboratives) that are internal to the very concept of a human action: for without knowing them, without knowing that agents are answerable for their actions and how they might bear that responsibility, then one simply does not understand what a human action is.

As we have seen, the grammar or logic of these elaboratives is one which creates a space within which individuals work to define the positions for which they are prepared to take responsibility, to determine what exactly it is that they have said and done and how they stand in relation to it; it is, in short, an impersonal framework within which the individual takes personal responsibility for who she is. To treat promising as a practice, and by implication to treat human speech as such as an institution or set of institutions, denies that element of personal responsibility, allowing us to think that our answerability for what we say and do is determined by objective rules or principles rather than by our weighing of the commitments and cares that speech and action exact – by logic rather than by ourselves. And the attractions of such a fantasy of absolution from personal answerability for what we do are, humanly speaking, all too obvious.

It follows that the strategy of opposing those who defend the is/ought distinction in the name of human autonomy by invoking a conception of speech which works to eliminate personal responsibility for what we say and do is fated to confirm the worst suspicions of those at which it is aimed. Cavell's strategy, by contrast, attempts to show that the true nature of the freedom which proponents of the is/ought distinction incoherently aim to capture is fully acknowledgeable only by jettisoning their sense that any such distinction exists. For, as Cavell describes them, the modes of reasoning that characterise moral debate actually make it possible for individuals to make themselves answerable for their actions in different ways without thereby exiling one another from a common world. The point is that that common world is a moral one, not a realm of pure fact.

This makes it far from easy to plot the nature of Cavell's critique in relation to that of Iris Murdoch. To be sure, there are many profound similarities between the two writers. Cavell shares Murdoch's suspicion of the picture of a gap between fact and value, and reiterates her denial of the existence of any peculiarly morally mode of inference that might be needed to license the use of evaluative terminology. Instead, he develops a vision of the grammar of human cares and commitments as articulating a field within which an individual can determine her moral position, helped by the honest perceptions and creative suggestions of others as much as by her own responsive construal of her responsibilities and opportunities. This vision clearly has much in common with Murdoch's conception of the moral importance of the human imagination, with its capacity creatively to interpret aspects of our experience into our moral life. Indeed, juxtaposing the two casts a penetrating light on both. For Murdoch's stress on the imagination highlights the fact that Cavell's conception of the grammar of cares and commitments as establishing a domain of personal responsibility acknowledges thereby not only individual freedom of choice but also individual creativity (the latter can, after all, be thought of as an aspect of the former); and Cavell's sensitivity to the normativity of grammar highlights the facts that Murdoch's conception of the open-ended reach of the human imagination is balanced by her concern that moral creativity should be responsive to the reality of the situations in which we find ourselves, and to the realities (the true conditions, concerns and potentialities) of human nature – that our re-imaginings of the world should and must make human sense. Furthermore, Diamond's account of Murdoch's version of this vision implies that any such version should tend towards a denial of the idea that moral discourse is a separate branch of language and experience, and so towards a denial of the common picture of moral philosophy as a separate branch of philosophy *per se*. And indeed, in his more recent work, Cavell has found himself emphasing a perfectionist dimension to morality, one which contests the departmental conception of moral discourse and moral philosophy, and which has led him to focus upon writers whose conception of their task as philosophers is essentially perfectionist.[6]

Against the background of these deep agreements between Cavell and Murdoch, however, certain disagreements acquire a new salience. One potential matter of contention is implicit in the care Cavell takes to contrast moral relationships with other types of relationship – political, religious, loving; for this emphasis upon the distinctness of the dimensions of human culture has a rather Enlightenment tone to it. Taken together with Cavell's interpretation of the moral dimension of that culture as enabling individual freedom in a shared world, and hence as giving liberals what they

[6] Cf. *Conditions Handsome and Unhandsome* (Chicago: University of Chicago Press, 1990).

mistakenly try to get from the fact/value distinction, it might be argued that his vision of morality chimes rather more neatly with protestant liberalism than do the main elements of Murdoch's Platonic perfectionism. Against this, it should be noted that Murdoch never disputed the importance of individual freedom, and indeed devotes much positive attention to it in *Metaphysics As a Guide to Morals*; she rather contested the philosophical tendency to present that commitment as the consequence of 'the' logic of all moral discourse, or of a clear perception of certain metaphysical truths about the realm of facts and its relation to human value – a view with which Cavell would, in general terms, hardly disagree. Nevertheless, a certain suspicion lingers that Cavell sees such liberal values to be rather more deeply embedded in, and rather more fundamentally determinative of, everyday moral discourse than Murdoch would wish to countenance. Whether one attributes this difference to Cavell's clearer perception of the lineaments of late twentieth-century culture, or to a lack of clarity about the reach of his own moral investments, is another matter.

There are at least two further respects in which Cavell's and Murdoch's writings on fact and value are differently inflected. First, Murdoch's vision of the perfectionist struggle is highly individual, focusing above all on the ways in which each of us struggles to purify and refine our own consciousness through a long internal labour that is aided by artworks, the disciplines of scholarship, and the challenge posed by the sheer existence of other people to perceive them as they really are; whereas Cavell's emphasis is rather more social, placing much (although by no means all) of its weight either on the individual's confrontation of others, or on the ways in which others can actively contribute to the individual's engagement with herself. Second (perhaps because of his greater inclination towards the values of liberal modernity), Cavell connects the motives of the fact/value theorist with the issue of scepticism in a way that Murdoch never does. Central to his treatment of the issue is the following claim:

> [I]t will be wondered why [the is/ought] thesis takes the form that it does; what, that is, the experience is of someone led to produce 'You ought to do X' in such a way that it will seem a reason for it to say 'You promised to do X' and then ask whether the conclusions follows from that reason as a premiss. In a sentence, the suggestion I would follow is this: I think it is a real experience which can produce such a surmise as 'Why ought I to do anything?' Given that as a question to be *answered*, the (generic) examples which present themselves will not, as in epistemological

contexts, be particular; they will, it seems, take the form, 'Why, for example, ought I to keep promises, pay debts, tell the truth, do my 'duty' etc?'. This, in effect, asks: Why ought I to honour the claims others make upon me? And, unlike … in epistemology, this is not a position which cannot coherently be maintained; it therefore leads to no sense of paradox when the philosopher is led by to his conclusion about the logical autonomy of ethical judgements. (CR, p. 322)

The detailed argumentative background to this diagnosis cannot be properly brought out here; but it suggests that a full assessment of the family resemblances between Murdochian and Cavellian perfectionism would require a detailed examination of their sense of the human significance of scepticism.

Index of Names

Index of Names

Nagel, T., 93, 198
Newman, J., 152
Nietzsche, F., 4, 15

Parfit, D., 165–8, 171
Plato, 65–6, 73, 77, 79, 105–18, 150
Platts, M., 152
Plotinus, 68
Posidonius, 66
Post, J., 97
Putnam, H., 20–1

Quinton, A., 64–6, 101

Raverat, G. 152
Rawls, J., 3
Reid, T., 241
Riefenstahl, L., 251, 254
Ross, W. D., 159–65, 169–70, 175–95, 208
Royce, J., 124, 132
Russell, B., 93
Ryle, G., 94–7

Scanlon, T., 162–7, 172
Scheffler, S., 175
Schopenhauer, A., 11, 16
Scruton, R., 103
Searle, J., 256, 273
Sellars, W., 101
Seneca, 66
Sidgwick, H., 175
Skinner, B. F., 129
Smart, J. J. C., 175
Socrates, 116
Speusippus, 105
Spinoza, B., 76–9, 83–8
Stebbing, S., 96

Weil, S., 248, 250, 258–9
Wiggins, D., 58–60, 63–4, 143, 150, 153–4
Wilde, O., 91, 152
Williams, B., 20, 21, 149, 175, 180, 256
Winch, P., 180
Wittgenstein, L., 104
Wordsworth, W., 35–7, 43
Wright, C., 20–1, 235–6

Zeno, 66